GARDENING AT THE MARGINS

GARDENING *at the* MARGINS

Convivial Labor, Community, and Resistance

GABRIEL R. VALLE

THE UNIVERSITY OF
ARIZONA PRESS
TUCSON

The University of Arizona Press
www.uapress.arizona.edu

We respectfully acknowledge the University of Arizona is on the land and territories of Indigenous peoples. Today, Arizona is home to twenty-two federally recognized tribes, with Tucson being home to the O'odham and the Yaqui. Committed to diversity and inclusion, the University strives to build sustainable relationships with sovereign Native Nations and Indigenous communities through education offerings, partnerships, and community service.

© 2022 by The Arizona Board of Regents
All rights reserved. Published 2022.

ISBN-13: 978-0-8165-4732-6 (hardcover)
ISBN-13: 978-0-8165-4733-3 (ebook)

Cover design by Leigh McDonald
Cover art by MHJ/istockphoto
Typeset by Sara Thaxton in 10/14 Warnock Pro with Adobe Caslon Pro

Publication of this book is made possible in part by support from the College of Humanities, Arts, Behavioral, and Social Sciences at California State University, San Marcos, and by the proceeds of a permanent endowment created with the assistance of a Challenge Grant from the National Endowment for the Humanities, a federal agency.

Library of Congress Cataloging-in-Publication Data
Names: Valle, Gabriel R., author.
Title: Gardening at the margins : convivial labor, community, and resistance / Gabriel R. Valle.
Description: [Tucson] : The University of Arizona Press, 2022. | Includes bibliographical references and index.
Identifiers: LCCN 2022008331 (print) | LCCN 2022008332 (ebook) | ISBN 9780816547326 (hardcover) | ISBN 9780816547333 (ebook)
Subjects: LCSH: La Mesa Verde (Organization) | Urban gardening—Social aspects—California—Santa Clara Valley (Santa Clara County) | Urban gardening—Environmental aspects—California—Santa Clara Valley (Santa Clara County) | Nutrition.
Classification: LCC SB454.3.S63 V35 2022 (print) | LCC SB454.3.S63 (ebook) | DDC 635.09794/73—dc23/eng/20220414
LC record available at https://lccn.loc.gov/2022008331
LC ebook record available at https://lccn.loc.gov/2022008332

Printed in the United States of America.
♾ This paper meets the requirements of ANSI/NISO Z39.48-1992 (Permanence of Paper).

Contents

List of Illustrations	*vii*
La Mesa Verde Community	*ix*
Preface: Hidden in Plain Sight	3
Introduction: "The only way to know I'm human is to share"	7
1. More than Weeds: Gardening in Spaces of Neglect	37
Interlude: Milpas at the Margins	*65*
2. Gardening as a Way of Life: Recipes from Grandma's Garden	69
3. Cultivating the "Good Life": "You're not gonna be rich, but who cares, you're gonna be happy"	97
Interlude: Chayote con Chile	*117*
4. Milpa-Based Cuisine: Cooking and Healing with Comida	121
5. "We're not just growing tomatoes": Cultivating Revolutionary Subjectivities at the Margins	139
Conclusion: Giving Back to the Body and Land	157
Acknowledgments	*165*
Appendix A: Home Garden Agrobiodiversity	*167*
Appendix B: Garden Agrobiodiversity	*169*
Appendix C: Recipes from the Garden	*189*
References	*195*
Index	*215*

Illustrations

1.	A typical La Mesa Verde home garden	5
2.	Harvest	11
3.	An all-too-common eatery in Washington-Alma	38
4.	Wide streets and very few large trees make up the landscape in Washington-Alma	39
5.	A typical tree-lined street in Willow Glen, a neighboring community of Washington-Alma	40
6.	Food emerges from the margins as a fig tree stretches over the fence	45
7.	Lucy's moving garden	56
8.	Grandma's garden	66
9.	Gardening as a way of life	70
10.	Sweet corn is a common crop grown in La Mesa Verde gardens	102
11.	The "good life"	111
12.	Chayote con chile	119
13.	Roasted tomatillo salsa	132
14.	A La Mesa Verde garden full of biodiversity	141
15.	La Mesa Verde gardens are about more than growing food	154

La Mesa Verde Community

La Mesa Verde (LMV) is a collection of home gardeners all working in different ways to cultivate food and community. At the center of this community is a labor process I refer to throughout the book as convivial labor. All of the home gardeners in this book are low income, and many are recent immigrants from Mexico, Central America, and Southeast Asia. Men and women home gardeners engage in convivial labor in different ways, yet what remains constant is how convivial labor facilitates the social reproduction of the community. Seed savers, farmers, ranchers, chefs, elders, activists, arborists, and even those new to farming and gardening all find ways to participate in the "social reproduction of the community." Women, however, do the bulk of the labor in this alternative food network. Men are engaged in the process, but they are rarely present at events, workshops, meetings, or home visits without their spouse.

Alfonso moved to San José, California, from Mexico City just over five years ago. He is in his eighties and is new to growing his own food.

Alma has been gardening with La Mesa Verde for many years. She is from southern Mexico, in her fifties, and lives with her brother Javi. She regularly volunteers and is an active member and supporter of the program.

David grew up in a small town in rural Jalisco, Mexico, where his extended family still resides. He is in his sixties and has extensive garden knowledge and grows many crops not commonly found in the United States. He has been gardening with La Mesa Verde since 2014.

Diana and Grandma (the name by which she is known in her community) are neighbors and share a garden. Diana is in her forties, and Grandma in her seventies. Grandma was born on a small farm in rural Jalisco and moved to the Santa Clara Valley in the 1950s with her husband, who was a bracero worker. Diana is Latinx, a single mother, and a great cook. At any La Mesa Verde event, you can find them together.

Diego was born in Peru and moved to the Santa Clara Valley several decades ago. In his mid-sixties, he continues to make trips home to Peru and to his brother's home in Mexico to gather seeds to propagate in his Santa Clara Valley home.

Evelyn is white, is in her late sixties, and lives alone. She grew up in the Midwest before moving to Northern California and later to the Santa Clara Valley. She is one of the longest-standing members of La Mesa Verde and remains a very active member.

Grace was born in the Sichuan Province of China. She is in her fifties, lives alone, and is always present at La Mesa Verde events. She began gardening in the program in 2013 and since then has transformed her backyard into a diverse and abundant garden.

Jessica is Cherokee and white. She still regularly visits friends and family in Oklahoma, where they live. She is a very active member of the community and a great advocate for La Mesa Verde. She and her husband have been a part of the program since 2010.

Karla was born and raised in the Santa Clara Valley. She is Latinx and in her fifties, and her family history goes back generations in California. She is a mother, grandmother, and *curandera*, or healer, and has been a part of La Mesa Verde since 2013.

Laura began with La Mesa Verde in 2013 and became one of its most active members. She is white, is in her mid-sixties, and can regularly be found organizing and advocating for the program.

Luis was born and raised in the Santa Clara Valley. In his late fifties, Luis identifies as Chicano and has witnessed the transformation of the valley. He has been a member of La Mesa Verde for many years and has become a leading advocate in the advisory committee.

Lucy was born in Manila, Philippines, and later moved to Singapore before she ended up in the Santa Clara Valley. She is in her sixties and has been gardening at La Mesa Verde since 2011.

Nancy is white and in her late fifties. She has been a part of La Mesa Verde since its early years and still volunteers even though she no longer has a garden. She is still a member of the advisory committee and can be regularly seen at events and workshops as well as volunteering when she can.

Oscar is a Latinx single father in his mid-thirties. He runs and operates his own landscape company. His "green thumb" can be partly attributed to the intergenerational knowledge passed down from his grandfather, whom he still visits in rural northern Sonora.

Rosa grew up in rural Durango, a Mexican state in northwestern Mexico. While her parents remain in Durango, Rosa continues to collect seeds and tubers (often sent through the mail or brought to San José by friends and family).

GARDENING AT THE MARGINS

Preface

Hidden in Plain Sight

It was early, sometime around six in the morning, on an October Saturday in 2012. Alma was outside tending to her crops. Her brother, Javi, invited me into their home. The sweet smell of masa and steamed vegetables engulfed the room filling me with a sense of nostalgia. The aroma of tamales transplanted me back in time to my grandmother's kitchen; the smell always meant something good was coming. Javi led us through the living room and into a galley kitchen where the tamales were cooking. A large steel pot sat on the stove, and the faint sound of its slow boil gave way to a steady flow of steam emerging from its lid. Javi explained how he and Alma make tamales from the vegetables grown in the garden and then sell them in the streets for a dollar each. Quite a bargain, considering most people are likely unaware of the high-quality vegetables, herbs, and labor put into this most humble of foods. Once outside, Alma showed me what she was growing. Pinto beans, green beans, heirloom beans, sweet corn, summer squash, arugula, verdolaga (purslane), basil, and kale, just to name a few, as well as lemon, lime, orange, nectarine, and peach trees. In the shade, she was husking tomatillos to make *salsa verde* for her family. She had a small chicken coop with several chickens, a dog that would wander the grounds, and two children to provide a helping hand.

She explained how her practice of crop rotation maintained healthy soil. She rotates crops; uses fava, pinto, and lima beans as nitrogenfixers; and makes her own compost to continually improve the tilth. Making efficient use of space, she practices vertical agriculture—scaling up rather than out.

The chickens ran about picking up insects and fertilizing the soil. "Todo comienza con buena tierra" (It all starts with good soil), she explained. Her daughter also gave me a tour of the gardens and showed me her favorite spots as well as the plants that produced the best fruits. In the distance, I heard Alma's cell phone ring, a subtle reminder that I was not in the countryside but rather in an urban environment. Alma's garden is immense, and more closely resembles a complex home garden found in Indigenous communities throughout the tropics, and yet is located within miles of major companies like Apple, Google, Adobe, and Cisco. In certain respects, it could not be farther away.

Gardens like Alma's are hidden in plain sight; if you are not paying close attention, you can walk right past them. There are many reasons for this invisibility, but most of all, it is because these gardens exist at the margins—in the overlooked, forgotten, and disenfranchised pockets of our urban cities. What is surprising is not that these gardens remain hidden but that they thrive. Gardens at the margins provide cover and opportunity for gardeners to gain control and autonomy over their lives, even if only momentarily.

Before leaving Alma's house, she loaded my pockets with cucumbers, summer squash, jalapeño and habanero chilies, and white peaches. She wanted to introduce me to her neighbor, Rosa, who grew several crops not commonly found here in the United States including *capulines* (or Mexican chokecherry; in Nahuatl, *Capolcuahuitl*), which is a relative of sweet cherries found in the United States, and Mexican plums, a wild plum found in northern Mexico and extending into central United States. As I walked with Alma to Rosa's home, she introduced me to several children playing soccer in the street, to neighbors in their yards, and to a couple who drove by. Alma has a reputation for knowing everyone and everything. She has a desire to share, help, and do what she can for her neighbors, even as she is struggling to get by herself.

Once at Rosa's home, Alma led me through a side entry gate where she introduced me to Rosa, who was weeding her plants in the far corner of her garden. When I asked about her garden, Rosa explained how she often traveled with seeds to and from Mexico. Over a decade ago she brought plum and corn seeds from her rural home in the Mexican state of Durango and remembered how her father cared for his crops. Rosa was simply revisiting the knowledge her father shared with her and modifying it to fit the environmental and social conditions of the South Bay. However, she stressed, "El éxito de esta jardín se deba a Alma" (The success of this garden is because of Alma). Alma excelled as a mentor, always willing to share her deep knowledge of growing food. As we left, Rosa gave me heirloom tomatoes, Mexican plums, capulines, and green figs. I visited four households that day, and while each home garden was different in terms of the crops grown and the spatial organization of the garden, the willingness to share the gift of food remained the same. Gardeners wanted to share their considerable knowledge of cultivation and their bountiful harvests.

My first trip to this community was a humbling experience. I walked in expecting to learn about how a home garden may help to reduce food insecurity and walked away with a different take on life. How is it that those with the least share the most? Each home I visited on that day was what sociologists call "low income." Several households were living well below the federal poverty level, and many individuals were undocumented. Yet, their willingness and desire to share remained constant. My initial reaction was that perhaps because of my own relatively privileged position as a visitor, gardeners wanted to share their harvests with me. It took me over four years of creating relationships with gardeners to learn that sharing is what gardeners do. As these acts become part of the social norms of a community, it binds them to

FIGURE 1 A typical La Mesa Verde home garden. Photo courtesy of the author.

their social relationships. It is both a strategy of resistance and a practice of cooperation, which encourages collective well-being and dignity. The stories of cultivating, cooking, eating, and sharing food in this book build off the rich history of food studies that explore how food and eating unify us and provide vivid examples of the material realities and cultural imaginaries that make up human life. This book is the result of over four years of participant observation, in-depth interviews, and garden conversations. And while it is informed by theory, it privileges the grounded knowledge and experiences of those involved. Without their open arms, hearts, gardens, and shared meals, this study would not have been possible.

Introduction

"The only way to know I'm human is to share"

Early one morning in the fall of 2014, I had a cup of coffee with Oscar, a thirty-four-year-old Latinx single father. His hands were rough and callused. He wore a long-sleeved flannel shirt, blue jeans, and thick boots. He pulled up in a white Ford F-150 with tools neatly lining the bed of the truck and explained to me how his grandfather had taught him how to farm. "I love the smell of wet soil," he told me with a smile, "it reminds me of him." The memory of Oscar's grandfather lives on in his garden and in his actions. "I know he would want me to continue his legacy and teach his great-granddaughter, my daughter, how to garden," he said. Cultivating the land, or tilth, is more than just something Oscar does; it is part of who he is. He attends agroecology classes, but much of what he knows about gardening he had already learned from his grandfather.[1]

The aspects of intergenerational learning and teaching are critical components to the strength of the home garden networks in this book. Oscar is a landscaper by trade, and as I have heard from countless gardeners, "He truly has a green thumb." The hours he works as a landscaper are long, and sometimes extend into the weekend, but he always finds time for the garden. "I don't like counting on the government for anything," he told me. "If I can do it myself, I will," he finished. Oscar explained to me his neighborhood and how he knew there were gangs and drugs around, but he always felt safe. Os-

---

1. *Agroecology* in this books refers to a holistic and integrated approach to farming and food systems (also see Silici 2014; Rosset and Altieri 2017).

car described his community as an assemblage of gardeners and gardens that produce food and security. Almost all of his neighbors had home gardens. "Everyone in my neighborhood grows different things, and when we can, we share. We're all just trying to survive." Oscar reveals a complex garden subjectivity that is held together through relational accountability because he understands that gardening is reliant on a variety of social and ecological relationships: "Growing food doesn't complicate things, it simplifies them. It's the small things that matter... you know, water, sun, soil, space, community, [and] life." The so-called "small things" Oscar refers to are by no means small. By caring for the land, the community, and the self, Oscar's worldview aligns closely with an ethic of care because he, and others in this book, recognize themselves as always interdependent beings.

Joan Tronto explains that an "ethic of care is an approach to personal, social, moral, and political life that starts from the reality that all human beings need and receive care and give care to others" (2009). It is by caring for others and the relationships that caring creates that make us human (Tronto 1993, 2012; Robinson 2011; Held 2006; Gilligan 1982). By sharing to survive, Oscar and his community recognize the strength of mutual interdependence. Oscar laughed as he described the most unlikely of gardeners—the twenty-something-year-old bachelors, the gangsters, the children, the single moms, and even the elderly. "You ever see a *vato* [homeboy] garden? It's a beautiful thing," he said with a smile. Oscar painted a mosaic of diversity that was connected through food and the stubbornly fierce, form-giving fire of emancipated labor. Gardening requires labor, and in the process of laboring, gardening creates a sense of autonomy that encourages home gardeners to live life on their own terms.

One evening after an interview with Oscar, I walked through his neighborhood toward my car. It was a warm September evening around eight. I expected the streets to be quiet and empty, but they were full of people walking and conversing with friends and neighbors. Kids on bikes teased each other as they raced down the road. Ranchero music blared from house to house, dogs barked, and the warm smell of roasted chilies and *barbacoa* permeated the air. As I turned the corner toward my car, I paused for a moment as a rooster crossed the street. I could have just as easily have been in rural Mexico, but this was downtown San José, California. This community is what James C. Scott (1998) referred to as a "thick" neighborhood because it is a place where people wanted to be, a place where people can make and partake in life together.

Later that week, I met with Oscar, and I asked him about the community. I was interested in the role food played in what I witnessed. He explained to me that growing food promoted self-sufficiency not just based on food production but because it helped to facilitate trust, and what I took to imply conviviality. "The only way to know I'm a real human is to share," he told me. My conversations with Oscar have led me to believe that the value of food is the agency embedded within it. In other words, food, as explained by Judith Farquhar (2006), allows us to collapse the structure/agency dilemma proposed by Anthony Giddens (1979) decades ago. We do make choices to eat what we do, and social structures do limit those choices depending on a variety of social, cultural, and economic factors, but as Farquhar insists, "maybe eating is not all about us" (2006, 155). The cultivation, preparation, consumption, and enjoyment of food make up the material realities in which human and nonhuman actors live out their daily lives. While we may not have complete control of everything around us, we can choose to live in ways that remind us how to be better humans and inhabit a world that is more just and joyful. Life may not always be pretty or easy, but depending on how we choose to live, it can be rewarding.

Food Value(s)

The material conditions of many low-income families force them to make decisions that are sometimes contradictory. In recent years there has been increased national attention on the prevalence of food deserts in low-income communities across the United States. Yet, coinciding with the raised awareness of food deserts, which is any neighborhood or community where a substantial number of residents have low access to healthy, fresh, and culturally appropriate food, is the rise of chronic, noncommunicable, diet-related illnesses like diabetes, obesity, and cardiovascular disease. These two seemingly oppositional forms present poor black and brown folks as both starving of hunger and dying of obesity, but the reality is far more perplexing (Patel 2007). As explained by Alisha Gálvez, "diet-related illness is different from other kinds of public health concerns in that its etiology—the way people understand the pathways for becoming sick—is rooted in personal behavior"

(2018, 5). In other words, the food choices people are able to make, which are reflective of the material conditions in which they live, matters.

Food is something all life depends on, but how one goes about acquiring and consuming that food is determined by a variety of social, biological, cultural, geographic, political, and economic conditions. Oscar's comments on how growing and sharing food are part of everyday practices for survival are great examples of this. These internal debates permeate every aspect of daily life for food-insecure people, where members of this precarious social group must find and create innovative ways to feed themselves by negotiating life at the margins. Their multiple, shifting, and often overlapping ethnic, gender, citizenship, age, linguistic, and socioeconomic identities are just a few of the variety of social categories and processes discussed in this book. Yet, the main theoretical thread that weaves itself throughout the book is the role food, and more specifically, *comida*, plays in how, and for whom, value is produced.

My argument is simple. The current neoliberal food system has the tendency to separate people from their very means of production. This process is damaging to our environments, our communities, and our bodies. This book details how displaced, marginalized, and oppressed peoples, those most impacted by the damaging effect of our food system, engage in the practices of growing and sharing food to envision and continuously work to enact alternative food systems that connect people to their food and communities. In the process of growing food, home gardeners work to transform society by transforming their means of production. Home gardeners grow food for various reasons, but central to all of their motivations is the objective to move from alienation to autonomy. Home gardens do more than produce food, they produce a variety of social relationships that contribute to both social and ecological resilience. In other words, at the heart of these home gardens in not just production but *reproduction*. Home gardens allow gardeners to engage in and define their own practices and process of reproduction through cultivation.

This book explores food values through a variety of social, cultural, economic, political, and nutritional contexts, but always with an analysis of social reproduction and the processes of alienation. To avoid confusion between the full range of terms; allotment gardens, dooryard gardens, kitchen gardens, house gardens, I use the concept of home gardens to represent "small-scale agroecosystems managed by individuals and households on private land, where households reside" (Egerer and Cohan 2021, 5). I argue that home gardeners reorganize reproductive work through both discursive and subversive practices that counter processes of alienation and remind them, and us, how to be human again. As Silvia Federici (2009, 2012, 2018) reminds us, the capacity to control our own reproduction is continuously under threat by global capitalism because capitalism "keeps us constantly on the move, separating us from our countries, farms, gardens, homes, and workplaces . . . [which] guarantees cheap wages, communal disorganization, and a maximum vulnerability in front of the law, the courts, and the police" (Federici 2018, 29). This book explores the various ways people use home gardens to literally root themselves, regain control over their means of production, re-envision communal organization, and move beyond the divisive logic of neoliberal capitalism by growing and sharing food.

At the core of this book is a quest to understand how and why people in the most precarious of circumstances grow and share food. This book contributes to the vast literature of scholars who seek to better understand how a labor theory of value may offer critical insight into how society is organized by providing hope for how we may transform society in more

FIGURE 2 Harvest. Photo courtesy of the author.

just and sustainable ways. Under capitalism, workers always produce more than what they receive, and this surplus becomes surplus value—the bedrock of capitalism. In this book, a labor theory of value understands this relationship (those who produce surplus value and those who accumulate surplus value) produces structures of inequality. These structures do more than create divisions between those who control the means of production (the tools and materials to produce value) and those who succumb to the means of production (those who work for a wage). It also draws a line in the sand between those who control the means of reproduction and those who do not. "Reproduction does not only concern our material needs—such as housing, food preparation, the origination of space, childrearing, sex, and procreation. An important aspect of it is the reproduction of our collective memory and the cultural symbols that give meaning to our life and nourish our struggles" (Federici 2018, 5). Perhaps there is no better place to see how these antagonisms play out than in the food we eat.

The food system has the profound ability to divorce us from how our food is grown, produced, and cooked, but as the people in this book so vividly portray, a homegrown food system can do just the opposite. In what follows, I present some key insights into the theories of value made by social scientists and then apply them to the context of urban agriculture, home gardens, and food. Discussions of "value" are often contentious, and this is not an exhaustive list; rather, I focus the key contributions that help to explain the lived realities and conditions of home gardeners in this book. While there has been a considerable amount of research done on community gardens, urban agriculture, and alternative food systems, there has been very little attention paid to home gardens and home gardening, especially within the context of the United States. The stories, narratives, and examples from this book provide the reader access to the often-unacknowledged spaces of private homes where home gardeners make sense of their lives by growing, sharing, and consuming food. These stories also provide insight into different ways value is called into being.

The Emergence of Convivial Labor

It has been said that Karl Marx can be read through a variety of lenses: as an economist (Rubin 2020), ecologist (Foster, Clark, and York 2010), humanist (Gramsci 1992), or revolutionary (Negri 1991). His work provides excellent insight into the dynamic relationships between production and reproduction presented in this study. And while Marx's and others' theories of value are articulated throughout this book, I am particularly interested in Marx's theory of alienation. Marx insisted that what distinguishes humans from nonhumans is our "species-being," or how we consciously and freely transform our world around us to better accommodate our needs. Marx, like the classical economists Adam Smith and David Ricardo before him, understood labor as the basis of what gives meaning, or value, to a community or society. Smith and Ricardo focused on labor because they believed it could tell them something about the prices of things. For classical economists, the value of any commodity is measured by the average number of labor hours necessary to produce it. That is, the amount of labor that goes into producing something is the source of its value. Marx, on the other hand, was interested in labor because he believed that how a society's labor was organized could tell us something about how power was also organized within that society.

My interest in labor is similar to autonomous Marxists who argue for a refusal of work. Yet, "the refusal of work does not mean the erasure of activity, but the valorization of human activity which have escaped from labor's domination" (Berardi 2009, 60). I refer to this type of labor as "convivial labor" because it occurs in the home gardens in this book as acts of celebration and resistance. My use of "convivial" builds of the work of Ivan Illich's *Tools for Conviviality*. Illich insists that common people need to take control of the tools and processes of production that shape their lives. In other words, people need more than the ability to obtain "things," they need the ability to create them. Illich explains that "the degree that he masters his tools, he can invest the world with his meaning, to the degree that he is mastered by his tools, the shape of the tool determines his own self-image" (2009a, 21). Central to my use of conviviality throughout the book is how people in the most unlikely of places use labor to create escapes from the oppressive nature of industrial capitalism.

Labor, in these instances, becomes what Antonio Negri (1991) and Harry Cleaver (1992) call self-valorizing. Within a capitalist system, labor is disciplined to valorize capital and increase the value of a commodity. Whereas labor that occurs outside a capitalist system is liberated from capital and valorizes those who practice it. In other words, self-valorizing labor is labor's escape from the clutches of capitalism and fulfills our species-being. As articulated by Bruno Gullì (2005), labor in these instances is not productive or unproduced but creative. It is an ontological reality, not a logical abstraction.

Throughout the book, I refer to labor as life's "form-giving fire" (Marx 1993, 361), because like Marx, I believe that labor can and should be liberating. However, work in our current economic model has the tendency to alienate workers from themselves, each other, the products they produce, and the very act of labor itself. "This is what essentially happens: the more the wage earner's energy is invested in productive activity, the more s/he reinforced the power of the enemy, of capital, and the less is left for oneself. In order to survive, in order to receive a wage, workers have to renounce their humanity, the human investment of their time and energies" (Berardi 2009, 37). Our souls, argues Berardi, have hardened because the conditions of work have changed. The industrial factory of the past that was ruled by the clock was only concerned about the body, whereas today's immaterial factory made up of digital capitalism seeks to depersonalize time by commodifying every aspect of affective and cognitive work.

These conditions do not escape home gardeners in the book. In fact, in Anna Tsing's words, labor in home gardens remains "haunted" by labor's historical legacy of alienation (Tsing 2015, 78). How, and for whom, value is produced in home gardens provide glimpses into how and why growing and sharing food enables home gardeners to invent and reinvent what it means to be human. From an anthropological standpoint, the theory of value helps us see how different people in different places and times have come to rationalize what is beautiful, worthwhile, and essential. Value is always a social phenomenon because it is created within a social context, and the value of something changes as the social environment also changes. Louis Dumont furthers the work of anthropologists who study value by exploring how human judgments of value within social systems are either holistic or individualist. That is, "either value attaches to the whole in relation to its parts" or "value attaches to the individual" (1980, 233). Another way of thinking about this through the lens of home gardens in this book is whether these value systems transform conceptions of personhood in which the social skin is stretched to "incorporate" other beings as part of the self through the "common substance" of the gift.

While the work of Dumont has furthered the thinking about social change and the role of cultural relativism in the creation of value, the work of Christopher Gregory (1997) sheds light on the role of the state in constructing and upholding a uniform standard of value. Values, insists Gregory, are the visible and invisible chains that connect people to things, but this does not happen outside of an already constructed value system. In fact, alternative values, those not pre-subscribed to the uniform standard, exist in opposition to the hegemonic values in a given society. Therefore, if value is vital for understanding a given society, then understanding "the power by which, from which, through which, and on account of which value exists" (1997, 15) remains paramount because people who hold alternative or counter-hegemonic values also often experience oppression and marginalization. Alternative values are not merely built through class consciousness (as Marx might insist) or through individual cognition (as the free market would have us believe) but also through reciprocal recognition with others. As the stories in this book reveal, home gardens shape and reshape value through the collective actions of growing, sharing, and eating food.

In a similar vein, David Graeber insists that how a culture interprets the value of something ultimately makes up the context and norms of that society. He suggests that value creates social norms because "everyone tends to lose track of the way their own actions contribute to reproducing and reshaping themselves and their social contexts" (2001, 258). The dominant social determination of the meaning of value helps to construct the foundation of societal norms. That means what we perceive as value and what we do with value can be liberating, because it can be counter-hegemonic and liberating. It can also be constraining because it may obscure and mystify the construction of value via commodity fetishism. In many ways, it is difficult for home gardens to overcome this relationship. When gardeners share things such as heirloom seeds passed from family to family, the value of growing those seeds can be counter-hegemonic because its value is no longer found in the material value of the seed, or perhaps even in the materiality of the seed. The value resides in the seeds' ability to contribute to the social reproduction of the community. Sharing has long been a feature of human societies because sharing ensures survival, as we are social creatures. Sharing predates most economic systems, but in the current system of privatized agriculture, carrying out acts of sharing de-linked from industrial capitalism are transformative.

Graeber, like Marx before him, recognizes the creative potential of labor to transform value through human action. Marx explains "labor as a liberating activity" (1993, 611) because value does not exist on its own but is called into being by the human potential to transform it, which is a political struggle rather than some universal and deterministic iron law of economics at the end of history. Labor is a necessary human activity that defines human history. However, environmental anthropologists might argue that this happens in a manner that is never de-linked from the interactive reality of shifting relations to the natural conditions of existence at a given point in time and space (Crumley 1994; Merchant 1989). Marx referred to labor as the "living, form-giving fire" (1993, 361) because the "world is nothing but the making and the having been made of labor" (Gullì 2005, 6). By sharing to survive, Oscar recognizes the ontology of labor, in which "labor is being" (Gullì 2005, 23). The labor that takes place in the home gardens in his community occurs to survive and are "neither-productive-nor-unproductive, but creative" (Gullì 2005, 61).

To situate the creative potential of labor into this discussion of value, it might be best to explore how home gardening encourages convivial labor. Convivial labor is the collective and celebratory process of growing, sharing, preparing, and eating food as an act of liberation (Valle 2017). Convivial labor does not disregard the violent reality of work for many food-chain workers (e.g., Carney 2015; Holmes 2013; Barndt 2008; Schlosser 2001) because many gardeners who engage in convivial labor in this book are also associated with life as food-chain workers. Instead, my goal is to celebrate acts of gardening, cooking, and eating as potentially emancipatory, although, as this book details, I am also well aware of its limitations. In the similar way that Meredith Abarca (2006) uncovers how *charlas culinarias*, or culinary chats, allow Mexican and Mexican American women to reclaim the kitchen as a site of agency and self-determination as they balance the historical legacy in which the kitchen has been projected as a site of oppression and liberation (Meah 2014), convivial labor reclaims the agency of labor, and its "form-giving fire," as it navigates the terrain between oppression and liberation (Gullì 2005).

The Context of Urban Agriculture Studies

An early study of urban agriculture conducted by Donna Armstrong (2000) found that urban agricultural projects promote community development and healthy lifestyle choices. She concluded that the common reason participants value urban agriculture is to experience its health benefits through access to fresh foods and being outside. Building on this, Saldivar-Tanaka and Krasny (2004) acknowledge that while urban agriculture projects are locations of food production, they are places of social reproduction because they serve as social and cultural gathering places where people share and create common values. Yet, sites of urban agriculture are not to be romanticized because they are always contested spaces as cities negotiate the competition between land and housing (Schmelzkopf 1995). As the world becomes more urbanized, the value of these spaces becomes more complex and contentious.

People are innovative and resourceful, so it should come to no surprise that people value space differently depending on their context. The garden setting allows for a critical lens to see how value emerges and transforms through the reciprocal recognition of growing, cooking, sharing, and eating food together. It was Thomas Lyson (2004) who introduced the concept of "civic agriculture" to the mainstream. He argued that a local place-based agricultural system has the potential to cultivate civic engagement through agricultural exchanges of growing, buying, and selling local foods. He insisted that civic agriculture is a flexible organizational form with a built-in "problem-solving capacity" (Lyson 2004, 63) because of the many ways civic agriculture can contribute to a region's social, economic, and environmental well-being. In the context of San José, California, the setting for this book, most studies of urban agriculture show that households that grow food increase their intake of fruits and vegetables generate substantial cost savings and enjoy the community benefits of added green space (Algert et al. 2016; Algert, Baameur, and Renvall 2014). These studies also seek to understand the potential of scaling up urban agriculture as a regional social movement (Gray et al. 2014).

Studies on urban agriculture and alternative food networks tend to fall into two camps—those who explore the progressive components of urban agriculture and insist it can restructure the agri-food system and capitalism all at the same time (Milbourne 2012; Travaline and Hunold 2010; Blay-Palmer and Donald 2006) and those who believe that urban agriculture is embedded within neoliberal forces that further subject the gardener or farmer to the exploitation of capitalism (Alkon and Mares 2012; Holt-Giménez and Wang 2011; Guthman 2011; Pudup 2008). While there are nuances between the camps, Nathan McClintock (2014) insists that such a frame invokes a false dualism and provides simplistic answers. Urban agriculture is messy because it has to be, and the contradictions associated with urban agriculture are inherent and internal to a given location. McClintock (2014) and others have shown that there is no one-size-fits-all approach to urban agriculture, and merely focusing upon urban agriculture's contradictions may actually undermine its transformative potential. As Lucy Jarosz contends, alternative food networks are "constituted out of multiple, contradictory processes and relations" (2008, 232) because such networks are always situated in specific places and times and informed by the contradictory processes inherent in capitalism (O'Connor 1991). This book is informed by that same contradictory process whereby "capitalism both creates opportunities for urban agriculture and imposes obstacles to its expansion" (McClintock 2014, 157).

This book is not alone in this regard, as there have been many recent studies that have sought a more nuanced understanding of how urban agriculture is both accepting and challenging of neoliberal logics (Ernwein 2017; McClintock 2014; Eizenberg 2012). Where this book diverges from previous studies lies in its attempt to come to terms with the way value (both use-value and exchange-value) intersect human subjectivity and what growing food has to do with it. All of this means that growing food is always about more than growing food.

The values of mental health (Broadway 2009; Armstrong 2000; Brown and Jameton 2000), or community development (Travaline and Hunold 2010; Blair, Giesecke, and Sherman 1991), or ecological literacy (Brown and Miller 2008; Holland 2004; Doyle and Krasny 2003) produced in the garden cannot be reduced to one or the other, because just as Marx, Graeber, and Lyson articulate, gardening and life are defined by human activity—a human activity that can be both liberating and disciplining. "As we organize our bodies, as living beings," insists Jeffery Baldwin, "we also work to organize the flows of matters which we value and add value to" (2016, 15). Baldwin imagines a paradigm shift that understands life, labor, and value in garden projects to reject the logic of exploitation, which "occurs when more value is taken than is returned" (2016, 17). He embraces cooperation, which often produces "more value than is consumed" (Baldwin 2016, 17). He calls these moments "affective food ecologies" (also see Barbiero 2014) where value is the result of "lively labor," similar to what I call "convivial labor." This shift can undo the logic of scarcity in favor of vitality and resilience. Still, it begins by thinking and acting differently about how we grow, prepare, share, and consume our foods. This book builds off these studies to better understand how the processes and practices of growing, preparing, consuming, and sharing food restore dignity, encourage autonomy, and reclaim the process of social reproduction so that gardeners can (re)learn to be human again.

A Critical Environmental Justice Studies Approach to the Study of Home Gardens

The environmental justice movement arose in the latter part of the twentieth century in response to the deterioration of the conditions of everyday life in communities of color (Pellow and Brulle 2005). Because of this, most early environmental justice cases focused on distributive justice, or the just allocation of environmental benefits and burdens (Kuehn 2000). In the 1980s and 1990s, three in five African Americans and/or Latinos lived near a hazardous waste site (United Christ Church 1987). By 2005, the conditions many minorities faced in the United States remained mostly the same (Bullard et al. 2007). Environmental justice studies demonstrate that the location of communities of color and the location of hazardous waste sites are linked (Brisman 2008; Holifield 2001; Gottlieb 1994; Bullard 1990).

Furthermore, these studies suggest an institutionalized pattern of inequality that persists in cities and towns across the country. This phenomenon became known as "environmental racism," which "refers to any policy, practice, or directive that differentially affects or disadvantages (whether intended or unintended) individuals, groups, or communities based on race or color" (Bullard 1993, 23). Contaminated land, and the people who inhabit that land, are considered "sacrifice zones" (Lerner 2010), and the people, land, and livelihoods are deemed expendable.

While environmental justice issues gained notoriety in the 1980s through the 2000s, the environmental justice movement splintered from mainstream environmentalism (Pezzullo and Sandler 2007). While the movements had both different and overlapping interests, the major distinction between the movements focused on how racism in environmental degradation was experienced by the urban working poor (Pellow and Park 2002; Chavez 1993; Fox 1991; Robinson 1991), on the one hand, and how large environmental issues such as climate change, global deforestation, and species extinction took precedence by mainstream environmental groups like the Sierra Club, the National Audubon Society, and the Wilderness Society, on the other (Peña 2005). As Randy Ontiveros explains, "The late 1960s was a crossroads moment when progressive activists could have linked ecological devastation to social justice as part of a coordinated campaign for a more livable, less profit-obsessed world. Some did, but not enough" (2014, 90).

For many communities of color, the struggle for environmental justice has been an ongoing struggle since the time of "contact" (Gilio-Whitaker 2019; LaDuke 2005). This is because environmental inequality is not merely the result of racist people but because racism is embedded in environmental policy (Pulido 1996) and conservation strategies (Dowie 2009). From the birth of settler colonialism (Whyte 2018) to the Treaty of Guadalupe Hidalgo (Almaguer 1994), as expansive as fishing rights (Norgaard, Reed, and Van Horn 2011), and as institutionalized as the ways certain schoolchildren experience the disproportionate burden of environmental hazards (Pastor, Morello-Frosch, and Sadd 2006), environmental policy is riddled with racial inequality. The problem, insists Pulido (1996), is that the environmental privilege many white people possess is so ingrained into society that they cannot see it (also see Park and Pellow 2011). Policies that appear to be fair and equal come across as natural for one group, but those same laws, policies, and ordinances can reinforce inequality and the subordinate status for many non-white communities. Much of the problem lies within a judicial system that purports to enforced blind justice. Yet, the manner in which the laws and regulations are applied have a disproportionally unequal impact on communities of color.

Building off this rich history, environmental justice in this book pertains to "any local response to a threat against community health" (Agyeman 2005). As previously noted, most early struggles for environmental justice focused attention on *distributive* justice (e.g., Mohai and Bryant 1992) because environmental justice movements build their base by framing "justice" in ways that mobilize impacted communities (Čapek 1993). Such "bottom-up" or "grassroots" movements articulate their struggle by reclaiming the rights that our social institutions have neglected to provide. Other environmental justice advocates have framed their movements based on *corrective* justice (e.g., Zimmerman 1994; Lavelle and Coyle 1992), and others have sought *procedural* justice (e.g., Lazarus 1993). In most cases, these movements address justice from a particular class-based or race-based position by arguing their disproportionate share of environmental risk is a result of their race or social class. This book takes a turn from that tradition by focusing on how people pursue dignity and autonomy by growing, sharing, and consuming food.

The people in this book are not seeking the "Trojan horse" of universal human rights, because what they are seeking extends beyond rights and can only be explained as the relentless and endless pursuit of dignity for life.² Similar to the work of David Pellow (2018), I believe traditional approaches in which environmental justice has sought "rights" have importance. Still, I think they are inadequate to address the complexity of issues confronting us today. In this book, justice refers to "a more respectful and egalitarian relationship with human beings to one another and to the greater more-than-human world" (Pellow 2016, 13). This lens deepens the understanding of home gardeners as interdependent beings tied up in webs of social relationships and allows us to move beyond a rights-based approach to a form of environmental justice that validates the everyday lives of human and nonhuman agents. The proceeding chapters highlight how home gardeners grow food in ways that validate their everyday lives because their practices allow them a means to control their social reproduction.

This book engages with what Wald et al. (2019) call "Latinx environmentalisms" to refer to the dynamic, multiple, evolving, and non-binary ways in which Latinx, Chicanx, Mexican, and Mesoamerican people experience and relate to the natural world. While not everyone in the book identifies as Latinx, I use the term throughout as "a placeholder that acknowledge forms of indigenous knowledge and practice that colonization attempted to eradicate" (Wald et al. 2019, 23). And while it is true that we may never fully recover all the knowledge lost during centuries of colonization, the "x" serves as a reminder that "Eurocentric epistemologies . . . are not the only ways of knowing the world" (Wald et al. 2019, 23).

Incorporated into the book are the four pillars of critical environmental justice studies (Pellow 2018), which allows us to come to terms with how home gardeners validate their everyday lives through the practices of growing, sharing, and consuming food. The first pillar pays close attention to the multiple forms of inequality experienced in the community, which allows greater insight into various social categories of difference at work. Many of the people in this book are recent immigrants from Mexico and Central America. Many others identify as white, African American, Chinese, Filipina/o, Latinx, and Chicana/o. There are women, men, and transgender folks

---

2. Gustavo Esteva and Madhu Suri Prakash call the universal human rights approach to social justice a "Trojan horse" because such an approach to equality assumes the universalizing truths of juridical power within the modern Western nation-state to uphold rights. This systematically denies the autonomy and "pluralversality" of juridical order in Indigenous communities (1998, 110–51).

who have United States citizenship, and others who do not. They range in ages from people in their eighties to others in their twenties and includes individuals who are retired on fixed incomes, and others who have one, two, or three kids and no job or multiple jobs. The positionality of each home gardener exemplifies the multiple and often overlapping forms of oppression they face on a daily basis.

The second pillar includes a multiscalar analysis of how people make use of home gardens to address critical issues and injustices. The role of scale in this book consists of a critical understanding of both its spatial and temporal dimensions—from the molecular (e.g., diet-related illnesses like diabetes), to the community (e.g., the prevalence of food deserts in communities of color), to the global (e.g., continual epistemological violence or erasure of traditional knowledge) and back again. The multiscalar approach of this book helps to illustrate how gardens at the margins make sense of the complex spatial and temporal causes, consequences, and possible solutions to the conditions they face. Throughout the book, I refer to the possible solutions as "escapes" because these escapes are ways in which different actors enact their gardens to create spaces to heal despite the many contradictions those escapes may create.

Key actors in the healing of communities are nonprofit or nongovernmental organizations (NGOs), and they frequently find themselves in communities like those in this book. Their goal is often to empower low-income and disenfranchised communities to take control of their own lives and communities. Yet, these good intentions can have unintended consequences. The third pillar of critical environmental justice studies this book explores is how racism (and speciesism) are deeply ingrained in society and often reinforced by state power. The very structure of society has the potential to be an obstacle to achieving environmental justice. Home gardeners use their marginality as a creative force to re-envision the state and to capture moments of autonomy through postcapitalist arrangements (Gibson-Graham 2006). They learn to negotiate the pros and cons of using state-sponsored interventions through practices of epistemic disobedience, which as Walter Mignolo explains, is a practice "de-linking from the magic of the Western idea of modernity, ideals of humanity and promises of economic growth and financial prosperity" (2009, 3).

As I noted earlier, several environmental justice studies have brought to light how low-income communities and communities of color inhabit "sacrifice zones," or places "where hundreds of thousands of [low-income] residents are exposed to disproportionately elevated levels of hazardous chemicals" (Lerner 2010, 2; also see Hedges and Sacco 2012). This coincides with recent scholarship that shows how communities and environments incurred risk in ways that illustrate their "dispensability" (Jalbert et al. 2017; Gómez-Barris 2017), but the fourth pillar of the critical environmental justice flips that logic to insist that these communities are in fact indispensable. From this frame, "indispensability demands dramatic change but does so from the perspective that all members of society and socioecological systems have something to contribute to the process and to our collective futures" (Pellow 2018, 27). The home gardeners in this study come from a variety of social positions, and their desire and willingness to grow and share food is a unifying practice that ensures all members of the community are indispensable because everyone and everything contributes something to the collective whole. Their strength is their common interests.

Situating the Valley

Humans rely on the function of healthy ecosystems for fresh water, clean air, and nutritious food for survival, and thus, we share a natural synergy or metabolic interaction with our environments. In this book, history is a series of "shifts and rifts" (Clark and York 2008) that explain how capital shifts around the ecological problems it creates and, in the process, creates rifts or disruptions in the metabolic interactions between humans and their natural environments. This is a history of violence and healing. As capitalism shifts geographically and in modes of production, the rifts, and in some cases, ruins (Hedges and Sacco 2012), created in its wake can be catastrophic. But that is not the end of the story because people actively work to heal their environments, communities, and themselves in innovative ways.

Located forty-five miles south of San Francisco, the Santa Clara Valley is surrounded by the Santa Cruz Mountains to the west and the Diablo Mountains to the east. Summer temperatures range from the mid-eighties to the upper fifties, and winter temperatures range from low sixties to the low forties. The average year will see over three hundred days of sun and a year-round growing season. Most of the fieldwork in this book took place in the communities of San José. Most of my time was spent in the communities of Washington and Alma, which I refer to throughout the book as Washington-

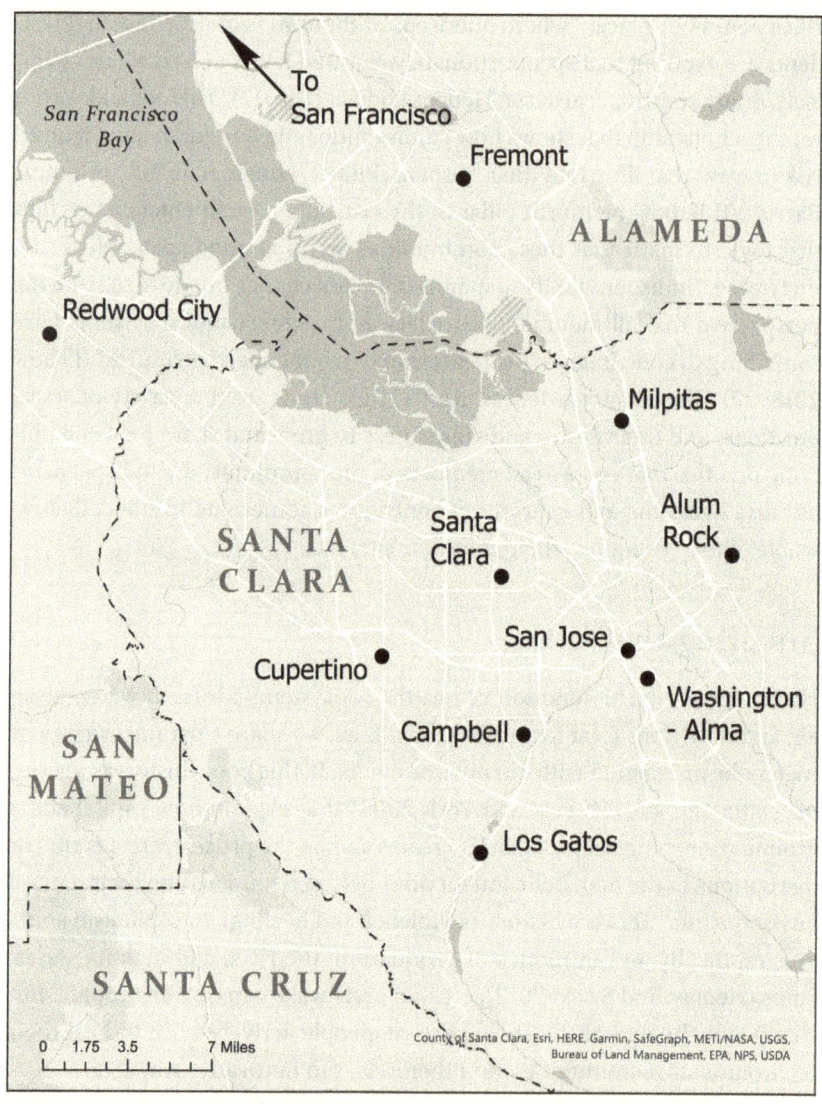

MAP 1 Santa Clara Valley. Courtesy of David Reis.

Alma because that is how the community referred to it. However, I also visited the communities of Campbell, Willow Glen, Spartan Keys, Japantown, Mayfair, downtown San José, and North San José, among others.

The irony of this story is that before the Santa Clara Valley became known as the "Silicon Valley," John Muir called it the "valley of your heart's delight."

Muir believed the valley possessed the richest soil, clearest water, brightest blue sky, and best well-tempered sun anywhere in California. Throughout the book, I play with the overlapping and diverging histories and geographies of the Santa Clara Valley and Silicon Valley. Similar to the work of Carolyn Merchant (1989), this book helps to explain the ecological revolutions, or the "processes through which different societies change their relationship to nature" (Merchant 1989, 273), of the region by bringing to light "how different ways of interacting with nature correspond to different types of societies" (Barca 2016, 133).

"Silicon Valley" is a name that evokes idealized, even romantic notions of a postindustrial city where the best engineers from around the world gather: A place where the palm tree–lined campuses of Google, Apple, Cisco, and Facebook form part of the American imaginary. The Silicon Valley is often presumed to be a post-racial paradise where anyone can be anything, but it is more of an imaginary than it is an actual place—a heterotopia not fixed to space but existing in the minds of the privileged few who have access to it (Ong 2006). This study takes place in the Santa Clara Valley and in Silicon Valley because home gardeners regularly navigate between both worlds. These two "spaces" are the same distinct geographical location, but they inhabit two separate material realities. Unlike the Silicon Valley, which has engineered its environmental and social relationships with its palm tree–lined streets and highly manicured corporate campus, the Santa Clara Valley is guided by the natural rhythms of the growing season and to the coevolution of people and places. This goes without saying that the hegemonic force of the Silicon Valley often continues to threaten the agricultural livelihoods of its residents by imposing economic and social systems that simultaneously produce extreme wealth and extreme poverty.

The latest data from the United States Census Bureau show the largest Santa Clara County racial/ethnic groups are Asian (39 percent) followed by white (30.6 percent) and Hispanic or Latino (25 percent).[3] Two-thirds the county's residents identify as "non-white," and according to Santa Clara County's "Existing Health Conditions Report," these same residents who identify as "non-white" or "Hispanic" are defined as a "vulnerable population" (2013, 2–10). The county's statistical maps of income, education, crime,

---

3. Census data provided from the U.S. Census Bureau and available for more detail: https://www.census.gov/quickfacts/santaclaracountycalifornia.

obesity, ethnicity, and diabetes show that the same area codes with high diabetes and obesity rates are the locations with lower incomes and education levels. These areas are predominately Latinx and have the highest levels of reported crime in the county. The detailed study of health trends of Santa Clara County demonstrates that the location of the city one resides is strongly correlated with economic mobility, educational attainment, and the probability of being obese and developing diabetes. This report emphasizes the political economy of health in the region by calling attention to the correlation between adverse health outcomes and its relationship to race, income, education, and geographical location.

In an ideal world, one could safely assume that the temperate weather and natural landscape of Santa Clara County would encourage most people to engage in outdoor physical activity. With close proximity to the Pacific Ocean and the Santa Cruz Mountains and an abundance of sunny days, there are endless opportunities for people to lead active lifestyles that are associated with improved health outcomes. Yet, we know that the "calorie-in and calorie-out" approach to health determinants is seldom played out in the living and working conditions faced by overworked members of the working classes (Ludwig and Friedman 2014). A focus on physical activity, especially as an amenity mostly afforded by people from the professional-managerial classes, distances the discussion of health equities away from the structural conditions that result in unhealthy outcomes and imposes the burden for a healthy lifestyle solely on individual willpower and choice (Otero 2018; Guthman 2011). For many working-class people in Santa Clara County, there are numerous compounding structural factors like racially segregated labor markets, and associated income inequality, that prohibit such positive environmental interactions and an extremely high cost of living.

Lisa Park and David Pellow (2011) refer to this condition as "environmental privilege." While much of the environmental justice scholarship focuses on environmental injustices shaped by the politics of race, class, gender, and citizenship, fewer studies address the "privileges" that other groups may have (also see Pulido 2000). Environmental privilege is an expression of "economic, political, and cultural power that some groups enjoy, which enables them exclusive access to coveted environmental amenities such as forests, parks, mountains, rivers, coastal property, open lands, and elite neighborhoods" (Park and Pellow 2011, 4). Environmental privilege is experienced in towns and cities around the world. Access to parks and green space, or the ability to go skiing or to the beach, are linked to the same structural conditions that limit access to medical care and health benefits. In fact, "for nearly every measure of health, affluent residents in Santa Clara County tend to be healthier than residents at or near poverty levels, and white populations have better health outcomes than Latinos, African Americans, and Asian populations" (Community Health Existing Conditions Report 2013, 1–2). One could also argue that the ability to have "leisure time" to carry out such activities also plays a significant role. In the Santa Clara Valley, the social determinants of health are determined based upon social status, race, income, gender, and education.

In addition to the significant health disparities between various ethnicities and neighborhoods in the Santa Clara Valley, the report does not account for the Latina/o health paradox whereby recent immigrants arrive in good health and the advantages of which significantly decline the more time immigrant households spend in the United States and assimilate to mainstream food and physical activity patterns.[4] The report does acknowledge the "healthy migrant effect," which is similar to the Latina/o health paradox, but they do not have a mechanism to account for it. Furthermore, the findings demonstrate that citizenship is also a factor in determining health, with just over 15 percent of the non-citizens surveyed reported excellent health (Community Health Existing Conditions Report 2013 2–22), although how long an individual has lived in the country was not taken into consideration. The determinants for adverse health in Santa Clara "often disproportionately affect vulnerable populations such as young children, the poor, and the elderly" (Community Health Existing Conditions Report 2013 1–2). Still, this story helps to show, people in the most precarious of situations can and do find ways to improve their health and their communities in the humblest of fashions.

This is a story of edges, of how the margins become centers, and centers become margins through creative practices of imagining what lies beyond

---

4. The Latina/o or Hispanic Health Paradox was first identified by LeClere, Rogers, and Peters (1997) to explain how high concentrations of Hispanic populations living in the United States experience better health outcomes and enhanced mortality rates in spite of residential segregation and poverty. Eschbach et al. (2004) refer to this as a "barrio advantage," while Calvo and Esquibel (2016) insist that the advantage is a result of traditional foods and meals. However, as detailed by Gálvez (2018), those trends are beginning to shift in Mexico as highly processed cheap foods are displacing traditional foodways.

economic orthodoxy (Gibson-Graham, Cameron, and Healy 2013). It is the story of how displaced people from Mexico, Central America, and Southeast Asia, as well as those United States citizens who have become displaced through histories of colonialism and capitalist expansion, grow food to return to the place-based practices of living and being. These place-based and displaced peoples navigate the interstitial spaces between the Santa Clara and Silicon Valleys to escape and resist erasure and enclosure. As Anna Tsing reminds us, "precarity is the condition of our time" (2015, 20). This implies that a sense of "rootedness" may be a privilege often not afforded to recent immigrants who are often also low income. Still, it does not discourage home gardeners for seeking that sense of deep connection with the places they inhabit. The power of modernity weighs heavily on people, especially those it has left behind. The hegemonic force of the Silicon Valley homogenizes the ideologies and value systems of our landscapes and foodscapes through its pervasive but alluring lust for wealth and power (see Pitti 2003).

La Mesa Verde Home Gardeners

This study was conducted as part of a Participatory Action Research project with La Mesa Verde (LMV), an urban gardening program of Sacred Heart Community Services located in San José, California. Sacred Heart is a California Nonprofit Public Benefit Corporation that receives financial support by way of contributions in-kind, government grants (both as cash and food), private contributions, United Way donations, and endowment investments. LMV, which operates within the branch of the Economic and Family Self-Sufficiency, identifies itself as "a network of urban gardeners who create access to healthy food in San José." The program offers garden workshops, classes, and one-on-one mentorship from the University of California Master Gardener Program. Each growing season, participating families receive several starter plants and seeds for the season. The program was initially conceived to teach as many low-income residents as possible to learn how to grow food. Their goal was to lower food bills and improve community health, but as this book details, the initial structure of LMV tapped into preexisting forms of knowledge, norms, and values. More than a program that merely teaches low-income residents how to grow their own food, for the gardeners themselves, it is a valuable resource that allows them to improve their well-being by providing the ability to recapture their social reproduction.

When I began working with La Mesa Verde in the summer of 2012, the program only served a small number of families—about 150. At the time, the program was made up mainly of Spanish-speaking recent immigrants to the United States. However, today, the program consists of a very diverse, multiethnic, multilingual group of gardeners that spans nationalities and age groups. Most of this study was conducted within the city limits of San José. In 2012, this study focused on the community of Washington-Alma, the location of Sacred Heart Community Services, where the majority of participants still reside. Today, LMV continues to expand its reach into other low-income pockets of San José, such as Gateway East and Mayfair in East San José as well as Spartan Keys in the south. It also reaches into areas of North San José, Campbell, and parts of Willow Glen.

The continual demographic changes that typify La Mesa Verde can partly be explained by its growth and by its revolving door of gardeners and organizers. Since 2012, I have witnessed the program change directors, organizers, participants, and even strategic missions. Many who garden in the LMV community want to be a part of the program, but just like everyone else, they too are subjected to the unpredictability of modern life. The LMV community consists of recent and long-standing diaspora immigrants from Mexico, Guatemala, Dominican Republic, China, Vietnam, and the Philippines. It also includes U.S.-born Latinx, Chicanas/os, white Americans, African Americans, and Asian Americans. Some people are new to gardening and others who grew up working and living on a farm or garden. The LMV home gardeners in this book are what Mignolo refers to as "border thinkers" (2011b). They do not completely reject modernity, nor do they completely ascribe to its norms, values, and ways of thinking. It is within these interstitial spaces where LMV home gardeners cultivate alterNative epistemologies of resistance that emerge when the concepts of alterity and indigeneity converge to produce decentering and re-membering subjects (Peña 2017a). This diversity is what makes the community so challenging to define and what allows for its continual transformation.

Finding Common Ground: Notes on Methods

Similar to other participants in this study, I have become what Roberto Rodríguez (2014) refers to as "de-Indianized" by modernity. I grew up in a household that attempted to balance between English and Spanish languages and Mexican and American identities. Over time, the weight of assimilation proved challenging to overcome. Part of this project is rooted in my attempt to "re-Indianize" myself by restoring my relationships with my closest connection to my Indigenous ancestors—my food. As Rodríguez describes, while many Mexican, Mexican American, Chicana/o, and Latinx peoples have lost their native tongues to colonial Spanish or English, they still cling to the cultural traditions of food and food preparation. Rodríguez insists that "our sacred maíz is our mother," and corn remains central to many Indigenous communities throughout the Americas. Part of my attempt to find common ground between the people in this book and me was to cede my privileged position as the researcher and to relearn the power and potential of food from those who remain connected to their Indigenous past in spite of migration, poverty, or modernity. I speak both English and Spanish, but my university accent and vocabulary were very easily recognized. While initially this may have been a cause for concern, as participants grew to know me as someone who aligned with their shared sense of commitment to improve health, community, and the environment, I became part of the LMV community.

This book is based on over four years of ethnographic fieldwork carried out between 2012–16 with a community of home gardeners living and working in the Santa Clara Valley. What began as a simple invite by the program director to see the program and meet the families developed into a fulfilling and rewarding Participatory Action Research project. Ethnographic research methods of participant observation, informal interviewing, and the sensory experiences of planting, harvesting, cooking, and eating with participants were central tools to the documentation of gardens at the margins. Yet, I do not take the "tools" of ethnography lightly, nor do I recognize them as "simple" and "objective." Rather, I use ethnography to engage in the decolonial option. Deepening the work of Linda Smith (2007), Walter Mignolo insists researchers have the option to "suppress the fact that you are Maori or Black Caribbean or Aymara" or Latinx in my case, or you can take the de-colonial option and "engage in knowledge making to 'advance' the Maori [or Latinx] cause" (2009, 14). I choose the latter. La Mesa Verde is a diverse, multiethnic, multilingual group of gardeners, activists, artists, cooks, and families, who stem from a long lineage of people who continue to force the hand of systems larger than themselves in pursuit of dignity and conviviality because oppressed and displaced peoples are not simply witness to history, they are makers of history (see Dunbar-Ortiz 2014; Cajete 1999; Zinn 1990).

In the field, I attempted to maintain an informal approach with the home gardeners who participated in the study. Participant observation, informal interviews, and hundreds of conversations at organized events, strategic planning meetings, family dinner tables, kitchens, and in the garden provided the bulk of the information presented in this book. In most cases, I was introduced to home gardeners by LMV staff while volunteering at Sacred Heart Community Services or by other home gardeners. Over the life of this research, I volunteered to help out for planting days, harvest festivals, building days, cooking workshops, and agroecology classes. At these events, I met home gardeners who expressed interest in being part of the Participatory Action Research project. After my initial introduction to home gardeners, I was often invited into their homes and gardens. As these relationships developed, I would often receive phone calls from gardeners to help them plant, harvest, or even cook. I do not make light of the relationships I have developed during this project, and I am guided by the Indigenous research methods of "relational accountability" (Wilson 2008) by ensuring that all the findings, data, photos, and transcripts are given back to the community.

This study has taught me a lot about humility, trust, and reciprocity. During each step of this research project—the conceptualization of the central research question, the activities generating ethnographic and observational narratives, and the interpretation of the results—the LMV community has collaborated with me. They have encouraged me to investigate deeper, listen longer, and relay the information to as many people as possible. When I began this research, the program director at the time wanted me to tell the story of how a group of food justice advocates and a community in need were challenging the commonsense logic of capitalism through the subversive act of growing and sharing food. She told me that for the LMV community, my study would say to the world, "we exist, and we matter." Along the way, these experiences have shaped me by providing an ethical framework to do research and live life. Shawn Wilson believes that "if research doesn't change you as a person, then you haven't done it right" (2008, 135). Well, this research has changed me; whether or not I got it "right" remains to be seen. I was fortunate enough to be given access to many home gardens and to document the agrobiodiversity of ten of them (see appendix B). Some of the stories from individuals with whom I conducted agrobiodiversity surveys are included in this book, but unfortunately, I was unable to include everyone's story.

In the field, my notebook was my primary tool for collecting data. As with many immigrant communities, there resides an initial distrust in outsiders, but my association with LMV helped me gain entrance into this community. My ability to speak both English and Spanish, and my knowledge of cooking and gardening proved to be a resource for many home gardeners. Regardless, many home gardeners, both documented and undocumented, distrusted the use of video or recording devices. This distrust was one reason I rarely used a voice recorder, the second was because of practicality. Since the majority of my conversations occurred while working with participants in their gardens, cooking food in their kitchens, volunteering at events, or even sharing a meal, the use of digital recording devices seemed obtrusive and inorganic. Because of this, I only use direct quotes when I can accurately convey exactly it is what people said and how they said it, or on the occasional instance when I was using a recording device. In other instances, my detailed and extensive field notes help me to paraphrase the context and discussions of home gardeners.

The majority of participants in the study were either English or Spanish speakers, and all interviews and conversations were conducted in the preferred language (English or Spanish) of the participant. However, there were occasional conversations with participants from non-Spanish or English-speaking backgrounds. In each instance, participants had good conversational English, and our interviews and conversations were done in English. Based on the knowledge of LMV organizers, I would be introduced to a home gardener in either English or Spanish, and from there, our conversation would sometimes shift from English to Spanish or from Spanish to English. As I got more acquainted with individual participants, the language they used often changed. In all instances, I attempted to use the language a given participant was most comfortable using at that particular time and place.

Finally, the aim of this book is to move beyond the figure of the "suffering subject" in writing about precarious and vulnerable communities and to draw attention to how people enact and live for the good. There is no doubt that in many cases global trajectories impact local lives, but what is often overlooked is how despite these global forces, local lives find and create spaces of autonomy to improve their communities, ecosystems, and health. The ethnographic narratives of home gardeners in this book highlight how they are not merely hopeless victims tied up in larger global projects of racism, oppression, and inequality but also transformative agents enacting change at scales far grander than commonly observed. An anthropology of good (Robbins 2013) does not ignore the fact that many people in the world are suffering from processes and structures beyond their control, nor does it romanticize people's ecological wisdom or sense of community by ignoring the lived realities of oppression and subjectification. The goal of an anthropology of good is to stress how people imagine better worlds and how they work to enact them. Throughout this study, my intentions have been guided by the action research ethics espoused by Gloria Anzaldúa, who urges that we perform work that matters "que vale la pena" (2009, 314) because, in the end, it is worth the pain.

Outline of Chapters to Come

This book introduces several influential gardeners who, often through circumstances beyond their control, find themselves initiating home gardens to preserve the cultural traditions of self-provisioning in order to foster well-being. Chapter 1 explains the emergence of gardens at the margins and how gardeners deploy their gardens to protect against uncertainty. Neoliberalism is a practice of privatization, deregulation, and free trade, accompanied by deep cuts in social spending for things like health care and education. Such practices have the tendency to create spaces of neoliberal neglect by deepening the structural process for uneven development, whereby creating the conditions from which gardens at the margins emerge. This chapter interprets the history of the valley's socioecological landscape as a process of "shifts and rifts" (see Clark and York 2008) to explain how the conditions of economic expansion shift around ecological problems and in the process generates rifts in the natural cycles and processes that keep humans and nonhumans happy and healthy. The prevalence of food deserts and diet-related illnesses are the result of capital's constant shifting, and movements for food justice are people's response to heal rifts in Earth's natural cycles.

Chapter 2 begins with a discussion about the historical roots of home gardens. While urban agriculture and community gardens have received high acclaim in recent years, there is a larger story here that is often overlooked by mainstream food movements. Home gardens are an ancient practice for many land-based peoples dating back millennia that has allowed land-based people to remain self-determining. I argue that gardening as a way of life is one way in which home gardeners in this book retain a level of autonomy while gaining control of their social reproduction. The home gardeners in this chapter shed light on how growing food at the margins can be a practice for environmental justice because it helps retain the elements of a way of life that works to counter the alimentation imposed on people by industrial society.

Chapter 3 introduces several home gardeners who live in pursuit of the good life. The narratives in this chapter reveal a garden subjectivity that interprets a communal form of property as relation rather than as possession. This interpretation appears to be a necessary precondition for the rise of any sharing system of reciprocal exchange. This chapter highlights how convivial labor allows gardeners to revitalize traditional knowledge, remake economic systems, and restore social and ecological relationships. Through their daily actions of growing, sharing, preparing, and consuming food, which helps to heal their bodies, traditions, and environments, home gardeners express the values of simplicity, sustenance, dignity, and respect for life. I argue that home gardeners hold "theories" of value that branch into the political and moral economy of material and vernacular culture. The value systems expressed by the home gardeners in this book articulate experiences that expand on the relationships between the human and the more-than-human world in ways that dignify daily life in all of its manifestations. This chapter builds upon an anthropological account of value (Dumont 1980; Gregory 1982, 1997; Graeber 2001; Sykes 2009) by exploring how different people perceive it through culturally distinct ways.

Focusing on health, chapter 4 demonstrates how home gardening encourages the creative redeployment of traditional healing techniques to counter the precarious reality of life at the margins. Health is the culmination of biological, cultural, economic, and social factors that must be placed within a broader historical context. Building on the work of Alisha Gálvez (2018), this chapter explores the tremendous potential of a "milpa-based diet" or "milpa-based cuisine" to reorient health and social relationships. Such a diet is reminiscent of a way of life and relies heavily on "ingredients, labor, and rhythms of life and mealtimes" (Gálvez 2018, 3) that are increasingly harder to come by. Regardless, gardeners at the margins continually pursue such a way of life because it is within these moments that the value of comida is (re)discovered and recovered.

Chapter 5 explores the potential emergence of radical political subjectivities from the margins. Home gardeners grow food for various reasons, but the true revolutionary potential of a garden subjectivity is that the measure of value is determined in relationship with others and as an exercise in social reproduction. Home gardeners do not use the margins by choice, but by choosing to use the margins to cultivate food, home gardeners strive for autonomy in pursuit of dignity. Many home gardeners in this book never wanted growing food to be a political act, but as each one of them articulates differently throughout the book, food is always political because the decisions about which foods to eat, the farming methods used to produce the foods we commonly have access to, and the distribution of healthy and unhealthy foods is determined by a variety of social, political, environmental, and ethical forces sometimes out of the control of the daily consumer. The home gardeners in this chapter show how gardening at the margins is an act of self-valorization because these gardens contain within them the essential elements for social reproduction and autonomy. Gardens at the margins produce and enable escapes from the mindless eating and living in which too many people are trapped by proposing different ways of being and seeing our human and nonhuman relationships.

The conclusion of the book contextualizes how home gardeners are doing far more than "growing tomatoes," they are fertilizing the soil with thoughts and values for future movements to come. They are growing food to strengthen relationships with each other and the land, they are sharing food to restore their bodies and communities, and they are generating new knowledge and propagating ancient ways of knowing to find escapes from the biopolitics of industrial capitalism. They are a "movement of many movements" (Holt-Giménez 2011) and actions at various scales. Many Indigenous and displaced peoples are not mimicking the social movements of the past, nor are they pursuing earlier forms of seeking justice, such as the civil rights or women's suffrage movements. Instead, they are pursuing what might lie beyond rights. The stories that fill the following pages are guided by an anthropology of good and emphasize how people imagine better worlds and then how they work to enact them. These narratives are not disconnected from the harsh reality faced by precarious communities. Instead, they are informed by those harsh realities and how, in spite of, or perhaps because of those realities, people create, innovate, and seek to make a better existence for themselves and their communities.

CHAPTER 1

More than Weeds

Gardening in Spaces of Neglect

> They [city officials] want to believe the city is thriving again, but it's not, it's dead. They traded food for silicon.
>
> —*Karla*

The historic center of old San José runs along First Street between East San Fernando and East Santa Clara Streets. The buildings date back to the 1870s and 1880s and stand as a monument to San José's historical past. The three-story Italianate Odd Fellows Building on the corner of Santa Clara and Third dates back to 1883, and the Pomeroy Building, known today as La Rosa Pharmacy, on South First Street, was built in 1870. Initially, the old core of the town ran up and down Market Street, one block from First. Slowly, as the city expanded, it shifted commerce toward First Street and eventually moved southward along the Guadalupe River, located just a few blocks west of First Street. Old San José was situated between the Guadalupe River on the west and the Coyote River on the east. In the past, these rivers served as a vital source of water for the residents of San José and their farmlands. As San José expanded, these rivers, and their seasonal flooding cycles, were subject to both control and extreme pollution. Today, the city's water no longer comes from the same sources used by the Ohlone, the original inhabitants of this land, but is pumped in from various sources including San Luis Reservoir in the southeast, Hetch Hetchy Watershed in the Sierra Nevada, and deep-water wells from the Santa Clara Valley Groundwater Basin.

Following South First Street, south of historic downtown, sits the Paseo de San Antonio where the Mexican American writer, poet, professor, and labor activist Ernesto Galarza is commemorated in a public monument installation with his words of wisdom are inscribed into the sidewalk. A glance to the west, just past the Fairmont Hotel, reveals La Plaza de César Chávez and a monument celebrating Quetzalcoatl, the plumed serpent of Mesoamerican legend sitting on the southern end of the park. Continuing south on First is the SoFa district. This renovated arts district is lined with outdoor dining, live music, and historical landmarks such as the California Theatre. Continuing south for two more blocks, South First Street merges with South Market Street at the Parque de los Pobladores. Adjacent to the park is the Movimiento de Arte y Cultura Latina America (MACLA), City Lights Theater Company of San José, San Jose Museum of Quilts & Textiles, and the San Jose Institute of Contemporary Art. Just past this lies Highway 280, which acts like a concrete curtain that blocks direct access to the cultural and historical amenities of the historic downtown for the Mexican, Central American, and working-class neighborhoods and districts.

Continuing south on South First Street past Highway 280, the streets widen, the trees become fewer, and auto-repair shops, car dealerships, and fast food become the norm. Sacred Heart Community Services is located on the corner of South First and East Alma Avenue in the community of Washington-Alma, a little over a mile south of the historic Odd Fellows Building in downtown San José. While only about one mile separates these

FIGURE 3 An all-too-common eatery in Washington-Alma advertising five burgers for $7.99, a price tough to beat. Photo courtesy of the author.

two establishments, they are worlds apart. The community of Washington-Alma is located just south of downtown San José. The community is made up of primarily Spanish-speaking immigrants from various parts of Mexico, although there are numerous different languages and ethnicities in the neighborhood. Willow Street, between Almaden and Lick Avenues, is a vibrant center of Mexican restaurants and shops.

Most homes are single-family, one- or two-story homes, although it is common to have more than one generation living under the same roof. Unlike many other parts of the city, very few of the homes in Washington-Alma have lawns. There are occasional groves of large oak trees, but most of those are found in more wealthy neighborhoods. For the most part, the homes in Washington-Alma get sun all day long. It took me months to figure out why this was. As many home gardeners told me, oaks trees create shade on valuable real estate, real estate that could be used to grow food. In wealthier neighborhoods, landscaping trumps food production. While many gardens in Washington-Alma have trees, they are often fruit trees used for the production of food. Every single-family home in Washington-Alma has a gated backyard, and many of those yards are large and remain out of sight from the street. One Stanford freshman volunteer told me in the summer of 2014, "Most people never come south of downtown, and if they do, it's on the freeway. They never enter this neighborhood." While there are many communi-

FIGURE 4 Wide streets and very few large trees make up the landscape in Washington-Alma. Photo courtesy of the author.

ties in South San José, the community of Washington-Alma, just south of Highway 280, remains hidden to the majority of those living in the South Bay.

There are many reasons why such a place would remain hidden, and much of that has to do with the historical patterns of disinvestment and uneven development that occurred in many low-income communities across the country since the postwar period. According to Nathan McClintock, "understanding the historical and structural roots of this urban landscape is fundamental to understanding the individual and collective agency that adapts to or resists its development" (2011, 93). In recent years, there has been a renewed focus on urban agriculture in cities all across the United States—from Detroit to New Orleans, Los Angeles to New York—where governmental and nongovernmental organizations have been finding and creating spaces to grow food. This, of course, is not inherently a just or inclusive process because the origins of urban agriculture in particular cities and communities have specific temporal and spatial dimensions that produce different outcomes for different people.

During the Great Depression, urban agriculture provided food, and in some cases, jobs to unemployed people (Lawson 2005). When World War II hit, and resources were in short supply, Victory Gardens took shape,

FIGURE 5 A typical tree-lined street in Willow Glen, a neighboring community of Washington-Alma. Photo courtesy of the author.

and women gardeners produced a substantial amount of food for the nation (Gowdy-Wygant 2013; Lawson 2005). The "back-to-the-land" movement of the 1970s saw urbanites escape the economic recession by relearning subsistence lifestyles. Most recently, urban agriculture has spread in response to the rise of food deserts, diet-related illnesses, and neglected neighborhoods (Gottlieb and Joshi 2010). In each instance, the discourse surrounding urban agriculture (e.g., community gardens, home gardens, Community Supported Agriculture, etc.), "has shifted from one of recreation and leisure to one of urban sustainability and economic resilience" (McClintock 2010, 192) depending on the given situation. In the Global North, urban agriculture has often been a response to the uncertainty and precarity experienced by urban dwellers.

Gardens at the margins emerge because as capital simultaneously produces spaces of high investment and abandonment (Davis 2006; Pellow and Park 2002), it effectively creates a "rift," or disruption, in what Marx (1990) called "social metabolism," which refers to the flows of materials between humans and their natural environments used for the purpose of social reproduction. "In an attempt to overcome natural limits, capital engages in a series of shifts to sustain production.... As a result, the social metabolism is intensified, as more of nature is subjected to the demands of capital, and additional ecological problems are created" (Foster, Clark, and York 2010, 82). These "ecological rifts" (Foster, Clark, and York 2010) are inherent in the system of capitalism. As systems shift to avoid an ecological crisis in one location and initiate crisis in another, they also generate "social rifts" that are a result of the commodification of land, labor, and food and "individual rifts" that alienate people from their environments and labor (McClintock 2010).

Gardens at the margins emerge in response to the "metabolic rift" (Clark 2006) created in the wake of economic expansion, and gardens at the margins are a means to overcome that very same rift. Gardens at the margins work to reverse alienated people, labor, and landscapes by becoming enacted spaces where labor's "form-creating fire" enables gardens to contribute to the social reproduction of home gardeners. These gardens provide access to not only food but also to health and well-being in a system where access to medical services is not easily affordable. Similar to the work of Nathan McClintock (2010), this chapter uses the framework of the metabolic rift to give context to the emergence of gardens at the margins in the Santa Clara Valley and to understanding their potential in healing environments, communities, and individuals.

In the historical transformation of Santa Clara Valley into the Silicon Valley, a metabolic rift is created in the economic logic that governs land use. This does not mean Muir's "valley of your heart's delight" is gone or lost, but that people engage in acts of growing food to restore their relationship to the valley of your heart's delight by healing the metabolic rift. On the one hand, this chapter describes the emergence of sacrifice zones (e.g., see Taylor 2014; Lerner 2010; Auyero and Swistun 2009; Johnston and Barker 2008; Bullard 1990) where landscapes, bodies, and cultures are sacrificed in pursuit of more wealth by the wealthiest of people, and on the other hand, it presents an account of how home gardeners are growing food to challenge the conditions of precarity and marginalization in pursuit of well-being and dignity. Their stories show that survival in the barrio, hood, or ghetto is not reliant on the pursuit of individual self-interest, but on the strength of relationships. The criminalization of migrants and the working poor have been initiated by a state-led, low-intensity warfare over whose bodies have value. The goal of this type of war is not to "win" or to eradicate immigrants and eliminate poverty, but to produce and make permanent the conditions of precarity and vulnerability (Rosas 2012). Yet, home gardeners resist such precarity and vulnerability by using their "marginality as an inventive force" (see Peña 1997) in counter-hegemonic ways.

Our contemporary economic system puts people at odds with their very existence because it reproduces the conditions of alienation from their environments, communities, and even themselves. Restoring individuals and communities to the fruits of their own labor (both literally and metaphorically) requires (re)connecting to the metabolism of their own environments (McClintock 2010). In other words, growing food mends our relationships with our environments because it makes labor meaningful and *convivial* again. This framework identifies newly emerging trends in alternative food movements whereby home gardeners work to create new worlds collectively in common without ever taking power (Holloway 2002; also see Hardt and Negri 2004, 85).

Shifting Landscapes: The Capitalist Industrial Transformation of the Santa Clara Valley

Karla is a Chicana in her mid-fifties who strongly identifies with her Indigenous roots. She is fun, outgoing, and personable. I had just finished an interview with her and was walking through her neighborhood, observing the surrounding home gardens when something came to mind. Much of the food security literature presents the idea that many low-income communities of color simply lack direct access to affordable, fresh, and organic fruits and vegetables (e.g., Winne 2008; Allen 1999). The neoliberal assumption is that with state-sponsored intervention, access to such amenities can be accomplished (Poppendieck 1998). This idea justifies the entrance of nonprofit organizations into communities to initiate change and also may lead to community organizations and individuals within the neighborhoods to push for change. There is no doubt that in many cases, neglected neighborhoods do not have access to healthy food options, but as I walked from block to block, I noticed something strikingly different in the homes that surrounded Karla. They did have access to fresh fruits and vegetables but did not fit the neoliberal social governance model of grocery stores, food pantries, soup kitchens, or food stamps.

As I walked, I could see orange, lemon, lime, and pomegranate trees towering over houses; pinto and green beans climbing up chain-link fences; and yerba buena, epazote, and verdolagas propagating around foundations. There were bees, hummingbirds, and ladybugs. Lorna Dee Cervantes's poem "Freeway 280," which is about this exact region, came to mind:

> But under the fake windsounds of the open lanes,
> in the abandoned lots below, new grasses sprout,
> wild mustard remembers, old gardens
> come back stronger than they were,
> trees have been left standing in their yards.
> Albaricoqueros, cerezos, nogales . . .
> Viejitas come here with paper bags to gather greens.
> Espinaca, verdolagas, yerbabuena . . .[1]

Unlike many communities where wealth is measured in monetary gain, the wealth of Washington-Alma could be measured in the diversity of escapes from capitalism that allows people to heal. This was a community of abundance, not scarcity. Many in the community do not hoard what they have but rather share what they can. These communities do not wait on

---

1. This excerpt comes from Cervantes's poem "Freeway 280," which she published as part of a collection of her works in Emplumada in 1982.

the assurance of state given rights and laws for their security but rather their mutuality is their security. Capitalist disinvestment in communities like Washington-Alma has opened opportunities to shift investment into other regions of the valley like Mountain View, home to the headquarters of Google, or Cupertino, home to the headquarters of Apple. The shifting nature of capitalism may have neglected communities like Washington-Alma by creating a neighborhood perceived to be neglected and dilapidated, but for those who inhabit it, the shifting landscape of capitalism has left spaces of neoliberal neglect where residents engage in creative participation with their environments and with each other (also see Cleaver 1989; Solnit 2009).

There is no doubt disinvestment has left many unmet social, environmental, and economic needs within the community that must be addressed by government officials. Still, the community puts their own marginality to use by innovating ways to resist and challenge their precarity. But precarity does not just happen overnight, it takes time to develop. In fact, "the spread of neoliberal calculation as a governing technology is thus a historical process that unevenly articulates situated political constellations" (Ong 2006, 3), and the spaces of neoliberal neglect that are discussed in this book are a direct consequence of those constellations. The transformation from the Santa Clara Valley to the Silicon Valley is the result of a series of shifts and rifts, whereby capitalism shifts around ecological problems, and in the process of "shifting," capitalism creates new ecological problems, or "rifts," which are disruptions in the environment's natural cycles or metabolism. Healing those rifts, or restoring the natural cycles of environment, is just as much a part of the story of the valley as the processes of urbanization and economic development.

Like many communities during the era of colonial expansion westward, the Santa Clara Valley underwent dramatic changes, and as early as 1800, it was known for agricultural production. Agrarian capitalism brought a series of shifts that transformed the region. Coinciding closely with California statehood in 1850, the rapid dispossession of Mexican rancheros from 1860–70 pushed generations of farmers off their lands. From 1870–80 the small-scale grain production and farmers that existed during the Mexican pastoral system crumbled, and by the turn of the century, intensive agriculture was widespread (Almaguer 1994, 90).

James Lick, who owned property in what is today the Alma neighborhood, became one of the wealthiest men on the West Coast by operating

FIGURE 6 Food emerges from the margins as a fig tree stretches over the fence. Photo courtesy of the author.

a flour mill, which he established in 1852. He brought countless seeds and starters and planted them on his land (Hylkema 2007, 43) and is credited for shifting the region's economy toward the fruit and canning industry. Both of these industries were highly racialized as immigrant men made up the bulk of low-paying agriculture workers, and immigrant (mainly Mexican) women made up the bulk of the labor force in the canning industry (Ruíz 1987). Lick's land became Muir's "valley of your heart's delight." The San

Jose Canning Company, which opened in 1919 in Washington-Alma, was the epicenter of the San José canning revolution. The irony here is that the community of Washington-Alma is literally located on top of Lick's orchards and Muir's valley. Today, the community continues the agricultural legacy of the Santa Clara Valley by seeking to mend these rifts through the unalienated labor of home gardening.

By the 1940s, the expansive farmland and fruit canneries that brought acclaim to the Santa Clara Valley began to shut down, and the regional economy shifted again, this time toward the microelectronics and information technology industries. This shift restructured the racialized workforce. The flexible male day labors that once worked the fields became the building custodians, outdoor landscapers, and maintenance staff. The women assembly-line cannery workers transitioned to fill assembly-line jobs for the booming microelectronic industry. The subcontracting of a few high-paid engineers alongside many "deskilled" low-wage laborers became the racialized order of employment still evident in Silicon Valley today (Zlolniski 2006). The shift in modes of production brought new concerns to the Latina/o and other immigrant communities in the region. Worst of all, many of the workers with the least amount of job stability also suffered disparate impacts of environmental racism in the workplace. Latina/o workers faced systematic exposure to higher levels of toxic contamination and other health and safety risks that extended from their workplace to their living environments.

The booming microelectronics and information technology industries, which began with IBM in the 1940s, expanded with Hewlett-Packard in the 1950s, and reached a crescendo in the 1980s, was the most significant contributor to environmental contamination. The hazardous materials of the industry have a tendency to accumulate in the body and cause severe health conditions such as cancer and birth defects. According to Pellow and Park, the toxic exposure affecting low-wage workers who handled the materials, of whom the majority were Latina, was also experienced in the nearby low-income communities of South and East San José (2002, 67), where several people in this book still reside. Santa Clara County has the highest density of toxic waste sites in the nation, and "more than twenty of the Valley's thirty-one toxic Superfund sites are directly related to the electronics industry's pollution" (Pellow and Park 2002, 94). Since the establishment of the North American Free Trade Agreement in 1994, the Silicon Valley's transnational companies have been able to offshore the production of highly hazardous products such as semiconductors and integrated circuit boards in the 1990s and externalized the environmental damages to countries like Mexico where regulation has historically been weak or nonexistent. Needless to say, decades of minimal local, state, and federal oversight of the technology sector have led to widespread pollution of the waterways and soils of the valley today. San José touts the Guadalupe River Park as the city's Central Park. Still, the river itself is one of the most mercury-contaminated rivers in North America (Park and Pellow 2004, 406).

To meet the needs of the growing population, new homes and communities spread across the valley floor as neighborhoods were carved out of the nearby hillsides, and farmlands were paved over. The rapid urban and industrial growth of the Santa Clara Valley had significant implications for the region. Settlement patterns and urbanization completely altered most of the native habitats, including the loss of 85 to 99 percent of wet meadows, oak savannas, and freshwater streams and destroyed alkali meadows and the vast willow groves that once flourished in the valley (Grossinger et al. 2007).

Many writers end up mystifying the valley's tumultuous history. Chris Benner characterizes the 1990s as an age of flexibility. According to Benner, "flexible work is an essential component of competitive success in the information economy" (2002, 5). While the agrarian community that gave rise to the "valley of your heart's delight" in the early part of the twentieth century was predicated on flexible labor, so too was the birth of the Silicon Valley, although the racialization of the labor force encouraged far different outcomes. The difference today is that neoliberalism has created a "new relationship between government and knowledge through which governing activities are recast as nonpolitical and nonideological problems that need technical solutions" (Ong 2006, 3). In other words, neoliberalism has re-engineered political space to reflect market demand as "market-driven calculations are being introduced in the management of populations and the administration of special spaces" (Ong 2006, 3–4). The rationality of neoliberal governments is to "optimize" both geographic space and physical bodies.

This plays out in the Silicon Valley in the form of flexible labor, which is predicated on resilient subjects, or workers who can withstand the ever-changing demands of the new work economy. Under the conditions of neoliberalism, argues Chandler and Reid, "the promotion of resilience requires and calls forth a much degraded subject, one defined by much diminished capabilities for autonomy and agency" (2016, 1). Coinciding with this was the rise of the "micro" electronics sector and the "amping" up to the personal computing and IT revolutions. Of course, often discounted in these stories is the fact that the microelectronics industry, while presented as a clean and light alternative to the old smokestack industries, has many unintended consequences. These "paperless offices" improve efficiency and increase consumption.[2] They have proved more than capable of accelerating the valley's landscape changes and the spread of environmental inequities. In the 1980s, high-tech companies began subcontracting employees to promote labor flexibility and reduce costs (Benner 2002). Such conventional analyses of the shifting capitalist organizational form overlook how this process of restructuring was a response to workers' struggles for union recognition, wage increases, pensions, and health care during the cycles of strikes in the industrial and manufacturing sectors over the course of the 1930s–40s and again during the radicalism of the 1960s and early 1970s (see Peña 1987).

Interpreting the "new work economy" is two-sided. The new work economy, which coincides with the neoliberalization of the valley, creates precarious workers who both actively engage in self-exploitation as precarious workers and actively resist self-exploitation (see Peña [1997] for examples on *maquila* struggles in Ciudad Juárez, Mexico). Karla epitomizes the contradiction embedded in the flexible labor present in the "new work economy." She is often underemployed and continually finds part-time work and odd jobs that force her to work outside the eight-hour day. When Karla began to restore her home garden, she was well aware that in the process, she would be participating in her own self-exploitation, but she chose to do it anyway. In fact, one could argue that Karla enacts the flexibility of her labor by consciously withdrawing her own labor from the marketplace to grow food. By actively removing her own labor from the flow of capital, Kara transforms what might have been alienated labor into unalienated labor, which is intrinsic to the process of self-valorization. Karla's agency disrupts the estrangement people commonly feel when working for a wage and demonstrates how flexible labor can be a source of self-valorization because she is in direct relationship producing food for herself and her family.

---

2. This is what John Bellamy Foster, Brett Clark, and Richard York refer to as "The Paperless Office Paradox" or "Jevon's Paradox" (2010, 183–91), whereby improvements to efficiency increase consumption and negative environmental externalities. The edited volume of JoAnn Carmin and Julian Agyeman (2011) also demonstrates the changing spatial dynamics of environmental inequality produced by modernity.

While people can and sometimes do choose to engage in flexible labor, many people are forced into flexible, low-wage work to pay rent and buy food. The growth of a "flexible" new work economy came about through workers' struggles to find value in both paid and unpaid labor. While flexible labor supports self-determination and autonomy, it does not happen without also producing at least a certain level of precarity. As much as Karla enjoys her work in her garden, and as much as the food she grows helps lower her weekly food bills, her "choice" to withdraw her labor form the marketplace furthers her precarity, yet she chooses to do it anyway. I believe this can partly be explained because her precarity encourages her to deploy her labor as convivial labor, or labor that is meaningful, rewarding, and perhaps even an escape for the oppressive norms of the "free" market. We cannot distance ourselves from the biopolitical reality the working class confronts, and the stories in the following chapters will further illustrate life and power are intertwined. The postindustrial economy driven by flexible labor is both an enabling and inhibiting feature of working-class struggles.

Where Weeds Are Life

Karla is one of many long-term residents of the region who told me about life in the valley before the booming years of the 1960s. Karla spent much of her early childhood years in South San José on a large piece of land owned by her great-grandfather. They hunted on the land and fished and swam in the nearby lakes and streams. As we sat in her garden, Karla explained her childhood:

> I hated school, I wanted to be outside. I remember how my family and I would often spend summers on the [Central] Coast crabbing and fishing with cousins and relatives. We would go to Año Nuevo beach, near Half Moon Bay, and work in the fields during the day, and crab in the afternoon. I remember lying together under the stars and listening to the waves as we slept. . . . I grew up with easy access to fresh fruit, vegetables, and fish. As a family, we would even make trips to the Central Valley to sell melons and apricots. . . . I hated those trips because it was so hot there. If I close my eyes, I can still see the Valley as it was. I used to be able to smell whatever was growing and know where I was in the Valley, and what season it was. Every part of the Valley was known for different fruits.

Her sense of smell and imagination would take her back to a time before semiconductors and freeways. Life in San José before 1950 was far more predictable. The seasons came and went, but people and traditions stayed. Today, this is seldom the case.

As the valley's economy and landscape shifted over the last half of the century, it unleashed a series of rifts that long-term residents, like Karla, continue to experience. The subsistence farming practices of Karla's grandfather provided direct access to fresh fruits and vegetables. As the sleepy agricultural town of San José shifted toward microelectronics, the need for more housing, roads, and infrastructure was at odds with open space. The open spaces she remembered as a kid growing up have been privatized and sold to the highest bidder. The rivers she swam and fished in have turned to creeks, and many of the lakes have become contaminated. "The last time I went by where my grandfather's house once was," she continued, "it was a subdivision with a golf course."

Within three generations, her family went from owners of land to workers of the land to having no access to land. The shifting political, economic, and environmental landscape of the valley changed enough to almost entirely disconnect Karla from her agricultural roots. The increased cost of living in the region, coupled with the lack of access to land to grow food, intensified adverse health and economic issues for her and her family. With few options left, Karla was forced to make some life-changing decisions and chose to restore the home garden she remembered as a child. Gardening has not only provided her with access to fresh, healthy, and organic fruits and vegetables, but it has given her a piece of her past back. Her garden produces enough food for her to be able to share its surplus with her neighbors. "We don't always do things by choice, oftentimes, we do many things out of need," she informed me.

Today, Karla uses her garden to restore the intergenerational aspects of home gardening by teaching her children and grandchildren about food, healthy eating habits, and self-provisioning. She also continues the family tradition of *curanderismo*, or traditional practices of healing and self-care. Almost everything produced in her garden is used for something. She uses the herbs from her garden for teas and household remedies. Leftovers become compost, and surpluses are shared. Always humbled by the stories and experiences of other home gardeners, Karla told me, "Gardening encourages you to give back, to share your knowledge, and to be a part of a community." Karla has networked herself with both home gardeners in La Mesa Verde and with her neighbors. She shares her harvests when yields are in abundance, and more importantly, she shares when times are tough. The ability and willingness to share broadens her social networks across class and ethnic boundaries.

Karla is fun, engaging, and almost always laughing. She loves to talk about what she is growing and what she is cooking. Every time we met, there was always food. In September of 2013, we met to catch up at her home, where she had prepared a light breakfast of tomatoes, berries, and cucumber-chia water. We sat at a table in the middle of her home garden as she traced her family history back to San José's Californio past. "I've spent most of my life in this house," she told me. No longer living in the house of her childhood, Karla's current home is located just west of the Guadalupe River in one of San José's oldest neighborhoods where large oak and maple trees line the streets. Karla's home is an old but beautiful two-story house that dates back to the 1930s. She has a small front yard where she has two raised garden beds. Roses line the walkway, which leads up to a small porch where she spends many afternoons with her grandchildren. While her house is small, she has plenty of space outside to grow several fruit trees, flowers, and crops. Across the street from Karla's home is a renovated mansion. "That house," she told me, "used to be a grocery store. They used to have sausages hanging and cheeses on display. Things you don't see anymore." Karla grew up within walking distance to a store where she could get locally produced fruit, vegetables, meats, and cheeses.

The owners, who lived above the store, had kids close to her age and they used to play in the store and in the streets. Her father even had a "tab" (line of credit) with the owner when he did not have the money to pay in cash. But the community that Karla grew up in is gone. Home values in the neighborhood have skyrocketed since the early 2000s. Yet, Karla and her family remain in the home she grew up in with her parents. When they passed away, she inherited the house and today lives there with her two daughters and grandchildren. In the latter part of the past century, people flocked to the Bay Area in pursuit of wealth and sunshine (see Davis [2006] for a similar analysis of Los Angeles), pricing the majority of people already living there out of the housing market. If Karla's family had not inherited the house, they too would have been priced out of the market.

Like many communities in California, the gentrification occurring in the upscale urban areas of San Francisco and San José has "suburbanized poverty" (Soursourian 2012). Today, the Silicon Valley is acclaimed as a meritocracy, but the reality is far different as it is the location for one of the highest income gaps in the nation (Benner et al. 2018). Hidden amongst the wealth of the valley are countless people living in poverty. In fact, the recent report for Santa Clara County's 2019 Homeless Census shows a continual trend of increased homelessness and a current homeless population over nine thousand residents.[3] One of the country's largest homeless encampments known as the "Jungle," which before its removal in December 2014, was estimated to have around three-hundred full-time residents. The encampment was within miles of some of the wealthiest people on the planet and only a few blocks from Sacred Heart and the community of Washington-Alma where the majority of this study takes place. The recent removal of people from this site has spread fear that those removed will simply end up somewhere else along the river (Emmons 2014). Recent pictures released by the *San Jose Mercury News* show men and women in white hazmat suits removing people, possessions, and debris from the encampment.

Throughout this project, I have spoken with several people who have either been homeless in the last few years or who fear it could be a real possibility. According to the Silicon Valley Real Estate and Marketing Group, the average cost of a home in Santa Clara County in June 2017, was $1.4 million. "It's not so much what is in this community [Washington-Alma] that sets it apart," a director at Sacred Heart told me one day, "it's what is not here that does." Trash cans, well-lit sidewalks, clean parks, grocery stores, bike lanes, things that are common in other areas of San José often are absent in the streetscapes of Washington-Alma and other similar communities where the home gardeners in this study live, work, and play.

In the closing stanza of Cervantes's "Freeway 280," she explains:

Maybe it's here
en los campos extraños de esta ciudad
where I'll find it, that part of me
mown under
like a corpse
or a loose seed.

---

3. For the full Santa Clara County Homeless Census Report see https://www.sccgov.org/sites/opa/newsroom/Pages/2019homelesscensus.aspx.

Many home gardeners in this study have articulated similar sentiments. The industrial development of San José has created the image of the Silicon Valley, but as Karla told me one day in her garden, "They [city officials] want to believe the city is thriving again, but it's not, it's dead. They traded food for silicon." Home gardeners in this study turn to their gardens to find the piece of themselves that has been "mown under" by freeways, managerial parks, and "progress." Where the neoliberal city sees a neglected ghetto, barrio, or hood, the people who inhabit such locations see an opportunity to enact spaces to grow food. Pointing to the verdolagas (also known as purslane) growing at edges of her garden, Karla stated firmly, "These plants are more than weeds, they're life." The so-called weeds growing in Karla's garden were carefully placed for integrated pest management. These annual crops add biodiversity to Karla's garden and to her diet. The high levels of omega-3 fatty acids found in purslane help her control her cholesterol by reducing the amount of LDL or bad cholesterol in the body (Simopoulos 2002). This helps to promote a healthier cholesterol balance in her bloodstream. Consuming foods high in omega-3 fatty acids help to reduce the risk of cardiovascular diseases while also providing plenty of fiber to help encourage healthy weight loss.

The racial projects that have occurred over the region's history are a result of the interplay between social structures and everyday life that normalizes inequality over time (Omi and Winant 1989). The production of race in the Santa Clara Valley, just like everywhere else, is a complicated matter, and the commonsense assumptions made about racial groups further normalizes wealth, health, and opportunity in the valley. Yet, Karla reveals a more nuanced understanding of how people are active participants in enacting alternative futures. Karla's home garden works to undo the racial projects that have produced her as a person reliant on an unjust, unequal food system by redeploying her labor as convivial labor through the active engagement with her home garden. Flexible labor practices that take place in the Silicon Valley place a heavy burden on individuals who are forced to navigate the uncertain terrain of underemployment, and yet, there exists a potential in flexible labor. Home gardeners like Karla, find that potential because their gardens allow them to heal the intergenerational traumas of shifts and rifts that industrial capitalism exposes. Her home garden does more than produce food, it provides her a means for social reproduction and a sense of autonomy. Just like the narrator of Cervantes's poem, Karla is planting seeds of change by gardening in the spaces of neglect underneath the freeway, in the cracks overlooked by city officials, and in the very halls of commerce that seek to maintain the racial projects of the past. It just may very well be "en los campos extraños de esta ciudad" (in the strange fields of this city) that new worlds are imagined and created.

Gardens that Move

I spent almost two hours with Lucy one Sunday afternoon in the fall of 2014. She showed me her garden while I took detailed notes on all the plants and herbs growing in it. She told me about what she shares with others and explained that some of the seeds she uses had been brought over from Southeast Asia by friends and how these plants would benefit her health. Lucy has an incredibly unique garden composition (see appendix B, garden 8). Her landlord, like so many others in the region, put a giant cement slab across most of her backyard several years ago to save water. This was great for him because it is far easier to maintain, but it provided Lucy with only minimal earth to work with. While this may have prevented some people from growing food, it only encouraged Lucy. With the help of La Mesa Verde, Lucy has two four-by-eight-foot raised garden beds lined with cardboard and filled with soil. Her three-foot-high beds are twice as high as traditional raised beds because the increased amount of soil is more resistant to the heat from the concrete below. Raised beds provide people with access to usable land, but under Lucy's circumstances, it makes it very difficult to expand garden projects. Lucy's solution to her modern problem was to hybridize traditional knowledge and expand her garden and improve her soil.

Lucy was born in the Philippine capital city of Manila, where she lived in a home with her grandmother and other relatives. Inside densely urbanized cities like Manila, there is very little access to good soil. In fact, Lucy told me the first time she had dirt in her backyard was here in the United States. Yet, somehow her grandmother in Manila was able to have a bountiful garden.

"How did your grandmother produce so much in an urban landscape?" I asked.

"With pots," she replied calmly.

"What do you mean pots," I continued with a sense of bewilderment.

Lucy smiled and then continued. "She collected pots, rotated them in her backyard throughout the year, and also made soil in the same pot while the plant was still growing." Lucy's grandmother used potted plants to make compost and grow food simultaneously, and Lucy continues to use this experiential practice in her home garden in San José. To understand fully, she gave me a one-on-one workshop on the process. First, depending on what she plans on growing, she chooses a pot of an appropriate size. Next, she uses cardboard and paper scraps from her house to create a one-to-three-inch layer at the bottom of the pot. She then puts a layer of dead plants and leaves to form the second strata. After that, she creates the next layer out of food scraps. Lastly, she adds the final layer, which is a combination of previously used soil and compost full of worms and insects. She then plants the seed or seedling. Depending on what she is growing, how the plant did the previous growing season, and the plant species, she uproots the plant after one or two years, takes the soil from the same pot, pours it upside down into another pot, and replants the same plant. What was previously cardboard has decomposed into nitrogen-rich soil. After two years of use, she uses the soil for other projects in her home garden or adds it to different pots.

She explained that the process of layering each pot is not an exact science, and the most essential part is to remember which plants were most recently flipped. She has a journal to write notes about how the plants are doing following the seasons. By moving plants closer or farther apart, Lucy practices integrated pest management by manipulating her backyard environment to suppress pests and encourage a healthy backyard ecosystem—a strategy of hybridized traditional knowledge she learned from her grandmother. Every few months or so, Lucy moves over forty different potted crops throughout the garden to keep her garden healthy. Her home garden is literally always in motion.

Lucy's garden is definitely labor-intensive, but she told me several times that she enjoys the labor because it keeps her happy and healthy. Some academics have critiqued the urban agriculture movement citing that individual actions and labor practices are self-exploitative and are limited by neoliberal constraints of self-help (McClintock 2014; Alkon and Mares 2012). In fact, Barbara Cruikshank argues that self-help is "emblematic" of liberal governments. As a tool, it can be used to reform both society and the subject by "indirectly harmonizing their interest" (1999, 48). She believes that self-help is a viable strategy to maximize citizenship because it can be used to address persistent social problems like hunger and poverty. Cruikshank's careful investigation into the study of empowerment reveals that "technologies of citizenship" encourage self-governing citizens, who,

FIGURE 7 Lucy's moving garden. Dozens of plants, most in pots, constantly in motion. Photo courtesy of the author.

through the everyday practices of voluntary association of "self-help," continually reproduce themselves. "Governance in this case is something we do to ourselves, not something done to us by those in power" (1999, 91). Governments and development agencies use the technologies of self-help to "empower" people to take control of their lives and communities as well as enable them to create positive social transformations. Technologies of citizenship have also "been adopted by mainstream development agencies as well, albeit more to improve productivity within the status quo than to foster social transformation" (Rai, Parpart, and Staudt 2007, 1). Such a "technology" moves to shift governmental responsibility to the individual and to create productive citizens.

The problem with empowerment, which is in keeping with Anthony Giddens (1994) and the so-called third way, is how it endorses a model that keeps (and in practice, privatizes) the state's "welfare" functions intact but fails to address and challenge the overwhelming asymmetries of power emblazoned in continued corporate domination through the increasingly unfettered institutional force of the capitalist market (also see Spies-Butcher 2002; 2003). In the context of the United States, what the "third way" has given us is an extreme "neo-regulatory" regime based on new enclosures, privatization, self-regulation of capitalist operations, and disinvestment in the environmental and social sectors, hence the neoliberal need for the "devolution" of the "welfare" function to the nonprofit industrial complex and the civil society associations intersecting with that sector.

In many ways, the critique of empowerment in low-income communities is fitting. Self-control can, and often does, reaffirm existing structures and institutions of power. Although, when I spoke with Lucy about her garden, she presented a different message. She and others were well-aware of the goals and intentions of self-help enterprises that are thrust upon vulnerable communities "for their own good." Many home gardeners in this study utilize the "good intentions" of governmental and NGO empowerment projects in their own communities to innovate and imagine new autonomous spaces. As James C. Scott (2012) notes, most of society's institutions are designed to control the masses, not to allow for autonomous communities. Home gardeners navigate this contested terrain. On the one hand, home gardeners like Lucy are doing exactly what neoliberal governments want by picking up where the government left off. The problem arises when self-regulation places the onus for well-being on the individual who now must assume a defensive posture in terms of limiting the risks that industrial food imposes. On the other hand, she deploys her own agency to encourage self-willing, self-defining, and self-organizing individuals and communities.

The first time I met Lucy was directly after La Mesa Verde's annual summer harvest festival in August 2013. We had been exchanging emails, phone calls, and text messages for several months, and when we finally met, Lucy gave me a hug. That is the way she is, inviting, humble, and warm. Lucy is many things; she is a gardener, an artist, an activist, a mother, a grandmother, and a cancer survivor. When feeling healthy, she spends much of her free time in the garden, and when she falls ill, she spends the majority of her time trying to be in her garden. "When I was sick," she told me, "keeping my hands in the earth was like stepping into a new beginning. I thought if this soil can squeeze out life, so can I." Lucy was referring to the symbiotic relationship she shares with her soil. As she heals the soil, the soil heals her. Lucy has been up and down with her health for many years. She helped organize a women's support group for cancer survivors. She encourages others in the group to use their gardens to help ease expenditures and to gain access to the most nutritional food around. Lucy has directly politicized gardening by merging her cancer survivor work with the promotion of the wisdom of having the personal space of a home garden and kitchen.

Home gardening is about two things for Lucy: sustainability and women's empowerment. But her definition of sustainability is complex. It is not merely sustainable development (as per the World Commission on Environment and Development 1987) or the triple bottom line (e.g., Elkington 1998). Instead, sustainability is a mindset that requires a complete restructuring of priorities. To achieve this mindset, she told me, "We have to change our perception of food." As we continued our discussion, it became clear that when Lucy referred to changing perceptions, she was referring to how we also need to change our understanding of life. Lucy did not merely happen to stumble upon this mindset; her life circumstances of precarity and the threat of cancer overturned her life and led her to make significant changes in her diet, livelihood, and, most importantly, relationships with others. Lucy uses her marginality as a source of innovation to "de-link" from the Silicon Valley and pursue a more rewarding life. "Cancer changes everything," she said. "What most people don't understand is that often women [who need to buy costly prescription drugs to control cancer] would rather die than let their kids starve."

Lucy is not the only person I have talked with who was told to go on expensive prescription drugs to control their illness. Many others, including the home gardeners discussed in chapter four, were told to take prescription drugs to control blood pressure, intestinal and heart diseases, arthritis, and diabetes. While many did take the advice of their doctors, others chose not to because they sought traditional remedies, or they simply did not have the financial means to afford expensive medicines. Lucy was the latter. "If my garden can support me," she told me, "then I can relax." Like many home gardeners in this book, Lucy's garden does more than produce food, it represented a social relationship, and the way she spoke of it reinforced that. While there have been many hard times during cancer treatments, she attributes much of her survival to the knowledge and social bonds she has gained through gardening. Growing up in Southeast Asia, she remembered that all her elders were always healthy because their garden provided them with life, both figuratively and literally. "I remember saying to myself, I want to be like that," she told me, referring to the elders she knew growing up. "Living here in the United States," she explained, "was the first time that I felt insecure with my health."

Lucy's experience confirms the existence of the immigrant health paradox (Calvo and Esquibel 2016; Gálvez 2011). She spent much of her life in so-called third-world countries, yet when she moved to one of the wealthiest nations on the planet, she was unsure about her ability to protect her health. "The problem in the United States is that it is tough to live healthy if you're poor" she explained, and then went to detail the meaning of health:

> It's not about making more money or moving from seven to ten dollars an hour. It's about changing a lifestyle. America is the only place I've ever felt insecure about health and food. We never had a lot of money [in Manila or Singapore], but there was always food. Here, we want to buy everything because we think it's better for us, but that's not true. Back home, people grow food on windowsills, porches, backyards, wherever they can, and they're healthier because of it. Gardening allows me to do what my grandma used to do, and it all starts with healthy soil.

There is minimal opportunity for such a lifestyle for her in the United States (also see Gálvez 2018). People do not have opportunities to create sustainable lifestyles, which is why Lucy believes gardening encourages sustainability and empowerment. Lucy offers significant insight because this suggests that gardeners are fully aware of how biopolitical power affects their status as United States residents and as members of the working class. They also recognize that gardening is a way to directly resist the biopolitical effects of modernity and to embark on the politics of self-enunciation by transforming the meaning and value of food through self-provisioning as part of the struggle for a more autonomous life.

Lucy follows the biomedical recommendations of her doctor to treat her cancer, but she uses her garden to heal from the cancer treatment physically, psychologically, economically, and spiritually. It took almost a year to get her hands on a durian tree (*Durio zibethinus*). The fruit, she informed me, originates from Southeast Asia and holds spiritual and physical healing powers. "Fruit of the Kings" is how it was often referred to in the past because of its large and formidable thorns. She uses several antioxidant-rich foods, including a variety of berries grown in her yard, to help purify her system after radiation treatments. What and how Lucy eats allows her to create a sense of self *in-place*. Lucy has spoken at San José City Hall about the need to support low-income cancer survivors and uses her garden as a platform to talk about the importance of eating and living well. She holds survivor group meetings in her garden and teaches about gardening. Her goal is to teach women how to use the garden to help lower bills, create community support, and alleviate the pressures imposed on people who take medication to survive. Her garden is a space for the conviviality of the "alterNative" (Peña 2017a) moral or social economy and a site of innovation against the continual expansion of the idea of the Silicon Valley.

Perhaps more importantly, Lucy's garden serves as an extension and piece of a larger "network struggle" (Hardt and Negri 2004, 79–91) against the demoralizing effects of the industrial food system. Home gardeners are resisting the imposition of an economic system driven by accumulation by transforming old ways (or maybe returning to the old ways) of socializing to meet their needs without remaining in the trap of the capitalist appropriation of value. These transformations are not the result of individuals demanding "rights." They are part of a larger project of people working together to define and meet their needs despite the imposition of the state and market systems. The linguistic and cultural diversity present within this group of home gardeners strengthens their bonds of relational solidarity.

There are moments where diversity emerges as a process of encounter through the exchange of different worldviews, value systems, agroecological knowledge, culinary practices, and self-provisioning skills from individuals of various origins. These "encounters" are both sites of tension and innovation. As Lucy's narrative illustrates, such encounters help support the diversity of the crops grown in gardens as much as it promotes a wide range of convivial social relationships that act as everyday forms of resistance and affirmation. This is exemplified through norms of convivial sharing of knowledge, resources, experiences, and food within the spaces of neoliberal neglect.

Revolutionaries at the Margins

When Lucy told me that living in the United States was the first time in her life that she felt uncertain about her health, it stuck with me. Her narrative typifies much of the food security literature whereby the industrial food system externalizes costs onto the most vulnerable and, in the process, creates suffering subjects (e.g., Wald 2016; Carney 2015; Holmes 2013; Guthman 2011; Harrison 2011; Barndt 2008). These narratives detail a food system that is more of a hyperobject than anything created and controlled by humans.[4] These stories can help to generate empathy for the "Other" to pressure governments and corporations to engage in more ethical and just practices. But in the end, if we are not careful, ethnographies that only project the "suffering subject" may simply fill Trouillot's "savage slot" (2003), or the objectified "Other." There are many ethnographies about the suffering subject, in fact, there are so many that Joel Robbins (2013) believes we need to move beyond this type of research and work toward an "anthropology of good." The reason Lucy's comment about her health stuck with me was not that she was a suffering subject but rather how she and others imagine better worlds and how they work to enact them.

Karla and Lucy pay close attention to the food they eat. After all, it has helped them overcome barriers of access to food and land. Therefore, reducing their "diet" down to an expression of identity would understate its complexity. Similar to Judith Farquhar's work in Beijing, the happiness of eating good food, and the nutritional health that results from it, is connected to the overall well-being of the human spirit. Farquhar's informants place "happiness at the center of a feedback loop linking 'body' and 'spirit' in a healthful cycle" (2006, 151). Both Karla and Lucy's healthy cycle includes the value of eating high-quality, nutrient-dense, and culturally relevant food and the practice of getting their hands dirty and growing that very same food. Gardening promotes strategies and tactics of everyday life that enable them to live a happy and healthy life and to validate that they are "doing something right" (Farquhar 2006, 153). As we begin to understand how the practices of eating structure our material and lived realities, the more we can appreciate how food enables us to bridge difference. "The closer we get to these processes that so resemble our own everyday lives the less useful a dualistic formation of victimhood and domination, repetition and creativity, becomes.

---

4. As explained by Timothy Morton, hyperobjects are "things that are massively distributed in time and space relative to humans" (2013, 1). They operate on such grand temporal and spatial scales that they blur the boundaries at scales considerably larger than we are able to rationalize. In many ways, they are invisible to humans and seemingly unreal because it is difficult to conceptualize the vast amount time such objects exist (e.g., the half-life of uranium is 4.5 billion years) and the vast ground they cover (e.g., deforestation in Brazil may contribute to melting glaciers in Greenland).

The kind of agency that builds the good life in Minnesota or Beijing cannot be attributed solely to those who (if only at times) escape domination or find original ways to bring significance to life. The conservative reproduction of culture is also a form of action" (Farquhar 2006, 154).

Karla and Lucy do not full willingly give into the hegemonic neoliberal ordering of the Silicon Valley. Yet, they understand their actions contribute to its potency, and they are not entirely autonomous individuals gracefully living in the Santa Clara Valley. In the modern city, home gardeners like Lucy and Karla use their marginality to innovate spaces that validate their existence in ways that further subjugate them to the oppressive nature of state power and in other ways that valorize their "right to the city" (Lefebvre 1991). David Harvey insists that the rights to the city do not come from "intellectual fascinations and fads," but rather, "they rise up from the streets, out of neighborhoods, as a cry for help and sustenance by oppressed peoples in desperate times" (2012, xiii). The urban poor have the power to transform the city through humble acts of everyday social interaction because "great emancipatory gains for human freedom have not been the result of orderly, institutional procedures but of disorderly, unpredictable, spontaneous action cracking open the social order from below" (Scott 2012, 141). This means there has never been an overarching banner of liberation, that local context matters. Local values, or what Ivan Illich (2009b) calls "vernacular values," matter because these types of values inhabit communities of shared values and interests (Bollier 2014).

Such a vernacular movement shifts perception from a political movement driven by ideology to one where people come to their own moral judgments based on something as simple as the reframing of the value of food. "Vernacular spreads by common use" (Illich 2009b, 71), which is why a vernacular movement such as home gardening has such potential—it expands on the human willingness to better the world.

Conclusion

Part of the reason people choose to grow food is because of the precarious conditions of modernity thrust upon them. That much is true. Yet, far more importance lies in the response of home gardens. This chapter illustrates that gardens at the margins emerged in response to a series of shifts and rifts initiated by the spread of industrial capitalism. Growing food is both radical and neoliberal. It challenges the commodification of land, labor, and food, and it accepts the neoliberal condition by providing a social safety net that governmental logics refuse to deliver. Similarly, home gardeners engage in the politics of recognition by demanding a more just and equitable food system, and they grow food in refusal of the politics of recognition. The demand for recognition by a social group (race, class, gender, religion, etc.) assumes that with recognition of another's humanness, equal rights will follow, but time and time again that has failed us. The problem with recognition-based social movements is that they are entirely dependent on being granted recognition because recognition can only occur within the contemporary conditions of the nation-state (Coulthard 2017). Whereas this group of home gardeners is less concerned about gaining recognition from the state and more interested in recognizing each other.

In the process of growing food, home gardeners run up against the limitations of the state and must envision what might exist beyond it—autonomy, anarchy, direct democracy, food democracy, sovereignty, socioecological resilience? So, while home gardeners grow food to ease their precarious working and living conditions, they also grow food to validate their ways of living and being for themselves, their communities, and their environments. This is not a retreat or surrender to the imposition of capitalism, but about imagining a more radical future grounded in self-valorization. Glen Coulthard believes the statist approach of recognition further subjectifies peoples and cultures to their own internal colonization, whereas "on-the-ground practices of freedom" made by real people in real situations "is less oriented toward attaining an affirmative form of recognition from the settler state and society and more about critically revaluating, reconstructing, and redeploying culture and tradition in ways that seek to prefigure a radical alternative to the structural and psycho-affective facets of colonial domination" (2017, 100). The rise of home gardens coincides with the increase, or perhaps resurgence, of a more radical consciousness that returns to the emancipatory potential of self-affirmation.

These home gardeners offer a unique insight into the emancipatory potential of growing and sharing food because the interaction in these spaces produces a convivial atmosphere and embedded within that atmosphere is a decidedly collective spirit. Mexican anthropologist Guillermo Bonfil Batalla (1996), insists that within Mexico's Indigenous communities, cooperation is based on long-standing customary rules of reciprocity. The philosophy of, "today for you, tomorrow for me" is what helps to maintain relationships within a community. While home gardeners in this study consist of recent Mexican immigrants who identify (or are identifiable) as Indigenous, others are United States-born Chicanas/os, Latina/os, recent and long-standing Asian immigrants, African Americans, and United States-born non-Latina/o whites. The shared labor practices and reciprocity norms within the community cannot be ascribed only to Indigenous peoples. I believe the "fiesta spirit" of communal labor that occurs within this community speaks to the power of food to create bonds that bridge social categories of difference.

The garden is a biophysical and sociocultural space promoting personal and communal transformation and a newfound or rekindled willingness to engage in broader collective action. More than sharing good food, seed, knowledge, or labor, home gardeners are sharing part of themselves and their culture by creating revolutionaries at the margins that celebrate and share the knowledge and experiences of everyday life. Collectively, home gardeners are participating in the meaning-making process of culture. The very mundaneness of gardens at the margins might be what allows home gardeners to retain autonomy and restore dignity. As James C. Scott (2009) has detailed, the "art of not being governed" has a lot to do with how cultural adaptations (i.e., social structures, language, farming knowledge) are designed to evade state capture and formation. Both the physical location of life at the margins and people's mobility or adaptation ensures autonomy in the face of precarity. So, while the transformation of the region from the Santa Clara Valley to the Silicon Valley has created an ever-widening chasm between wealth and poverty and an ever-increasing "precariat" class (Standing 2011; also see Polanyi 1944), gardens at the margins continue to emerge as escapes from neoliberal governmentality. Spaces of neglect and marginality are also spaces of innovation. They offer the opportunity for a way of life that values social relationships over material wealth, subsistence over dependence, and diversity over uniformity.

INTERLUDE

Milpas at the Margins

On a fall afternoon in late September 2013, I met with Diana, who was to give me a tour of the garden she shared with her neighbor. I arrived at the small house near Empire Gardens Elementary School, just north of downtown San José. Diana is a short and assertive Chicana with a warm personality and a friendly smile. I parked my car and began to walk toward the house as she waved me over while holding the gate. Diana is a single mother in her early forties who spends much of her time cooking and, more recently, growing food with her neighbor. Diana walked me into the shared backyard where Grandma, her neighbor, was already hard at work. We continued into the garden that seemed to go on for miles. We walked past a display of several flowers in clay pots that were hanging from the wooden fence that surrounded the yard. Iris, hibiscus, Easter lily, and *mastuerzo* were arranged near the entrance. Just beyond the flowers, the garden opened into a display of diversity and innovation.

The first time I was introduced to Grandma, she told me that she had lived in the community longer than anyone else in the neighborhood. On their walk home from school, neighborhood kids would often say "Hola abuelita" (Hello grandma) as they passed, and eventually, the name stuck. Today, she is known throughout the neighborhood simply as Grandma. She lives in a simple two-bedroom home that sits on an oddly shaped rectangular lot that measures about fifty feet wide by two hundred feet long. We could see Grandma on the far end of the yard and walked over to greet her. Diana explained to me that ever since they started to garden together, Grandma had shared with her a

FIGURE 8 Grandma's garden. Photo courtesy of the author.

deep understanding of the land. Diana's daughter, who was in junior high at the time, was even gaining an interest in growing food and healthy eating. Diana described how the garden serves to bridge the generations from Grandma to her and then to her daughter. Gardening provided her and daughter access to a profound garden subjectivity that recognizes the interrelationships between physical, social, mental, and environmental health.

On our way to the far end of the garden, we walked past serrano, jalapeño, and yellow peppers. Diana pointed to how the cherry, beefsteak, Sungold, and several varieties of heirloom tomatoes were intercropped with basil and Mexican marigolds to help with pest management. Green beans, snap peas, and pinto beans climbed a homemade trellis along the fence behind the tomatoes. We passed two Meyer lemon trees, two Mission fig trees, as well as one white peach, Gala apple, pomegranate, guava, and a Valencia orange tree. "Grandma has fruit all year round," Diana told me. She also told me that her daughter's favorite part of the garden was the many summer and winter squash flowers that bloomed throughout the year, which she picks to put in quesadillas. "That girl," Diana told me, "could live off quesadillas."

One thing that struck me as we continued to walk toward the far end of the garden was how the scattered bunches of tomatillo plants looked haphazardly placed. Wondering why, I asked, "Why are there so many different places with tomatillos?" Diana replied with a smile and chuckle. "That's how Grandma does it, milpa style." She explained to me that Grandma rotates crops over time, which is one reason, the other helps to explain Grandma's unique knowledge set. As the tomatillo plant grows throughout the year, she harvests particular fruits prematurely to allow for others to ripen bigger and more flavorful. She then tosses those prematurely harvested tomatillos into particular places to provide nutrients to other plants as it decomposes. Sometimes this method results in a new tomatillo plant the following spring. This explained Grandma's intensely farmed and regenerative garden; it also explained why Diana has one of the best roasted tomatillo salsas in the neighborhood.

CHAPTER 2

Gardening as a Way of Life

Recipes from Grandma's Garden

The increasing speed and power of global capitalism have led to the homogenization of daily life and has forced countless people out of subsistence farming. The transition has disrupted the lifestyles and daily routines associated with "milpa-based cuisines" commonly found in rural communities where fresh and local vegetables form the bases of the local diet (Gálvez 2018). The technological changes of industrial agriculture have reduced the diversity of options we see at the grocery store and increased the range of diet-related illnesses people are now exposed to (Winson 2013), coinciding with the simplification of global diets is the simplification in the production, preparation, and consumption of food. But there is a growing resistance to the homogenization and degradation of our food and health (Winne 2010), and as Sandor Katz (2006) explains, such a revolution will not be microwaved.

There is an assumption that the industrial model of food production is the best way to feed a growing population. However, recent research provides evidence to the contrary (GRAIN 2014; FAO 2021). The industrial agro-food system disenfranchises people by making them dependent on a system of food production that damages the earth, impairs their health, and centralizes wealth (Shiva 2016; Gálvez 2018; Otero 2018; Lowder, Sánchez, and Bertini 2021). These social conditions are most strongly felt in the sacrifice zones of our urban and rural communities (e.g., Bullard 1990; Lerner 2012; Nixon 2011; Taylor 2014), but this is also where we see a discursive resistance forged through the "struggles of the common man" (Esteva 2005).

70   Chapter 2

This chapter uses Grandma's garden as a gateway to gardening at the margins. Home gardens are indispensable for people like Grandma because growing food is never just about growing food; it is also about self-constitution and autonomy. Yet, while there has been an increased interested in urban agriculture in recent years (e.g., Carpenter 2009; Ladner 2011; Cockrall-King 2012; Reynolds and Cohen 2016), there exists very little recognition that home gardens are part of a long cultural tradition in Mexico, Latin America, and Southeast Asia. Indigenous and Mexican peoples have historically used home gardens as a means to remain self-determining (e.g., Salmón 2012; Peña et al. 2017), yet this part of the narrative is often erased, and erasing that portion of our history normalizes our dependence on the industrial food system. While urban agriculture and community gardens have received high acclaim in recent years, there is a larger story here that is often overlooked by mainstream food movements. This chapter offers a more nuanced perspective of urban agriculture through the lens of home gardeners.

Furthermore, the same people who have experienced the effects of erasure have historically faced various forms of enclosures. The removal from their ancestral homeland, the privatization of common land, and the re-

FIGURE 9 Gardening as a way of life. Photo courtesy of the author.

stricted access of fishing, hunting, and seed saving are only a handful of ways colonized people have experienced enclosures. Yet, enclosure is not a one-off event; it is a reoccurring process of events (see Harvey 2001), and the continuity of home gardens is an expression of self and communal determination against enclosure. This chapter brings some context to the Santa Clara Valley by drawing attention to its history of repeated enclosures and the resistance to those enclosures as experienced by its people.

The home garden is often a place where people in this study find peace and purpose because it is a site of communication between the self and the more-than-human world. The garden is an "agentic assemblage" (see Bennett 2010) whereby the metabolism exchanged between gardeners like Grandma and the plants grown and consumed helps to bridge the "ontological divide" (Bennett 2010, 51) between self and Other. Food, and as I argue, the garden, is an "actant" (see Latour 1996) because it "enters into what we become" (Bennett 2010, 51). For many gardeners like Grandma, the intergenerational aspects of gardening have been passed from generation to generation through cultural transmission. The garden is indispensable for people like Grandma, who passes her library of knowledge to others through the humble act of gardening. Culture, language, values, and health are embodied practices that gardening helps to maintain and restore.

Following a similar vein, many gardeners in this study are recent diaspora immigrants and displaced peoples who have been forcefully removed from their homelands and find themselves in the Santa Clara Valley. Yet, their home garden allows them to literally and metaphorically root themselves to cultivate a sense a place through an ethic of care. I argue that home gardens offer an often-overlooked example of the commons, or what Gustavo Esteva (2005) refers to as "the new commons." This frames home gardens as a collective process of "commoning" (see Linebaugh 2009), or the act of creating together with others, because such spaces are enacted through a cooperative placemaking process (Blomley 2008, 320). Enclosure is a step toward the homogenization of space *and* value(s), while commoning is a practice shaped by local, use-value oriented norms (Bollier 2014). The goal of commoning is to generate a "spatiality of difference" (Sevilla-Buitrago 2015, 3). For people like Grandma, the home garden common is more important than ever. As capitalism continues to gain its wealth through the seizure of the common (in terms of land, markets, norms, values, knowledge, and bodies), only by reclaiming what is created "in common" can people create new and awaken old alliances across difference as sites of conviviality and social reproduction. The home gardens presented here are enacted socio-environmental assemblages that help to enable the formation of autonomy.

Gardening Milpa Style

A milpa is a traditional style of agriculture common throughout Latin America. The most common crops found growing in a milpa are corn, beans, and squash. The "three sisters," as they are commonly referred to by many Indigenous communities, are perfect examples of the relationships and interdependencies present in traditional farming methods. Milpa-style agriculture is an intricately designed and managed practice that stems from a deep understanding and awareness of the land. Farming a milpa requires the rotation of annual crops with a variety of perennial shrubs and trees. The success of the milpa originates from the "synergistic effects" of intercropping and rotation (Cajete 2000, 142). Corn provides shade and a trellis for beans and squash to grow. As the squash grows and spreads itself, it offers ground cover and reduces the competition for water and soil nutrients from potential unwanted weeds. While expanding, it also shields the ground from rainfall, thus preventing erosion and capturing the maximum available rain. Beans also provide vital nutrients to the milpa as they fix nitrogen in the soil through their roots to improve soil fertility. But more than a regenerative farming method, I gathered from Grandma that a milpa is a way of life, or way of thinking about life, and a clear example of the dynamic nature of how home gardens are tailored to the experiential knowledge, history, and circumstances of a family.

While Grandma no longer grows corn, she uses legumes throughout her garden as nitrogen fixers. She creates living compost throughout the growing season, a method she learned from her father. She uses cover crops and intercrops plants, flowers, and even fruit trees to maintain and restore soil nutrients. Grandma maintains her garden mainly through direct seeding, which is a planting method done with no prior tillage and minimum soil disturbance. Grandma's garden retains most of the crop residues on the soil surface, builds topsoil, improves overall soil health, and increases productivity. Her garden landscape influences her ideas about herself and her sense of community. Part of her identity is written into the garden landscape, and maintaining its health is also about maintaining her well-being.

We toured the garden and discussed the ethnohistory of each crop until we reached the foot of four nopal cacti. Grandma explained that there used to be a lot more of them, but over the years, she removed them, or they died. Grandma described how to harvest and prepare nopal with conviction, but Diana's facial expression relayed a different message. "Es un arte" (It's an art), Diana assured me. Her garden is an autotopography (see Mares and Peña 2010, 2011), a place transformed by her identity, history, and sense of place. Grandma's garden is her story, an expression of who she is, and this autotopographic oasis assured Grandma and Diana a pathway to self-determination. Standing at the foot of one nopal, Grandma said, "Todos mexicanos tienen un nopal. Lo más tiene, lo más mexicano" (All Mexicans have a nopal. The more Mexican one is, the more nopal one has). Diana laughed in agreement. "¿Tierra y libertad, no?" (Land and liberty, right?) Looking at the cactus, Grandma simply nodded her head in agreement.

"Tierra y libertad" was the battle cry of the Mexican Revolution (1910–20). As the *Porfiriato* sought to seize up land for the aristocracy, the peasants struck back in resistance, claiming only with access to land could they achieve liberty; the two were wed. During his dictatorship (1876–1911), Porfirio Díaz understood that without land to grow food, peasants would be forced into a wage economy, which was controlled by the Mexican elite. The battle cry was also used by the South Central Farmers in resistance to the foreclosure of the downtown garden in Los Angles in 2006.[1] Throughout my conversations with home gardeners, the same awareness was present; access to land can enable a level of autonomy and contribute to one's social and ecological resilience (also see Peña et al. 2017; Trauger 2017).

For people like Grandma, a garden is a repository of knowledge, and while "gardening" is something people have always done throughout time and may seem inconsequential to many, what makes the home gardens in this study so important in our current world, is the diversity of ways growing food offers escapes from the homogenization of industrial capitalism. When a gardener

---

1. South Central Farm (SCF) was a fourteen-acre urban farm in Los Angeles, California located at East Forty-First and South Alameda Streets. Between 1994 and 2006, SCF was considered one of the largest urban farms in the United States and provided food to over 350 families. The City of Los Angeles evicted gardeners in 2006 and forcefully removed gardeners and destroyed their crops. Over the years, the farm provided valuable resources to the community (see Juárez 2017). Today, the fight to restore the farm continues through the efforts of many people working for food justice.

plants an heirloom seed passed down from an ancestor, she is doing far more than planting a seed or "growing a garden." She is actively participating in the continuity of culture, knowledge, language, and even agrobiodiversity that is often marked for erasure. By growing food, Grandma engages in environmental justice by illuminating the indispensability of traditional knowledge. Not only does her garden increase the organic matter that feeds soil microbial activity and results in healthy soil, but her garden, and the practices that take place in her garden, also enhance social and ecological diversity.

Diversity is perhaps a precondition for the rise of the very self-regulating ecosystems and peoples that are now threatened by anthropogenic climate change. In fact, Soule and Piper believe diversity to be "the currency of adaptation" (1992, 17) because cultural diversity enables biological diversity. Aldo Leopold (1949) understood this in the 1940s when he observed in the *Sand County Almanac* that biodiversity is essential to the health of the "land organism," and cultural diversity is vital to the health of society. The coevalness of biological and cultural diversity has shaped the trajectory of ethnoecology—as can be traced in the scholarly work from Conklin (2008) through Shiva (2010) and Nazarea (2005). The link between cultural and biological diversity, or "biocultural diversity" (see Posey 1999), refers to "the diversity of life in all of its manifestations: biological, cultural, and linguistic, which are interrelated (and possibly coevolved) within a complex socio-ecological adaptive system" (Maffi 2007, 269).

We live in a world with ever more degraded ecosystems and ever more culturally and environmentally destructive social systems. Historically, we have looked to baseline norms to inform us of environmental conditions before our current era. Still, the baseline norms that Darwin or McC. Netting once observed are far different today. And furthermore, we may never be able to, nor want to, go back to those same norms (see Marris 2011). Diversity is our lifeline, and both cultural and biological diversity feed off each other to ensure the evolutionary process. How we influence one of these will significantly impact the other. Modernization and efficiency have created what Vandana Shiva (1997) refers to as "monocultures of the mind" because the monocultures of industrial agriculture extend beyond the homogenization of the landscape into the homogenization of farming practices, value systems, and ways of knowing. This has negatively impacted our epistemologies, environments, diets, and social systems as such a worldview rejects plurality and self-organization in pursuit of uniformity. Yet, as groups such as the Zapatistas and La Via Campesina have shown us, there are alternatives. Embedded within these alternatives is the concept of autonomy, which encourages the self-constitution of those who practice it. Forms of conviviality lie in spaces just beyond the reach of the circuits of the expanded reproduction of capital. Growing in Grandma's garden is far more than food. In fact, food that originates in Grandma's garden and ends up on her table is the end product of a process that is continually under threat. The continuity of Grandma's garden, and more importantly, the continuity of Grandma's way of life that is enabled because of her garden is a form of resistance because her agency is de-linked from capitalist enclosure. Grandma's urban milpa escapes the trap of industrial agriculture and offers an alternative way of life.

Huertos Familiares: The Legacy and Erasure of Home Gardens

"Tenido un jardín todo mi vida" (I've had a garden all my life), Grandma told me. "En México, éramos muy pobres, pero siempre teníamos comida suficiente" (In Mexico, we were very poor, but we always had enough food), she continued. Grandma is from *el campo*, or the countryside, and has been around food and farming her entire life. Growing food was not a novelty, but a way of life. Growing up in a rural community in the state of Jalisco, her family, and the families around her, all had home gardens, or *huertos familiares* as she referred to them. Yet, while the food produced in these gardeners circulated throughout the community, it rarely reached the marketplace. The food of her childhood was food of subsistence. As a child, much of the food she consumed was already de-linked from the global food supply chain, and when she moved to the United States, she continued this subversive way of life. Grandma is not alone in her actions; in fact, generations of Mesoamericans, Latin Americas, Africans, Asians, and Indigenous folks have continued to cultivate home gardens as a means of cultural determination and survival. As Enrique Salmón explains:

> This knowledge is a reflection of a way of being or what may be considered a way of life. This is not so much a lifestyle, which often suggests choice, but just being. It is not a movement that can be joined, but rather a resilient worldview from which the people draw whole thinking approaches to every action and choice related to people and place. (2012, 161)

The legacy of home gardens is deeply rooted in the norms and cultural practices of many land-based peoples whose history of resilience and determination is often disregarded, or even erased.

Recently, two well-trained permaculturists, Eric Toensmeier and Jonathan Bates (2013), published a book documenting their experiences in attempting to create a "permaculture paradise." In the process, they filled their backyard with low-maintenance edible plants. They were able to intensely grow (some better than others) almost two hundred varieties of edible plants on one-tenth of an acre. This is about three times the size of Grandma's garden. While Grandma's garden might not offer the same agrobiodiversity (for Grandma's agrobiodiversity index, see appendix B, garden 5) as Toensmeier and Bates's, they incurred very little risk. Both of them held full-time, well-paying jobs, and their garden was not so much a way of life as it was an experiment into diversity. Most of the home gardeners in this study do not grow diversity merely because they can but rather because they must. Toensmeier and Bates give no mention of how countless home gardens around the world also grow high levels of biodiversity on even smaller pieces of land, with far fewer resources, and with plants better suited for local environmental conditions and cultural contexts. Nor do they acknowledge the deep biodiversity they are able to achieve is because centuries of home gardeners have intentionally selected and cultivated diversity. This is not to discredit the importance of experimentation for Toensmeier and Bates but instead to draw attention to how such research can often disregard and effectively erase centuries of traditional knowledge and practice.

Huertos familiares, or home gardens, have historically been an essential feature for peasants and immigrants alike to assure diversity and to navigate uncertainty (Peña 2005; Eyzaguirre and Linares 2010; also see Valdovinos 2017). Ramón Méndez believes "el huerto familiar es el espacio de reproducción social, cultural y simbólica que da sentido a la identidad de quien lo cultiva y lo habita" (the home garden is a space of social, cultural, and symbolic reproduction that gives meaning to the people who cultivate and inhabit them) (2012, 4). These plants are valuable because of the diverse social, cultural, and symbolic value ascribed to them. Not only do the huertos familiares described by Méndez carry far more diversity than that of Toensmeier and Bates, but they also transmit the living cultural memory of seed saving and sharing. It is for reasons like this that people like Virginia Nazarea ask, "If seeds and memories are important to people who are rooted in place . . . , how critical are these 'resources' to people who have uprooted from their place of origin and settled in a foreign land or, for that matter, who perpetually negotiate two worlds, never completely belonging to one or the other?" (2005, 98). The agrobiodiversity present in huertos familiares helps people to mitigate risk. Whether those risks are crop failure, social networks, cultural determination, economic opportunity, or diaspora, home gardens provide opportunities for people, plants, and places to form coeval relationships of resilience (Altieri and Hecht 1990; Gliessman 1990; Brescia 2017). The handpicked seeds selected to be passed down were chosen on their effectiveness and ability to withstand the local conditions such as soil fertility, soil diseases common for that area, insect infestations patterns, availability of water, and even taste.

The adoption of such coeval relationships is the result of generations of the "sophisticated cultural engagement" of place-based peoples (Ford and Nigh 2010, 184). Research on home gardens and milpa farming documents how polyculture farming in pre-Columbian America enabled high levels of crop diversity, which were accompanied by complex social systems (Cajete 2000; Gliessman 1990; Altieri and Hecht 1990). To understand the role of huertos familiares in the daily lives of gardeners, one must consider the structure (spatial organization), composition (plant and species diversity), and function (use-values provided) of these gardens (Lope-Alzina and Howard 2012). Yet, perhaps the most essential attribute of home gardens is that they are dynamic; each garden is distinctly different in its structure, composition, and function. So, while the current trend may focus on the composition or structure of these gardens (e.g., Toensmeier and Bates 2013), the actual function, or what the garden *actually does* for the people that grow them, is far more complex and nuanced. Leading scholars acknowledge the need for more detailed research on the functions of home gardens and how the use-values of these gardens may contribute to their biological structure and composition (Lope-Alzina and Howard 2012; Howard 2006).

Many assume the urbanization and development of rural and peri-urban landscapes have resulted in a loss of agrobiodiversity. However, research by Poot-Pool et al. (2015) reveals that while this may be true for certain tree fruits, it is not valid for harvestable herbs. In fact, "agrobiodiversity does not decline along the rural-peri-urban gradient, but differentiates" (2015, 203). People tend to grow crops in home gardens that are not easily found in markets or that cannot be easily and packaged and shipped. These plants are often passed on via seed or cuttings, which means they're more often heirloom varieties. Home gardens are modified to make practical use of space and resources. Furthermore, recent research by Ávila et al. (2017) has shown that urban areas in the Global South are hotspots for agrobiodiversity, and more importantly, such agrobiodiversity varies depending on the level urbanization. Medicinal and food plants are mainly found in the home gardens of communities with high to intermediate levels of urbanization, while ornamental plants are more common in rural community home gardens. These findings disrupt the idea that the highest levels of agrobiodiversity are found in rural settings and highlights the need to focus attention on how and why urban home gardeners cultivate diversity.

While these studies are very informative and add to the discussion of home gardens, they do not focus on how migration (both voluntary and forced) may enhance or disrupt agrobiodiversity. There is no doubt that when migrants move, they often carry with them seeds, rootstock, or tubers to plant in their new locations (Crow 2017; Mares and Peña 2010, 2011; Komarnisky 2009). In fact, Heraty and Ellstrad (2016) argue that contemporary germplasm conservation tends to focus attention on ex situ and in situ forms of conservation management. Transnational migrants disrupt this as they adapt landrace varieties to new locations. Home gardens become sites of in vivo conservation (see Nazarea 2005)—or the coevolution of people, places, *and cultures* (also see Nabhan 2013, 2017). The transnational dispersal of people and seeds creates an opportunity for the maintenance of genetic diversity beyond its recognized centers of diversity.

While these studies highlight the structure and composition of home gardens, they leave the function unresolved. Some studies that have attempted to grasp at the use-value of home gardens to reveal more of its complexity. Taylor et al. (2017) finds that with the growing interest in the ecosystem services of home gardens, many researchers have overlooked how different ethnic groups consider the uses of their gardens. Home gardens produce ecosystem services such as cleaner air and water, as well as green space and aesthetics (e.g., Calvet-Mir, Gómez-Baggethun, and Reyes-García 2012; Barthel et al. 2010), but gardeners often choose plants based on their uses rather than their ecosystem services alone. The agency of the gardener is critical because the choices one makes reveals much about what one values.

Similarly, Chan, Pennisi, and Francis (2016) argue that gardening can cultivate resilience by serving as a "social-ecological refuge," or a safe, restorative community that not only enables gardeners to reconnect with themselves, each other, and the local environment but also functions as biocultural refugia that foster community food security by preserving and transmitting adaptive cultural and ecological memories, skills, and resources related to growing food and managing local urban environments. In this way, "growing food at home" enables migrants to construct identity through reshaping the landscapes in which they inhabit. These hybrid landscapes embody both traditional and new practices and corps. This argument further confirms the multiple, shifting subjectivities of recent immigrants (Gerodetti and Foster 2015; Mares 2012; Mares and Peña 2011; also see Anzaldúa 2007).

In this chapter, I am particularly interested in the function or use-value of home gardens and the influences of place-based cultural practices. There is no doubt that many of the gardeners I have worked with throughout this study have a tremendous garden composition (see appendix B for agrobiodiversity survey data) and highly sophisticated garden structure (see figure 1 for an example), but to understand the legacy of home gardens in Mexican, Latinx, Chicana/o, Indigenous, and other diaspora and displaced communities, we must pay close attention to their value. Reflecting on her home garden in eastern Washington, María Guillen Valdovinos describes both a nostalgic past of her ancestors in Mexico and a continued struggle for cultural survival in her new home in the United States. She states, "This led me to recognize and appreciate resilience as a living labor capacity to create spaces that reaffirm a sense of place and a sense of belonging in places far from our homelands" (2017, 175). What is missing from much of the literature on home gardens is how they can create spaces that must remain hidden. In fact, as explained by Valdovinos, "Kitchen gardens have historical links to our [Mexican and Indigenous] communities and are an essential component to our identity, in particular in creating autonomous spaces" (2017, 182).

Autonomous spaces are often sites of contestation because they exist outside of the reach of capitalism (Scott 1998, 2009) and are always at risk of enclosure. Yet, enclosure is far more complicated than the seizure of material resources (i.e., land or natural resources) because it often coincides with the dispossession and deprivation of "the autonomous capacities for self-valorization" (Sevilla-Buitrago 2015, 5). The goal of enclosure is to create heteronomous value regimes and to establish the submission of life forms to the rule of the marketplace (also see De Angelis 2007). Yet, for people like Valdovinos and Grandma, who unearth essential components of identity through the intergenerational practices of gardening and farming, the home garden is a subversive practice against the homogenization of modern life.

Gardening against Enclosure: From *Gerguensun* to the Silicon Valley

Enclosure is a process that occurs when common land, or land that people use in common for subsistence farming, herding, fishing, or foraging, is taken and privatized. Often, enclosure is discussed within the context of the English enclosure movement of the 1600s, where elites seized common land for their own pursuits and wealth. Embedded in the idea of enclosure were the promise of individual wealth, autonomy, and freedom, but as Peter Linebaugh explains, the opposite is true. "*Enclosure*, like *capital*, is a term that is physically precise, even technical (hedge, fence, wall), and expressive of concepts of unfreedom (incarceration, imprisonment, immurement)" (2014, 142). Enclosure is not about democratizing land ownership but controlling land and access to it. While the 1600s marks the particular period of the English Enclosure Acts, enclosure by no means started or stopped during that era. They are still very much alive and well today. Similar to Linebaugh, my use of enclosure refers to "the complete separation of the worker from the means of production" (2014, 32). This means that I am not only concerned about access to land but also whenever and wherever the means of production are separated from the worker.

Like most sites of colonial conquest, the Santa Clara Valley has a long history of separating the worker form their means of production, and while the social, ecological, and economic makeup of the Santa Clara Valley is far different today than it was at the time of "contact," much is still the same—namely, the recurrence of enclosure confronted by those deemed "nonwhite." This occurs for various reasons. First, in the Marxist sense, enclosure operates to remove people from their ability to provide for their own means of production and reproduction (i.e., live off the land) by creating a marketplace where labor can be sold and goods can be bought to support an economy. The so-called primitive accumulation first occurred at the emergence of capitalism and has since expanded and evolved through time and space. Marx explained primitive accumulation "as a process which divorces the worker from the ownership of the conditions of his own labour" (1990, 874) and thus forces one to enter the marketplace to earn a wage to eke out a living. Second, in the Foucauldian sense, enclosure operates as a means of social control whereby standardizing juridical order, emergent markets, social norms, written languages, and forms of social organization (also see Byrd 2011). Dispossession is nothing new, but since the birth and expansion of capitalism, it has become highly methodical (Sevilla-Buitrago 2015).

More than nine thousand years before the arrival of Europeans in the Americas, various Indigenous groups in western United States lived enmeshed in the vast oak savannas that flourished in its many valleys. According to M. Kat Anderson, "Oaks and hands interacted in a myriad of ways as people in each of the many ethnic groups went about their daily routines of gathering, tending, and preparing oak parts: acorns, bark, leaves, and branches" (2007, 1). These early agroecologists farmed and gardened on such a grand scale that it was beyond anything the new "arrivants" (see Byrd 2011) could comprehend. Indigenous peoples of California farmed entire ecosystems (Anderson 2007; also see Bowman and Haberle 2010; Keeley 2002). However, the oak savannas were of paramount importance. Their agroecosystem spanned from the oak-dotted canyons in the Sierra Nevada foothills of California to the oak savannas in the Willamette Valley of Oregon. Stretching from the Pacific Northwest to the American Southwest, various Indigenous peoples used and managed oak trees for food, resources, and guidance.

This part of history is often overlooked by historians, as Leventhal et al. (1994) acknowledge. Yet, the reality is that Indigenous peoples were not merely "hunters and gatherers" but also managers. Before Europeans created *wilderness* (see Cronon 1996), Indigenous peoples farmed *wildness*. While Indigenous groups in California did forage for readily available wild foods, mainly shellfish and other small game, they also tended the forests through various agroecological and agroforestry practices, such as burning and tilling (Leventhal et al. 1994; Anderson 2007). In fact, "the production systems of native Californians provided reliable food surpluses for large populations located in the myriad micro-ecosystems distributed around the Bay Area" (Leventhal et al. 1994, 303). The food surpluses helped to forge strong networks for economic exchange between various groups in the region and encourage ecosystem resilience.

The protected waters of the Bay Area proved to be a great asset to the Indigenous inhabitants called the Ohlone, as they traveled throughout the region for commerce and trade in their canoes. The high grasses common in the South Bay provided cover for the Ohlone. They navigated the vast mazes of the surrounding marshes and wetlands to hunt and fish for marine mammals like sea otter and harbor seals that were once abundant. The California horned snail, bay mussel, oysters, and clams were central aspects of the Ohlone diet, and all were readily available in the South Bay marshes. Shorebirds such as gulls, pelicans, cormorants, egrets, and great blue herons were also common in the marshes and used by the Ohlone (Hylkema 2007).

Along with the diverse foods available to the Ohlone through foraging and hunting, the most important food was the acorn. "Making acorn," as it is commonly referred to by many Indigenous groups, was primarily women's work (Anderson 2007). Women made acorn by collecting and processing the acorn into mush, which serves both as a diet staple and a critical component in rituals and ceremonies. The Ohlone also tended to the oak tree for a variety of medicinal uses. The Ohlone would use the bark for treating infections and internal disorders, boiling down the inner bark of the blue oak to form a drink that helped relieve arthritis and treating indigestion with a concoction made from the ashes of the green bark of coast live oak soaked in water. Oaks served as critical components of maintaining the health of the Ohlone throughout the Bay Area.

While the health and well-being of the Ohlone depended on oak trees, the health and well-being of the oak savannas were reliant on the co-management of humans. "Native Americans in the West were well aware that to have the most diverse, healthy, and productive oak woodlands, they had to intervene and actively care for the oaks and the surrounding ecosystems" (Anderson 2007, 11). By burning the underbrush, the Ohlone could keep the grass from getting too high, which increased the visibility of fallen acorns. This form of agroforestry contributed to the health and diversity of the understory. "These understory plants were in a sense crops, because they were managed with the techniques of tillage, seedbeating, sowing, weeding and/or burning for many products" (Anderson 2007, 15). Tilling and sowing the oak understory provided wildflowers and edible bulbs for food.

The vast oak savannas that once flourished in the South Bay were a result of human co-management. The Ohlone did not just forage acorns; they also farmed them. They managed the forests to produce a consistent surplus of food and resources while also managing the forests to promote ecological health and increase biodiversity. The environments and social organization of the many Indigenous groups in precontact California were of surplus, not one of scarcity (also see Sahlins 1998). The logic of scarcity was brought on by the enclosures initiated by European settlers as they misread the landscape through their colonial lens. Burning contributed to the production and abundance of various resources while also helping to control the spread of disease. Today, the spread of Sudden Oak Death has been reported in the oak savannas throughout the Bay Area, much of it a result of a lack of coeval human co-management.[2]

The Ohlone and other Native American groups who made their homes in the oak savannas understood how agroforestry practices could manage and restore native landscapes, build biodiversity, improve forest health for different plant and animal species, and stop the spread of disease. Contact, colonialism, and the enclosure that followed changed much of the traditional practices of the Ohlone as they were forcefully removed from their ancestral lands. As Anderson acknowledges, "the decline in the eating of acorn and other traditional foods is closely linked to a rising incidence of health problems among Native Americans in California and elsewhere" (2007, 5). What began as a land enclosure resulted in the loss of a way of life, decline in biodiversity, loss of forest resilience, and a disruption in cultural health.

Hylkema (2007) believed the Muwekma Ohlone, the name of the Ohlone who once lived in what is today the community of Washington-Alma, chose the site for strategic purposes because it is located along Guadalupe River at the convergence of many creeks and drainages, which include Stevens, Calabazas, Saratoga, Los Gatos, Canoas, Silver, Coyote, and Penitencia Creeks. The meandering nature of the Guadalupe River created a natural levee and protected the community. The vast oak savannas that the Ohlone help to manage created what they referred to as *gerguensun*, or "the place of the oak trees" (Hylkema 2007, 17). Oaks provided protection from predators and illness, they contributed to the spiritual and physical well-being of the people, and they enabled the biological and cultural diversity of the region. The colonial transformation of "the place of the oak trees," which is today the site of Mission Santa Clara, serves as a repeated theme whereby enclosure inhibits the health of a people and the landscape.

---

2. Sudden Oak Death refers to the spread of the plant pathogen *Phytophthora ramorum*. This pathogen has had a devastating effect on oak diversity and population throughout California and Oregon. Also see http://www.suddenoakdeath.org/.

The leading cause in the decline of the Ohlone population after European settlement to the region was disease. Smallpox, measles, syphilis, and tuberculosis all contributed to the fall in population. The second-leading cause was malnutrition and starvation (Almaguer 1994, 130). These two interlocking factors demonstrate the divorcing of the worker from the means of their own production and the dramatic effects of enclosure. For generations, the social and environmental health of the valley was reliant on the coevolution of humans and their environment, but the metabolic rift (see Foster, Clark, and York 2010; Marx 1990) initiated by settler colonialism set in motion a series of events that continues to degrade the health of the land and its people. Foster's notion of metabolic rift works off his reading of Marx's *Capital* volume three, where he insists that capitalism creates an "irreparable rift in the interdependent processes of social metabolism" (1981, 949). The ecological disruption inherent in industrial capitalism contributes to our alienation from nature.

Like many early Spanish and Mexican settlements across California, San José has a long history of colonization. Recent success stories featuring high-tech companies making billionaire fortunes in the Santa Clara Valley are touted as the latest silicon-gilded version of the "American Dream." But the lust for wealth, power, and fame on display in San José is not a recent trend, and the settler-colonists who first approached and encroached on this valley were also driven by the lust for wealth and power (Pitti 2003). Ever since its founding in 1777, the quest for accumulation and conquest has remained the apparent aspiration.

The racialized class warfare and violence of the successive waves of invading settler colonialists presents a continuous thread throughout the history of the Santa Clara Valley. One has only to recall the conditions facing the so-called Mission Indians (the Ohlone in this case) during the 1700s to get a sense of the deeply rooted nature of this assault and the similarities it shares with the conditions and circumstances faced by Mexican workers in the same valley since the nineteenth century. Leventhal et al. (1994) describe the environmental, cultural, and health degradation unleashed by the mission system:

> As agricultural laborers, missionized Indians were largely separated from the seasonal rhythms of their own food production practices. At the same time, the growth of mission farms and rangeland for cattle initiated an environmental transformation of the Bay Area and the entire coast that destroyed much of the resource base of the indigenous economy.... The demographic

collapse of the Ohlone populations held captive at Mission Dolores at the tip of the San Francisco peninsula, Missions Santa Clara and San Jose in the South and East Bay respectively, the Amah-Mutsun at San Juan Bautista to the south, and the Esselens at Mission San Carlos on the Monterey peninsula occurred because of the horrendous effects of European-introduced diseases, exacerbated by the unhealthy diet and over-crowded living conditions at the missions. Birth rates plummeted from disease, mistreatment of women, and from a psychological phenomenon now recognized as post-traumatic stress. . . . As the populations of Ohlones both inside and outside of the missions decreased, survivors tended to congregate around the missions, seeking solutions to their seemingly unsolveable [sic] problems from the missionaries who were causing those same problems. Under the circumstance of socio-cultural holocaust, many Bay Area Ohlones identified with their oppressors, who seemed to have overthrown and taken control of all of the old systems of spiritual and earthly power. (1994, 305–6)

Conquest and settler colonialism set in motion a series of socioecological transformations that degraded the health of the land and the environmental conditions facing both Indigenous peoples and new arrivals. This is a process that continues to unfold in the present. Ironically and tragically, in this transit of empire, the imprint and wisdom of Indigenous peoples are mostly recounted by environmental anthropologists, like Anderson who laments:

The memories of Native American elders, the diaries of early Spanish explorers, old anthropological accounts, and archaeological research all provide evidence that native peoples were actually accomplished managers of their oak environments who actively manipulated plants, populations, and habitats to increase yields, sustain production, and improve the quality of natural raw materials. They did so with an impressive breadth of knowledge, keen observational skills, fine-tuned horticultural techniques, and judicious harvesting. (2007, 1)

However, even this account can ultimately obscure contemporary Ohlone struggles ongoing today to intervene as political actors in the protection and restoration of the oak savanna life zone, which retains potential as an essential component of the native agroforestry mosaic, alongside a return to heritage cuisines based on judicious and mindful use of that habitat. This happens because contemporary conditions of liberalism assume a postcolonial and post-racial world where multiculturalism actually promotes the spread of empire (Byrd 2011).

The conditions of struggle and violence experienced by Indigenous peoples, immigrants, Chicanas/os, and African Americans are normalized through such logic. Success stories such as these are often coded with ideas of "prevailing against the odds" in pursuit of freedom. They accomplished the so-called American Dream. Worse yet, liberalism does not provide proper attention to how colonialism and racialization have historically worked simultaneously to create order. This, argues Lisa Lowe, is the "violence of forgetting" (2006, 206).

When people experience the violence of forgetting, remembering becomes an act of healing, resistance, and self-valorization. Like many Mexicans, Grandma comes from a complicated history of mixed European and Indigenous blood. Conditions beyond her control forced her to migrate north, but conditions within her control have allowed her to maintain a garden based on preexisting norms from her dislocation and resist the violence of forgetting. This is why home gardens, like Grandma's, are so crucial in today's world. The enclosures of the past are not over. They are merely different. Industrial farming, the patenting of seed and knowledge, and the commodification of water are all forms of enclosure that the modern farmer and home gardener must confront. The privatization of the land completely altered the landscape and the Ohlone relationship to it, and their removal has reconfigured the social order of the region and negatively impacted the health of Indigenous groups in the region. While Grandma is not Ohlone, like many Mexican-origin peoples, she descends from a similar history of enclosure. She remains caught in the same colonial matrix of power (see Quijano 1992, 2000) that continues to impose enclosure. Grandma's garden remains as a site against the transit of empire because it rejects the homogenization of enclosure. With each gardener that takes up the responsibility of home gardening, the legacy of resistance continues.

"Frijoles de mil manera": Garden-Centered Recipes for Life

Grandma learned how to cook when she was about thirteen or fourteen years old. On a small rancho, her family herded cattle and grew corn, beans, chilies, and squash. "Comimos frijoles de mil manera" (We eat beans a thousand ways), she told me with a smile. Grandma explained that living on a ranch is hard work. In fact, she never completed her schooling because she needed to devote her time to the rancho. As we discussed her childhood and young adulthood, it became clear that gardening, farming, and cooking are essential in influencing her worldview and ethics. When I asked her who taught her how to garden, she replied with a short, simple, "Nadie. La vida me enseñó" (No one. Life taught me).

Grandma's home garden influences her ability and desire to adapt. It also demonstrates her ability and willingness to create and transform. In fact, that is exactly what an "enacted space" is. Rojas (1991) articulates how enacted spaces are a result of the interactions between physical space and social space. For home gardeners, the interaction between their physical environment (i.e., the home garden) and their social space (i.e., history and culture) create autotopographies, or spaces of "self-telling through place-shaping" (Mares and Peña 2010, 258). Grandma's place-shaping is done with her food both on the ground and in the kitchen. Life is, has been, and always will be unpredictable, especially for people living life at the margins. However, this does not mean people willingly give in to their precarious circumstances. Grandma's ability to remain resilient while continuing to learn is guided by her humility and the indispensability of a variety of human and nonhuman interactions.[3]

Norms of humility are common values shared by home gardeners. Alfonso is a gardener in his eighties who grew up in the surrounding farmlands of the Bajío region of Mexico, not too far north of Mexico City. His presence is unmistakable as his personality demands the room. He loves to chat, tell stories, and explain his next project going on in his garden. He always wears a Panama hat with a black trim and a long-sleeved collared shirt, and uses a dark wooden antique cane. He told me about his childhood, the move north, his family, and his loving wife, Rocío. His stories had a nostalgic feel, and in a deeply felt way, he reminded me of my own grandfather.

On a fall afternoon in 2013, Alfonso informed me how growing food was not just about growing food. "Para ser un jardínero, es para estar en comunicación. Comunicación con la comida, familia, comunidada, y tierra" (To be a gardener is to be in communication. Communication with food, family,

---

3. According to Melissa Nelson (2008b), humility is a core value for those living in accordance with "original instructions," or a set of instructions about how to live well in a particular location given to us by the creator.

community, and land). Alfonso moved through his garden as if in concert with its rhythms. His dry, aged hands gently touched each tomato before selecting the perfect one to pick. He handed it to me and gestured to his mouth. Without saying a word, he contently smiled and moved on. Alfonso's sentiments demonstrate a profound understanding of the indispensability of human and nonhuman relationships. Growing food means nurturing lines of communication with the plants, the land, our bodies, and each other. His sentiment has two levels of meaning to it. First, Alfonso believes that growing food is part of a self-provisioning experience that requires strong norms of reciprocity. On another level, he believes the simple act of growing food requires mutual recognition of the Other. The function of Alfonso's garden is far more than the food it produces or the biodiversity it creates. If fact, the very mundaneness of gardening forces us to reconsider the use-value of daily actions. When we grow food, we enmesh ourselves into a world of social interactions where human and nonhuman actors collide to create new possibilities and new values.

This is what Jane Bennett (2010) means by an "agentic assemblage." She insists that it is easy to understand how we act on the environment, but it is far more challenging to come to terms with the ways the environment works on us. We need to give up attempting to disentangle the relationships between human and nonhuman actors and embrace the interaction as a coeval relationship. The environment is just as much an actor in the drama of life as we are. It is far more complicated than realizing that "wilderness" can stir emotion in the human spirit as people like Muir or Thoreau have described. Such a shift requires an ontological turn that is removed from human exceptionalism. Alfonso's awareness of his coeval relationship and responsibility to that relationship demonstrates such a shift. As Alfonso showed me around his garden, he continued the stress that gardening is about communication. He did not speak of his garden as a collection of plants, but as an assemblage of life forms inhabiting and creating space together with him.

Removing human exceptionalism allows gardeners, like Alfonso, to collapse the ontological divide between himself and his food. "To the extent that we recognize the agency of food, we also reorient our own experience eating it" (Bennett 2010, 51). Alfonso reorients his relationships and his accountability to those relationships by acknowledging the lines of communication between plants, community, food, and self. This broadened perspective of "self" and "Other" encourages us to rethink the forces of human and nonhuman agency because it does not project assumptions about hierarchical order and process. Devon Peña refers to this broadened realization as the "relationality of wildness" because it involves the "dissolution of the boundaries of the self" (2017b, 90). Alfonso's awareness of the Other is at the same time his suspension of the Cartesian boundaries that are often assumed within Western epistemology and his recognition of his relationality to the Other. This recognition allows him to develop "kincentric landscapes" (Salmón 2012, 22) between himself, his plants, and the more-than-human world within his home garden to cultivate a sense of place wherever he finds himself.

The ability to use the home garden to both adapt and create is a theme expressed by many in this book. Luis is a gardener in his fifties who has spent his lifetime in the Santa Clara Valley. He told me stories about growing up in the valley and his connection with the farmworkers' struggles of the 1960s (I introduce him further in chapter 5). Luis has been a part of various social justice organizations throughout is life, and when I asked him about his garden, he expressed similar sentiments. "Your garden is a reminder of how to live well," he said. Not only does it produce food, but it also provides a sense of shared values and goals sought and accomplished. "When you share the food from your garden you greet your family, your friends, your community—you greet life!" he concluded. While Luis's words resemble those of Marcel Mauss (1990), who believed that living well assumes the ability to share, they extend beyond Mauss because Luis has embedded himself into the "metabolism" of the land and community. By greeting his garden, he is confronting Agamben's (2004) "anthropological machine" and collapsing the "openness" between humans and nonhumans by engaging in the "open whole." Both Alfonso's and Luis's garden subjectivity forces us to think differently about how language and relationships are commonly conceived and discussed (also see Kohn 2013).

These conversations have led me to believe that part of the ontological turn that enables people like Grandma, Luis, and Alfonso to reimagine their positionality as part of a more complex whole occurs when growing, preparing, and eating food becomes a celebration. In fact, Diana said one morning in Grandma's garden, "Food is always about celebration." Throughout this project, I have witnessed Diana prepare food several times, and each time her meals bring life to those who consume them. On one occasion, she prepared me *empanadas de calabacita* (or baby squash empanadas), a rare treat made with baby winter squash. These delicate squashes come about once a year, so to share them with me was quite an honor. Her approach to cuisine acknowledges the vitality of food from production to consumption because she is committed to making real food that brings life to people that matter. This is what Luis meant by "you greet life." Acknowledging the vitality of food in all its manifestations means accepting that food is not just what we eat, but "what we become" (Bennett 2010, 51).

Luis told me that he thinks he comes into contact with at least sixty different people that he would otherwise not come into contact with for each crop he grows. Whether it be telling a neighbor about a plant, describing how he cares for a plant at a La Mesa Verde event, or sharing and cooking it with loved ones, Luis is deeply embedded into the social relationships of his garden that make him who he is. This forms part of the relational accountability present for many home gardeners. As explained by Native scholar Shawn Wilson, "Rather than viewing ourselves as being *in* relationship with other people or things, we *are* the relationships that we hold and are part of" (2008, 80). This means moving beyond seeing oneself as an isolated individual who exists *in* relation to other people and places. Instead, we *are* mothers, fathers, sons, daughters, friends, neighbors, and we *are* from places. The agentic assemblage of the garden allows Luis, Grandma, and Alfonso to orient, inform, and solidify their relationships.

Throughout the life of this study, the celebratory aspects of growing, preparing, sharing, and eating food have remained constant. I have witnessed sicknesses and death in many families. I have seen people evicted from the homes, fired from their jobs, and even deported. Yet, when people are able to pick up the pieces of their life and put them back together again, the garden is almost always one of the first parts they restore because it provides the means for social reproduction and resists the alienation of modern society.

This happens because a garden is a tool for the home gardener, and similar to Ivan Illich's "tools of conviviality," the garden is a tool that actually works for people. In many ways, "community-based" organizations are really "community-placed" organizations, meaning that despite the good intentions of these organizations, their agenda often does not align entirely with that of the community. But the garden is different. Illich asserts, "Individuals need tools to move and to dwell. They need remedies for their diseases and means to communicate with one another" (2009a, 11). Above all, people need "the freedom to make things among which they can live, to give shape to them according to their own tastes, and to put them to use in caring for and about others" (2009a, 11). Tools of conviviality are tools of practicality. Illich uses the concept of conviviality because he believes it to be the opposite of "industrial productivity." But more than that, tools of conviviality support diversity because there is no one approach or outcome.

The function of home gardens, or what gardens actually do for home gardeners, greatly varies depending on the circumstances of gardeners, the materiality of gardens, and their history. When gardening enables one to live a certain way, the act of growing food moves home gardeners closer to self-valorization and autonomy because it heals the alienation imposed on gardeners by systems and institutions outside of their control. Gardening becomes a way a life. As land and our relationship to it becomes a way of life, we develop "place-attachments" that could never have monetary value (Taylor 2006). Place-attachment helps to generate an "ethic of care" (Tronto 1993) that facilitates social and ecological interactions that rethink our place in the world. Grandma, Luis, and Alfonso communicate *to* their garden through their daily interactions *with* their garden. Perhaps the attachment to place, food, people, and community that these gardeners support through their daily interactions is a first step in moving toward a more just, sustainable, and convivial food system.

The Home Garden Common and the Spatiality of Difference

For home gardeners and their extended relationships, growing food is a political act in that their garden networks strengthen their capacity to improve well-being and create their own version of community values outside the spheres of control under the neoliberal privatization of social government. The "commoning" of home gardens described in this chapter is quite different than regularly perceived. The discourse on the common often refers to physical space, but Sevilla-Buitrago urges us to avoid such imprecision, rather, "use the notion of 'enclosure' to designate capitalism's mobilization of diverse configurations and significations of space to deprive people of what they create in common" (2015, 2). So, while Grandma, Alfonso, and Luis might not be commoning physical space, they are commoning knowledge, history, and norms because they work to create them "in common" with each other. Hardt and Negri also attempt to push the discourse in a similar direction in *Common Wealth*. They insist, "Love provides another path for investigating power and productivity of the common" (2009, xi–xii). This further solidifies the agentic assemblage of home gardens and asks profound questions about the revolutionary potential of creating "in common." Enclosure is more than the seizure of geographic space, it is also the dispossession of the autonomous capacity for self-valorization. In fact, much of the research on the commons focuses attention on common-pool resources (CPRs) but does not address how enclosure is also the disciplining of social organization through market expansion.

Luis told me one day, "My garden works for me because it provides me what I need." We did not talk too much about what he meant by "need," but I insinuated from our many conversations that Luis's conceptualization of need was very complicated. "I never wanted to be a part of the 'food thing,'" he told me, "But the funny thing is, everything branches out." For Luis, food is just the beginning. When Luis says, "when you greet your garden, you greet life," he is referring to the plurality of ways in which his garden allows him to greet life from the micro to the macro. By greeting his food, he is addressing the biopolitical reality faced by many low-income communities of color who inhabit food deserts. Diabetes, obesity, and high blood pressure are only a few of the common noncommunicable illnesses that many of the home gardeners in this study share. By greeting his food, Luis is questioning the normalization of diet-related illnesses in communities of color and challenging inequality at the molecular scale. The nutrient-rich and culturally appropriate foods grown in his garden allowed him to lose weight and for others to stop taking prescription drugs to control blood sugar. By greeting his community, Luis confronts inequality on a more human scale by continuing the intergenerational sharing of knowledge, creating community, and helping to spread norms of the common. And lastly, by greeting life, Luis's garden empowers him to challenge inequality on the macro scale by challenging the epistemological violence of forgetting. Enclosures happen at various scales at all times, and home gardens continually work against those enclosures at various scales at all times. This is what Hardt and Negri mean by "Empire is materializing before our very eyes" (2000, xi). The complex spatial and temporal positions of enclosure make addressing the real ramifications of enclosure both challenging and incredibly important. Greeting the garden may lead to better health, increased self-awareness and remembering, greater autonomy, the sharing of traditional knowledge, and the ability to resist empire and enclosure.

Grandma, Alfonso, and Luis work to create what Gustavo Esteva refers to as the "new commons" (2005, 20). The world we live in is quite different than it was two hundred, one hundred, or even twenty years ago. Just as "enclosure adopts diverse materialities and morphologies that vary through different stages of capitalist development" (Sevilla-Buitrago 2015, 17), so too does the practice of commoning. The "new common" "celebrates the adventure of common man" (Esteva 2005, 22). It is the bricoleur de-linked from the logic of capitalist accumulation. This way of life is vital for people like Grandma, who is reliant on her garden for more than food, but also the social relationships with community, land, and self. In a world where just about every aspect of domestic life has been commodified, taking care of oneself and one's community through the convivial labor of growing, sharing, preparing, and eating food is an act of liberation. This type of labor has been referred to as *self-valorizing* (Negri 1991; Cleaver 1989, 1992; Valle 2015) because it offers new hope and new spaces despite, and possibly because of, marginality (also see Trauger 2017; Anderson 2010; Peña 1997). In these new spaces lurks a diversity of options and opportunity because such spaces are self-organizing. Sevilla-Buitrago refers to this as the "spatiality of difference" (2015). When spaces emerge autonomously and organically "in common" with others, they are bound to be different than other spaces (also see Ostrom 1990). The home garden common offers opportunities for those working in common to create, transform and enact labor that is self-valorizing because it is part of a "self-defining, self-determining process, which goes beyond the mere resistance to capitalist valorization to a positive product of self-constitution" (Cleaver 1992, 19).

The autonomy practiced by these home gardeners is a positive project of self-constitution because of the creative intercourse between persons and their environments. Through the sharing and enjoying of food, Grandma, Luis, and Alfonso reconfigure neoliberal capitalist value framings and participate in the experimental aspects of self-organization based on their enjoyment of food and labor (i.e., gardening). Their acts are against the industrial capitalist productivity of food and labor and for the self-constitution of home gardeners and their communities.

When Luis shares his food and greets his food, community, and life, he is valorizing his labor and "de-linking" it from the capitalist accumulation. According to Esteva, "for people on the margins, disengaging from the economic logic of the market or the plan has become the very condition for survival. They are forced to confine their economic interaction . . . to realms outside the spaces where they organize their own modes of living" (2005, 20). By disengaging from orthodox economic logic, Luis does not sell his labor on the marketplace for a wage to valorize capital. He chooses to enact the self-valorization of his labor and remain self-determining by engaging in convivial labor. Within these spaces, people and groups enact autonomy to define their own needs, and with the tools of conviviality, they have the practical tools to act upon those needs. Home gardeners often work collaboratively to determine needs, and having a garden remains a vital resource to meet those needs.

Conclusion

One evening, at a faculty event in 2017, I had a conversation with fellow faculty members about home gardeners. Many faculty members thought it was exciting to grow food and that these home gardeners were examples of empowered people taking control of their own health and community. While all that is true, much of the lived reality of home gardening was lost to this group of faculty. In fact, one person told me, "I don't get it. So what? I mean, my family has always had a garden. How much change can really happen with a backyard garden?" What this person was unable to grasp was that for colonized peoples, growing food has always been about far more than growing food. Sure, the raised awareness about food deserts has struck a chord with people across a diverse political spectrum, but it is more than that. The reason South Central Farms was shut down was not that it was providing food to poor people of color, but because of what it represented—a way life de-linked from the logics and institutions of capitalism (Tezozomoc 2017).

For Grandma, Luis, and Alfonso, growing food represents an escape from the oppressive histories, norms, and institutions that continue to work against communities of color. While the home gardens discussed in this chapter might not be the same as a traditional commons, they operate in a very similar fashion because they support self-determining ways of living. There is no doubt the marginalization experienced by many home gardeners is restrictive because it furthers financial hardships, but it also offers cover and opportunity. By rejecting Western structures of association, home gardeners make an ontological turn that enables radical, and perhaps even revolutionary garden subjectivities. For most people living in the "modern" world, the value of money structures just about all of our social relationships. Yet, for these home gardeners, the universality of money does not make exchange easier but threatens the very distinctiveness of who they are. Home gardens and home gardeners are networked together through a common set of values, but each garden is distinct in its escape from the conditions of capitalism's oppressive nature. Home gardens are tools of conviviality that produce food that is de-linked from capitalist accumulation and an opportunity for a way of life that is inclusive, not exclusive.

CHAPTER 3

Cultivating the "Good Life"

"You're not gonna be rich, but who cares, you're gonna be happy"

In the fall of 2012, I met with Jessica, who descends from a mixed history of Indigenous and European bloodlines. Every few years, she travels back to Oklahoma to visit and reconnect with her Cherokee relatives. Growing up in the Lower Midwest, Jessica learned deep ethnoecological and ethnobotanical knowledge about the wild foods of her ancestral homeland, but today reviving that same knowledge in the Santa Clara Valley remains difficult. "I wish La Mesa Verde offered classes about how to forage native plants, herbs, and medicines," she told me. "Walking into my garden is like walking into a grocery store. Now," she continued with a smile, "I'm working on my drug store."

Jessica's home garden is filled with medicinal herbs she remembers from her childhood, including lemongrass, stinging nettle, yerba buena, watercress, wheatgrass, wild oregano, aloe vera, and pokeweed. Along the south-facing side of her home, she grows blackberries, blueberries, and raspberries to support a healthy immune system. She also grows verdolagas and quelites (lamb's quarters) to help provide her with vital nutrients needed for optimal health. Jessica practices what is known as a companion planting by growing mutually beneficial plants next to each other. This strategy maximizes growth and yields while maintaining optimum plant and soil health.

Jessica is in her mid-fifties and stands about five and a half feet tall with long brown hair and warm brown eyes. Her deep plant knowledge draws the attention of fellow home gardeners. She speaks mostly in English, but her knowledge of plant names and their uses is recounted in broken Spanish.

Jessica lives in East San José, a community that has a history of struggle and activism going back to its Mexican past (see Pitti 2003). It is a multiethnic community made up primarily of Mexican and Chicana/o residents. We met at the Mexican American Heritage Plaza on the corner of Alma Rock Road and South King Street. This vibrant corner was well documented in Art Rodriguez's novel, *East Side Dreams* (1998). The plaza stands as a tribute to the community's deep Mexican roots and as a place for the celebration of the Mesoamerican cultures and the traditions of dance, music, theater, and the visual arts. When I met with Jessica, we discuss her history of advocacy in East San José and how she shares those experiences with fellow home gardeners. As we talked, she reflected on the 2008 recession as if it was yesterday. "Within a matter of days, we [her and her husband] lost both of our jobs, our health insurance, and almost our house," she told me. Like so many middle-class families, Jessica and her husband were living paycheck to paycheck. They had to pay off their home and car loans in addition to regular bills and buying food. And just like that, everything came crashing down. "Our garden saved us. Without it, who knows where we would be," she said. The 2008 recession forced many middle-class families into poverty, compelling them to make dramatic changes in their lives just to make ends meet.

Jessica and I sat in the plaza for close to two hours that day. She explained to me what life is like for people like her who live below the poverty line in the Santa Clara Valley.

> The people around here are more than my neighbors, they are my community. There are a lot of problems facing poor communities, but to me, the biggest problem is that people don't know each other anymore. We have to get back to the way things used to be. We have to get to know each other again, and our gardens can play a huge role in that.

Jessica attempts to return to "the way things used to be" by using her garden to support her community in a variety of ways. She shares food from her garden to battle the prevalence of food insecurity, she makes tonics and herbal remedies for those in need, and she walks door to door to provide her own labor and knowledge in the garden to help those who are too old or sick to do it on their own. "As a [home] gardener," she explained, "you're not gonna be rich, but who cares, you're gonna be happy."

The precariousness felt by the urban poor has today expanded into many middle-class families. Jessica confronts that precariousness with a heartfelt sense of experience and pain, but as she explained to me, "This is reality. This is where we are headed." While the valley's wealthy residents are getting richer, the valley's poor are getting poorer, and they must find and cultivate ways to mitigate risks associated with the "new norm" of ever-deepening economic inequality. Jessica's home garden is one such option that allows her to navigate uncertainty. It became evident in my conversations with Jessica that the ability to grow food coincides with the wellness and ability to transform the value of food through labor's "creative fire." The decoupling or de-linking by Jessica of wealth and happiness from the norms of Western consumer culture is an example of a revolutionary subjectivity enunciating epistemic disobedience whereby she *values* sociality over material accumulation.

Jessica's home garden is part of the "new common" because it is as much a physical space as it is an aspect of the cultural imaginary that recovers epistemological and ontological wisdom of how to live well. She produces food for herself and her husband, and she shares much more than surplus with her neighbors as they, too, use its resources. Similar to the work of Marcel Mauss (1990), gift-giving societies and communities such as Jessica's are tightly woven together through responsibility and obligation. Jessica is a "precapitalist" gift-giver precisely in the sense that the fulfillment of mutual social obligations is also experienced as the source of her own personal well-being. Her sense of community is based on the memory of how it was in the past and how she would like to recreate the past in the present.

The "Good Life" at the Margins

When Jessica explained that as a home gardener, "you're not gonna be rich, but . . . you're gonna be happy," she was actively engaging in what Fabiola Cabeza de Baca Gilbert (2005), and much later, Priscilla Solis Ybarra (2016), call the good life. As explained by Gilbert, "Life as I grew to know it [in rural New Mexico] . . . was rich but simple. People drew their sustenance from the soil and from the sprit. Life was good, but not always easy" (2005, v). Much of the world that Gilbert grew to know in the first half of the twentieth century has been lost, yet pockets still remain. In fact, part of the uncertainty people feel in the valley may very well be the repeated collision between the Santa Clara Valley, where *life is good, but not always easy*, and the Silicon Valley, where *life is easy, but not always good* (also see Berlant 2011). These seemingly oppositional worlds are where many low-income people find themselves as they negotiate their modernity with rural and traditional knowledge. The world presented by Gilbert exists not only in memory, but also as explained by Ybarra, in "the values of simplicity, sustenance, dignity, and respect" (2016, 4).

This chapter uses the work of Gilbert, Ybarra, and Anzaldúa to articulate a way of life that exists not in opposition to modernity but alongside it as an alternative. Such a way of life is not a romanticized pre-capitalist utopia, but a way of life that exists as a form of "border thinking" that occurs when colonized peoples disengage from Western assumptions of wealth, happiness, and value. This is what Walter Mignolo (2011b) and others refer to as the "decolonial option," whereby colonized bodies, economies, ecologies, and ways of life break free from the constraints of Western epistemologies, which project a "dichotomy between humans and nature and make space for Indigenous practices and narratives that have survived colonization and that preserve and adapt traditional environmental knowledge" (Ybarra 2016, 15). In this chapter, the narratives of Jessica, Laura, Diego, and Davíd demonstrate how people in the most precarious of situations utilize home gardens to navigate uncertainty by forging new and revisiting ancient value systems to create spaces for the "good life."

There is no question that an academic discussion of value cannot occur without a basic understanding of the insights of thinkers such as Karl Marx, Adam Smith, and David Ricardo. In fact, such thinkers have historically held a monopoly over the concept of value. The goal of this chapter is not to discredit any of these theorists but to offer insight into how gardeners at the margins hold "theories" of value that have existed far before any labor or class theory of value. The value systems expressed by these home gardeners articulate experiences that move beyond individualistic human rights and toward a relationship between the human and the more-than-human world that dignifies daily life in all of its manifestations. As explained by Ybarra, this turn is deeply rooted in the Chicana/o, Mexican, and Mexican American relationship with the more-than-human world. "This departure from individualist rights also shifts the focus from justice based on equality and toward justice based on dignity and respect" (Ybarra 2016, 17). By emphasizing a value system based on dignity and respect, home gardeners find themselves with the ability to navigate the interstitial spaces between the Santa Clara and Silicon Valleys.

It is important to not glorify or romanticize the good life of home gardeners because there is no question that while it may be good, it is most definitely not easy. Foregrounding the experiences of people living in the heart of modernity better explains how they make use of their marginality in pursuit of dignity. Furthermore, such an understanding best articulates how individuals and communities enact positive value transformations through their social relationships with each other, their labor, and the places they call home. Such transformations disrupt norms of modernity (e.g., consumerism, individualism, and accumulation), but they do not destroy them. That is not the intent. These two value systems are both products of modernity, but they diverge and coexist, inhabiting similar, yet vastly different worlds.

The border thinking practiced by the home gardeners in this book is part of "a specific epistemic response from the exteriority of Western modernity, a response from the outside created from the perspectives of the inside" (Tlostanova and Mignolo 2012, 7). This is fundamental for understanding how people define and articulate their own political struggles. In other words, "while we are all in the colonial matrix, not everyone belongs to its memories, feelings, and ways of sensing. Many of us have been 'trapped' in the colonial matrix but do not 'belong' to it" (Tlostanova and Mignolo 2012, 7). Many home gardeners are trapped by the colonial matrix of power and, in turn, use their home gardens as "escapes," but as these narratives suggest, there is far more to it. Home gardeners do not just "de-link" from coloniality to escape capitalism to participate in sharing economies that reduce their cost of living. Instead, they create escapes by navigating between worlds to validate ways of being and knowing that coloniality often suppresses. To survive the "darker side of modernity" (see Mignolo 2011a), colonized people must, as Anzaldúa so aptly points out, "live *sin fronteras*" (2007, 217) by navigating the liminal spaces of the borderlands.

The home garden is a political statement because it is a self-reliant activity against an industrial food system that alienates us from our social relationship to our food. By growing food, people can mend the wounds of alienation caused by a food system that damages our bodies, environments, and communities. The collective response to alienation is conviviality. These home gardeners are not a politically driven revolutionary army rising up against racist neoliberalism. Instead, they are people whose lives (and bodies) are

FIGURE 10 Sweet corn is a common crop grown in La Mesa Verde gardens. Photo courtesy of the author.

enriched through a newfound connection (or reconnection) to the production of food. They are engaging in the revolutionary act of recovering human dignity through the fruits of their labor, or through what I have been calling convivial labor. Their collective subjectivities give rise to the transformative potential of growing food.

Anthropologists have long sought to understand value because it helps us to see how different people in different places and times have come to perceive what is beautiful, worthwhile, and essential. As anthropologist David Graeber suggests, "value . . . can best be seen in this light as the way in which action becomes meaningful to the actor by being incorporated in some larger, social totality" (2001, xii). Value is an elusive concept because it is always in the process of being remade. Thus, "everyone tends to lose track of the way their own actions contribute to reproducing and reshaping themselves and their social contexts" (2001, 258). The elusiveness of value is what might actually offer the possibility of producing an alternative to the market theory of value, or it may merely reaffirm economic hegemony.

What we perceive as value and what we do with value can be liberating because it may offer new subjectivities and ways of living. They can also be constraining because it may obscure and mystify the construction of commodity fetishism. Value does not and has never existed on its own. It is called into being by the human potential to transform it, and this is a political struggle rather than some universal and deterministic iron law of economics at the end of history. Nancy Munn has suggested that "actors create value through effecting positive value transformations," and through the navigation of these transformations, a "community creates itself as an agent of its own value creation" (1986, 20). This would suggest a continual struggle by communities who seek to enact positive value transformations in the face of outside, often antagonistic forces. The constant negotiation by home gardeners to navigate between the Silicon Valley and the Santa Clara Valley is just one example of the antagonistic forces ever-present in the production and protection of value.

The Moral Economy of the Home Gardener

Several months after my first meeting with Jessica, I received a phone call from her asking if I would like to accompany her and her neighbor to glean for fruit, a process in which fruit is taken from the property of vacant homes, city streets, and public parks. This was an excellent opportunity to learn how people made practical use of urban spaces as a commons. Obviously, not everyone can have an orchard in their backyard, which makes gleaning a rational adaptation by anyone seeking to improve self-sufficiency in an environment territorialized through enclosures that block such efforts.

I met Jessica and her neighbor at her home early on a weekday in the late summer of 2013. Before we left her home, we prepared by gathering water bottles, garbage bags, and a light lunch consisting of fruit and veggies from her garden. As we drove around San José, Jessica pointed out fruit trees she had either already gleaned with her friends and neighbors or would soon glean. With each tree, they demonstrated their ethnoecological knowledge of the valley's seasonality and their deep awareness of each tree's many uses. Jessica explained to me where several different wild boysenberry and marionberry patches were scattered across the Santa Clara Valley, and she knew which berries would be ready during their May–September harvesting window. In addition to understanding their seasonality, Jessica explained how berries are one of the best foods in the fight against diabetes because they are high in fiber and help improve blood sugar levels. Jessica was particularly excited about a large area almost ready for harvest along the edges of Lake Vasona, which is part of a county park located in Los Gatos, southwest of San José.

Driving with Jessica changed my perspective of the city. Her city orientation was guided by the location of harvestable fruit trees and berry patches, not the well-known names of buildings. Most people living in the valley are entirely unaware of the abundance of fruit that is literally "ripe for the picking." Jessica and her neighbors would often go scouting for possible places to glean. At times, fruit trees were on vacant land or abandon homes, and others, Jessica and her group would ask the homeowner (sometimes leaving a note) if they could harvest unwanted fruit. As Jessica informed me, they almost always said yes.

On the day I accompanied Jessica and her neighbor, we stopped at several places. The first house we stopped at had two peach trees. The house was a foreclosure and looked as if it had not been lived in for years. When we got out of the car, we walked up to the house and took out our plastic bags we had brought with us. Immediately, I reached for the peaches on the ground, assuming that we should not take hanging fruit from someone else's tree. "Don't take those," Jessica said, "they might make you sick. Who knows how long they've been there?" Together we began taking peaches from the tree until we had our bags full. She taught me how to tell when the fruit was ripe enough to pick. From there, we moved onto the next house and harvested plums. Again, we left once we had full bags. Next came figs. By the time we were on our way home, we had more plums, peaches, and figs than any one of us could eat in a season. "What are you going to do with all of this," I asked her. "Freeze, preserve, and share," she said. Throughout the summer and fall months, Jessica gleans from these unattended trees, and each time she shares what she gathers. Her belief that keeping trees healthy and not letting their fruit go to waste reflects a principal social value. The chaos of capitalism is partly to blame for the abundance of unused fruit trees in the region. While the 2008 housing bubble forced many foreclosures and nearly knocked Jessica off her feet, she uses the chaos left in its wake to cultivate spaces of innovation and opportunity by using the fruit trees on vacant home lots to help sustain her community. Littered across the Santa Clara Valley are countless empty houses, and many have an abundance of fruit trees. While the everyday resident of the valley might not notice the wealth of food growing just feet above their head, Jessica and her neighbors are keenly aware of the waste that the numerous unattended and unused fruit trees produce across the valley. Village Harvest is one of many formal organizations that operates throughout the greater San Francisco Bay Area that gleans unused fruit from backyards and small orchards and then distributes them to local food agencies to help feed the hungry and improve food insecurity. Even still, there are plenty of trees that go unharvested within the valley. For this reason, Jessica and her neighbors go gleaning every few weeks. Jessica learns the location of these trees through websites, Facebook, and listservs, but mostly by word of mouth. Every few weeks, Jessica collects pounds of fruit to share with her family, friends, neighbors, and the broader community.

When we returned from our trip, we began to unpack the fruit by placing it into bins Jessica had prepared. She had planned to share the ripest fruit with her neighbors while the other fruits ripened to make preserves to share at a later date. When I asked her why she shares so much food, she simply said, "It's my role as a community member to do what I can to help my neighbors." Jessica does not have much, but what she does have, she willingly shares. Like many others in this book, the reasons for sharing are complicated. Jessica's comments suggest that the desire to share is influenced by the memory of the past good life. Her willingness to help neighbors is a conscious decision to act on these values. The sort of agency that gardeners like Jessica and her neighbors enact seems quite different from the idea that Mauss proposes in his notion of "the gift" because they give without expecting to receive. Jessica informed me that giving is less about obtaining and more about maintaining a healthy and connected community. "I don't want my neighbors to go hungry. We can't do this [survive] alone, *we have to work together.*" Jessica's garden subjectivity finds solidarity in the mutuality of others. It closely resembles the timeless knowledge and community strengthening practices of the commons (see Bollier 2014), and the convivial labor of Jessica and her neighbors reaffirms the vernacular values of simplicity, sustenance, dignity, and respect. Her garden subjectivity illuminates the cooperative and convivial labor practices that may harbor escapes from the oppressive and constrictive norms of economic orthodoxy. This close-knit community gives to maintain its survival and to find moments of the good life. "I'm like a farmer's wife, I spend hours in the kitchen every day," she continued.

Sure, communities like Jessica's can survive. In fact, that is exactly what the technological fixes of the Silicon Valley enable them to do. When food is scarce, food pantries and emergency food can help fill the gap. When money is scarce, cheap processed food can temporarily fill our bellies but not nourish our bodies. Yet, Jessica's actions demonstrate that she wants more for herself and her community then the quick fixes and conveniences of our current food system. So, while we can survive off the standard American diet, also referred to as SAD (Winson 2013), home gardeners like Jessica choose to flourish. The idea of "flourishing" rather than "sustaining" is nothing new. Ybarra insists that Chicana novelists who have documented the Chicana/o experience through story and poem have historically been at the forefront of challenging Western assumptions, norms, and values by writing and validating the experiences of what lies just beyond survival in the form of "joyful communion" (2016, 156).

The garden subjectivity articulated by Jessica transcends the individual egoist who acts on her own self-interests, a basic tenet of neoliberal capitalism. The world that Jessica holds together through her extensive sharing network challenges the biopolitical reality of neoliberal capitalism while influencing positive value transformations through acts of sharing. The idea of happiness is part of a larger project of relational accountability. Jessica does not exist by merely being in relation to those in her sharing network; instead, she is her relationships, and she holds herself accountable to others who also make up that social bond. Unlike the Western notion of individualism, the good life that Jessica pursues cannot be accomplished alone, but only as part of a "complex whole."

Embedded in the market economy is an assumption that with enough money, one can purchase all that is needed to live. This idea influences the consumer culture that makes up much of the modern world. What we do not have, we can simply buy. In his study of Southeast Asia, James C. Scott (1976) uncovers a contradiction embedded within this market-based ideology. He finds that the market economy passes the burden of economic unpredictability on to the most vulnerable, which is exactly what Jessica and her community are experiencing. Scott's study takes place at a particular moment in history when the governments of Southeast Asia were imposing the market economy on rural peasant communities. This transition sought to "civilize" peasants while also modernizing the nation-state and making it more competitive in the global market.

Peasants were forced to grow crops to sell in the marketplace; however, if the harvest failed or did not sell, the burden of the economic loss was on the peasant. Scott argues that this logic goes against the peasant subsistence economy because their traditional economy is based on "risk avoiding behavior" (1976, 15). In other words, the subsistence economy is an ethical lifestyle that brings together a range of networks and institutions that act as "shock absorbers during economic crisis" (1976, 27). These strategies range from trade, craftsmanship, casual wage labor, and, in some cases, migration. For home gardeners and farmers, this risk adverse behavior also consists of planting a diversity of corps to account for uncertainty and to retain pieces of the subsistence economy.

This logic is also present in the risk-avoidant behavior of Jessica and her community. Rather than turning to the market economy to fulfill her needs, she turns to community; she turns toward culture to protect her against vulnerability. E. B. Tylor (1920) noted that culture is a powerful tool for human survival because culture forms a "complex whole," which includes the knowledge, values, morals, customs, and norms needed for an individual to be a member of society. The market economy may place the burden on those most vulnerable, while the moral economy extends relations of accountability to protect the most vulnerable.

Similarly, the moral economy of the home gardener operates to maintain social solidarity and improve health outcomes for the most vulnerable in the face of structural conditions that increase precarity. Home gardens share for various reasons, but the recurring theme is the relational accountability to others. Generosity operates as a core value within the community, but people do not give and expect something in return. Instead, they give to promote the conditions of social reproduction and autonomy embedded in the moral economy. Growing food reminds us of our place as mothers and fathers, as daughters and sons, as nurturers, and as community members. These relations of accountability hold their world together. As Jessica informed me while we were separating fruit on her kitchen table, "Food is a happy medium, it is something we all share." Her ability to use food as a medium coincides with her acknowledged responsibility to others. Food as a medium also contributes to the recomposition of the working class because by growing and sharing food, gardeners are contributing to their own self-valorization and the positive value transformations of their communities.

"It really is therapeutic to weed"

Labor is an instrumental aspect in human life, yet whether it occurs organically as life's "form-giving fire" or as an extension of estrangement and alienation depends upon people's pursuit of self-determination. People always have and always will continue to use their human labor for a variety of projects. However, how labor is perceived is often called into question. According to Marx, labor "is a condition of human existence which is independent from all forms of society; it is an eternal natural necessity which mediates the metabolism between man and nature, and therefore human life itself" (1990, 133). Labor was and is the source of value. However, in drawing attention to this phrase, it is not my intent to discuss the origin of value but rather Marx's use of the metaphor of "metabolism" to illustrate how self-valorizing labor can reverse alienated labor and heal the metabolic rift. Marx believes labor to be a natural condition of the human experience, which exists independent of the particular social forms in which this necessity is organized and controlled.

Throughout Marx's work, he is careful not to confuse labor for work (also known as labor power). While the two are closely related, they are also drastically different. Labor is what sets in motion the metabolism between humans and nature because it involves transforming the world and the self in ways that alter the conditions of human existence. Work, on the other hand, generates a system of social control, which alienates the worker from the means and results of his or her own productive activity. This is a pivotal moment to invoke Marx's famous, but often overlooked, distinction between the working class *in itself* and the working class *for itself*. A working class *in itself* sells its labor to capital and thus becomes labor-power. A working class *for itself* "asserts its autonomy as a class through its unity in struggle against its role as labour-power" (Cleaver 2000, 83). How and why one exerts labor not only helps to structure one's position in society but also allows people to use their creative potential to enact their own agency in everyday lived "escapes" of varying degrees from the power and control of capital.

Labor for the home gardener is quite different than labor for the factory or office worker. While the factory worker is forced to sell his or her labor to the capitalist to survive, the home gardener asserts his or her own autonomy over work to produce his or her own means of subsistence. Throughout this study, I had countless conversations about the labor used in gardening, and never once did anyone say they did not enjoy it. The earlier examples of Grandma, Alfonso, and Oscar clearly demonstrate this as well. Sure, there were days when someone was too sick or too tired to be in the garden, or perhaps there were parts that they did not enjoy as much as others. But every person I spoke with enjoyed the labor of gardening.

"You know," Laura, a white woman in her late fifties, told me as we worked in her garden, "the garden is hard work, especially at my age, but it really is therapeutic to weed." This statement sums up much of the experiences of many gardeners. Weeding is one of the most disliked tasks of gardening, yet it offers an opportunity to get on your knees and get your hands dirty—to be closer to the land as it is. "Working in the garden allows you to think," she continued as she momentarily paused from weeding and looked toward me. "It allows me to be outside, to get away from the TV." Much of the alienation imposed on the worker can be mitigated by the garden. Laura does not look for TV to fill the void created by industrial society. Rather, she puts her hands in the soil, and by engaging with its metabolism, she participates in the positive value transformation of her community.

Yet, simply turning to the garden to counter alienation labor is often not straightforward. At the end of the day, we need to work. This is part of the contradiction embedded in urban agriculture. As Silvia Federici argues, capitalism must conquer the body to continue to valorize itself. She positions the body and the labor-power of the body as the original site of primitive accumulation. She finds that "the body had to die so that labor-power could live" (2009, 141). Through the imposition of work, the body was disciplined and denied its creative potential so that labor-power could live as the object of capitalist desire. Marx often refers to this process as "vampirelike" (see Marx 1990, 1993) because being forced to become labor-power slowly destroys the body.

Laura counters the "vampirelike" aspects of work in at least two distinct ways. First, by confronting the biopolitics of work through the substitutability of their labor, gardens offer "escapes" from the industrial capitalism and have the opportunity to heal and nurture their bodies and communities through the growing, sharing, and consuming of healthy, nutrient-dense, and culturally appropriate foods. Second, she extends Federici's argument of primitive accumulation whereby "the body had to die for labor-power to live." Federici does not mention that land also had to die—it too had to be conquered and deemed disposable. In this case, the home gardeners in this book confront the historical legacy in Santa Clara Valley, whereby industry positions the land as expendable. Through agroecology and bioremediation, home gardeners are healing the land by healing themselves. The coevalness and co-production of health further engrain a revolutionary subjectivity of relational accountability between land, people, and food.

Over several years of this study, I spent a lot of time with Laura and her husband, Diego, a Peruvian in his mid-sixties. They are both retired and live in the community of Willow Glen, a more affluent neighborhood than Washington-Alma located just west of Highway 101. But as Laura told me one day while we were in her garden, "Don't let that fool you, we're willow gleaners. We repurpose everything." Just because they are both retired does not mean life comes easy to them. In fact, because they are retired, and on a fixed income, they are forced to stretch their dollars more than many others. Yet, they do not see their age as a disadvantage; in fact, "Our advantage is our age," she told me one day as we sat in shade in their garden and shared a pitcher of homemade lemonade. "We're patient gardeners," Diego finished with a smile. "A lot of people forget that growing a garden and learning to garden doesn't happen overnight." Diego got up from his chair and walked over to point out several crops that simply failed. Their garden was not perfect, and despite decades of gardening, they are always learning more. As Diego put it, "Our garden is perfect in its imperfection" (see appendix B, garden 6).

One day on a visit to their garden, Laura was trying something new. She was drying bay leaves that she would use in cooking and share with her extensive networks. Laura told me that she had dried herbs such as oregano and epazote in the past and thought she would give bay leaves a try. "We have lived here for a while now, and our garden continues to evolve," Laura informed me as she sat back in her chair and took a sip of lemonade. "While we don't have a lot of land, we've used it well," she finished while smiling at Diego. On any given day, you can often find Laura and Diego enjoying the "good life" by working in the garden.

FIGURE 11 The "good life." Photo courtesy of the author.

During one of our conversations, I asked Laura, who has been able to control her type 2 diabetes without going on prescription medication, how she would define what healthy living and eating was, and how or if, she and Diego were living such a lifestyle. She did not say anything for a while; she just looked at me as if she was looking beyond me. Then she turned to her garden and said, "Healthy living is when you can go outside and pick a few blueberries off the bush in your own garden, put them in your yogurt, and eat it right then and there." She then recounted a story of watching Diego from her kitchen window collect blueberries from the garden in his pajamas. Her awareness of the interrelationships between health, well-being, and food reinforces Gary Nabhan's project of coming home to eat, where he says food "should be valued less for its caloric content and more for what it expresses about our relationships with the world" (2002, 18). These relationships come in many forms, and for Laura and Diego, asserting their own labor in the garden is a subtle way home gardeners were taking control of their health by restoring the metabolism of life's form-giving fire.

A Garden Is Always More than a Garden

During one of the last agrobiodiversity surveys I conducted, I met with Davíd. He is a jovial man in his late sixties from Michoacán. He grew up on the edges of Lake Pátzcauaro in the small village of San Andrés Tziróndaro. His family still lives in the region and continue to work the many avocado fields that line the hillsides. His once dark black hair is now full of streaks of gray. His Chivas Guadalajara baseball cap was worn from the sun, yet he wore it proudly. Highway 280, one of the nation's busiest freeways, is located just beyond his backyard. Davíd explained to me that twenty years ago when he moved to the United States and into his home, Highway 280 was still there, but its presence seemed less prominent, intrusive, and far less busy. When he first moved into the home there were several hundred feet of open space from the end of his property to the freeway, and the only thing stopping one from crossing was an old barbed-wire fence, which still sits in his yard. Today, a twenty-five-foot cinderblock wall lies just beyond his apple, avocado, and pomegranate trees, and is a constant reminder of "progress."

As we sat on his porch in the shade, the Silicon Valley began to melt away as the fertile Santa Clara Valley emerged. Hummingbirds and butterflies were constantly moving in and out of the garden. Davíd pointed out several different species of birds that entered and exited the garden. We could hear them sing over the constant hum of the freeway. Wind blew through the trees as it gently stirred his wind chime. He showed me his grandson's favorite tomato plant. Davíd explained to me that it was his favorite because the fruit tasted the best. I could not believe that tomatoes would taste so different simply based on where they were in the garden, so Davíd set up a taste test. I closed my eyes, chose my favorite, and sure enough, it was from his grandson's favorite plant.

Davíd's garden was one of the most complex of all those I visited (see appendix B, garden 9). His pomegranate, apple, loquat, *naranja agria* (sour orange), kiwi, avocado, guava, and white and red peach trees have been there for over fifteen years. Yet, he knows that when he is forced to move, the new owner will not value those trees in the same way he does. More likely, he will not pass the house down to his children or grandchildren. The house will be bought, remodeled, and those trees will be replaced with grass or, worse, concrete.

Like so many migrants that move, sometimes forced, form place to place, Davíd has developed a unique sense of place that is both physical (found in his love and care of growing his fruit trees from seedlings) and part of the cultural imaginary. If our attachments to "things" or to "land" are what allow individuals to develop a sense of place and engage in some sort of "land ethic," than one would expect that when Davíd is forced, once again, to leave his home his sense of place would be lost. But for Davíd, and many others in this study, his attachment to place moves beyond ownership and toward relationality. His attachment to place is not fixed in place but instead continually evolving in the living cultural memory of seed saving and sharing. The heritage commons of seed saving is continuously reinforced by Davíd's actions and relationship with his food. Davíd's radical garden subjectivity de-links from the Western notion of *ownership of* nature and embraces a more nuanced *relationship with* nature. But this is nothing new, in fact, Priscilla Ybarra traces this part of Chicana/o history by interpreting how land and relationships are discussed in Chicana/o literature. She insists that "[m]ore radical than reclaiming lost title to lands, these writers declare that our communion with nature ranks higher than any legal document, even if we are the only ones who recognize it" (Ybarra 2016, 117). When Davíd shared seeds from his garden with me, he was sharing more than seed. He, like Mauss insists in *The Gift* (1990), was sharing part of himself and his attachment to place.

Marx provides some clarification on this in his posthumously published, *Pre-Capitalist Economic Formations*:

> Where [value] derives from the individual families which jointly constitute the community, they are independent owners co-existing with him, independent private proprietors. The common property which formerly absorbed everything and embraced them all, then subsists as a special *ager publicus* [common land] separate from the numerous private owners . . . In both cases, individuals behave not as laborers but as owners—*and as members of a community who also labor*. The purpose of this labor is not the creation of value, although they may perform surplus labor in order to exchange it for foreign labor—i.e., for surplus products. Its purpose is the maintenance of the owner and his family *as well as of the communal body as a whole*. The establishment of the individual as a worker, stripped of all qualities except this one, is itself a product of history. (1964, 1; emphasis added)

Here Marx is alluding to the communal form of *property as relationship* rather than as possession, which seems like a necessary precondition for the rise of any gift-giving system of reciprocal exchange. Mauss ignores the property relation in precapitalist societies and so ends up obscuring the dynamics of the very institutions of collective action that sustain such a system.

In the *Grundrisse*, Marx also argues that "[a]n isolated individual could no more possess property in land than he could speak. At most, he could live off it as a source of supply, like the animals. The relation to the soil as property always arises through the peaceful or violent occupation of the land" (1993, 485). Here, Marx is pointing to the social quality of labor in precapitalist formations, a point he shares with Mauss. Moreover, he recognizes that the violent process of primitive accumulation disrupts the communal nature of the social bonds that holds this precapitalist system in place. The loss of the social embeddedness of labor is obscured and devalued in the transition to capitalism and the tyranny of the commodity form of labor it imposes. David's garden subjectivity exemplifies that while we no longer pass "things" from one generation to the next like we once did, through acts of sharing and cooperation, we can continue to pass on something far more valuable than a piece of land—our relationship with it.

Finding the "Good Life" in Conviviality

Convivial social relations surface regularly for this group of home gardeners. On a spring afternoon in 2014, I sat with Diego at a La Mesa Verde event. I asked him why he continues to come to events when he is already a very successful gardener. He told me, similar to Jessica, that a home garden can never exist in isolation. "I love that each year there are more and more people to get to know," he told me with a smile. "Es una extensión de nuestra familia" (It's an extension of our family). Home gardeners like Jessica, Laura, Diego, and David all demonstrate that in gardens at the margins value is never a given and the community itself takes an active role in the positive value transformation of their community and their relationships through their actions. Jessica's home garden presents a site that moves beyond possession. She gives not because she expects to receive something in return but rather because that is what community members do. Deeply rooted in relational accountably, she insists that no one exists on their own, and as such, we need to work together. While she admits that by being a gardener, "you're not gonna be rich... but you're gonna be happy," she de-links from the assumption that wealth equals happiness. This logic goes against just about everything modernity has taught us. The decolonial option of rearticulating the equation that financial wealth equals happiness opens new worlds of possibility that exists outside a rational choice framing of the world.

Michael Taylor (2006) argues that rational choice theory (RCT) is an overbearingly economistic way of thinking of the world. In the RCT argument, individual self-interests are pursued in all contexts, even in the group or collective action setting. Therefore, what appears to be a selfless act is really an act to protect the group's numbers and its overall safety, which ultimately benefits the individual. But as we see in news accounts every day, the race and gender of the person suffering distress is filtered by ideological presuppositions and dominant constructions of the "Other" and can precondition one toward action or the refusal to act. Taylor argues that RCT is an ideology that "denies to its subjects' capacities and dispositions that are part of what makes us human" (2006, 55). If this were not the case, we would be as receptive to the health needs of the "shelterless" (homeless is a problematic category) as we are to the wealthy Silicon Valley barons with second, third, and even fourth and fifth homes at their disposal. Are the gardeners' actions of gift-giving based on the assumption that they have something to get from it? Is Jessica assuming that someday she may need help so she might as well help others now? Or, do her actions simply remind her of a particular kind of human being?

While we might not ever honestly know these answers, Juan Estevan Arellano believes that growing and sharing food is what has allowed Indo-Hispano communities in New Mexico and southern Colorado to survive for generations. *Convide* is a concept that merges the Latin *con* (with) and *vite* (life) to express the sharing of food and life. "Conviviendo, helping each other as community, instead of simply 'sustaining' to save and then invest somewhere else, is what has blessed us with '*una vida buena y sana y alegre*' [a good and healthy and joyful life] because we have followed the simple philosophy of sharing the water, food and work and that has made our lives festive" (Arellano 2010, 3).

These sentiments are deeply felt by Laura and Diego, whose labor in the garden reminds them of their humanness. The therapeutic nature of weeding that Laura mentions is more than contemplative moments; it begins with sharing the earth's natural metabolism and extends into an ethical framing of how to live well. The "extension of community," explained by Diego, represents both his human and more-than-human communities that are held together with dirty hands. Their home garden offers countless "escapes" where they can cultivate the good life and heal from a variety of historical traumas initiated by enclosure, expanded by colonialism, and materialized in contemporary society. This emerging revolutionary subjectivity is not one-dimensional, but multidimensional because it is an intersubjective experience that connects people like Laura and Diego to a whole host of human and more-than-human communities. In the same way that Jessica shares with her neighbors out of relational accountability, Laura and Diego maintain their relationships through the experiences of convivial labor.

Within the practical and mundane activities and uses of homegrown food, home gardeners like David take the "decolonial option" by de-linking themselves from colonial epistemology (i.e., materialist accumulation) by cultivating relationships that resist being alienated from the land despite migration. His attachment to place exists through the living memory of seed saving and sharing. As he passes the seed and his knowledge of his grandson's favorite heirloom tomato plant, he continues the legacy of his ancestors by maintaining accountably to his relationships through a revolutionary subjectivity embedded in moral economy of the home gardener. In his own way, David is rejecting the commodification of food, which often renders food devoid of meaning, by filling the food he grows with his own set of values that have their own ecological, social, economic, cultural, spiritual, and technological dimensions ascribed to them. The confident voices of these home gardeners testify that the value of growing food lies in its creative potential as a tool of conviviality. This is a rational response to the conditions of precarity imposed by the regime of neoliberal governmentality and may prefigure the appearance of more radical, actively political, and perhaps even militant subjectivities.

INTERLUDE

Chayote con Chile

Ingredients:

2–3 chayotes, peeled and sliced

1 onion, roughly chopped

1–2 jalapeño, diced

2–3 ripe tomatoes, chopped

Olive oil

Cilantro for garnish

Salt to taste

Directions:

Over medium heat, warm olive oil. Add onions and cook until fragrant for about 3–5 minutes. Add chayote and cook until soft, about 8–10 minutes. Add garlic and jalapeño, and cook for 3 more minutes. Add tomato and reduce heat. Cook until tomato thickens. Serve on a warm plate and garnish with cilantro. The perfect complement for this dish is fresh pinto beans and warm homemade corn tortillas.

It was a hot, dry day in late August 2014. Before Lupe gave me a tour of her garden, she wanted to prepare a simple meal of *chayotes con chile* with me. Lupe is a mexicana from central Mexico in her mid-fifties who always has a smile and good food to share. On that day, every window in the house was open to create a cool breeze that moved through the rooms. Her home was small and full of life. Plants soaked in the sunlight on windowsills, handcrafted tin-silver crosses typical in Mexico were hung over doorways and next to pictures of the Virgin of Guadalupe. Old black-and-white family photos sat on end tables next to more recent color pictures of her family and friends. She led me into her kitchen to explain and demonstrate each step of this traditional dish. On her kitchen table, there was a place setting for three, a bowl of cherry tomatoes from her garden, and a pitcher of homemade *limonada*, made the Mexican way with limes rather than lemons. She pulled out two cast iron pans and set them on the stove, switched on one burner, turned to her cutting board, and began to explain how to cook.

Lupe began by preparing the chayote. She cut both ends off and delicately peeled the skin with a peeler. Once peeled, she sliced the chayote lengthways and carved out its thick seed. She then proceeded to chop the chayote into bite-size pieces. She explained to me that so many people are afraid of chayotes because no one knows how to cut and prepare them, let alone cook them. For people like Lupe who have been diagnosed with type 2 diabetes, chayotes are a powerful weapon in the fight against processed food. They are low in calories and low in fat, but they are incredibly high in fiber, which for people with diabetes means you stay fuller longer, and blood sugar levels can remain more consistently low. Chayotes also contain trace minerals such as zinc, magnesium, calcium, phosphorus, and potassium to help encourage proper metabolism and to maintain a healthy immune system while also supporting strong bones.

At this point, the pan was plenty hot, and Lupe placed the chayotes in the hot oil, stirred them a bit, and began to cut the onion. While slicing the onion, she explained to me how hard it was being low-income and getting her son to eat healthily. Almost everything she provides for him in his lunch is homemade, and much of it comes from her garden. But once he is out of the house, he wants what other kids have. He often reaches for processed chips, cookies, soda, and sweets. It felt ironic how Lupe was discussing the difficulties low-income people face when trying to eat healthy while she was slicing the onion, which themselves carry phytonutrients, or naturally occurring compounds found in fruits and vegetables that react with the human body in ways that trigger healthy reactions, quite the opposite of the processed food she was discussing.

Once the chayotes had softened, Lupe tossed in the onion, and within a minute, the delicious aroma of sizzling onions filled the house. She then grabbed two jalapeños, sliced and deseeded them in what appeared to be one motion, and then diced them into pea-size pieces. She explained to me that

FIGURE 12 Chayote con chile. Photo courtesy of the author.

everyone likes different levels of heat, but in her house, she likes it hot. As she told me, "la especia es buena para la salud" (spice is good for health). And she is right; in fact, aside from the benefits of vitamin A and C that jalapeños provide, they also naturally carry a chemical called capsaicin, which according to some studies, has been shown to have natural pain-relieving properties (see Nabhan 2013). With each added ingredient, I was beginning to understand why this dish was so crucial to the maintenance of Lupe's health.

At last, Lupe took three heirloom tomatoes, which only minutes earlier were growing in her garden, diced them, and added them and their juice to the pan. Tomatoes have long been known to be a vital part of a healthy diet, less well known is how the often-limited access to fresh fruit and vegetables, like tomatoes, chayotes, jalapeños, and onions, in communities like Lupe's can have everlasting effects of the people who live there. In fact, the growing field of epigenetics, which seeks to understand the relationship between active and inactive genes within a person, has made groundbreaking discoveries on how the decisions our grandparents made about their health may actually affect our health today (see Francis 2011). As our genetic code is passed from one generation to the next, different traumas or stigmas, such as poverty, can trigger genetic reactions and stimulate noncommunicable like diabetes, obesity, and high blood pressure. In other words, life circumstances can turn specific genes on and off. This means that what Lupe eats and has access to today has a lasting impact on her future generations. While Lupe was finishing the preparation of the meal, it became clear that by returning to a milpa-based diet like the dish of chayotes con chile, Lupe was doing far more than cooking to control her own diabetes, she was, in fact, working to reverse a historical trauma caused by systems, institutions, and choices sometimes out of her control. Lupe turned the pan to a simmer. "Y ahora," she said, "el jardín" (and now, the garden).

CHAPTER 4

Milpa-Based Cuisine

Cooking and Healing with Comida

Health, like wealth, is both a material reality and a social construction. This is because health is the result of variety of complex and often overlapping factors that may include social, cultural, spiritual, psychological, and even environmental well-being, and for colonized and oppressed people, heath extends well beyond the physical body (e.g., LaDuke 2005; Mihesuah 2005; Nelson 2008c; Mohawk 2008; Barreiro 2010). Many participants in this book were told by their doctors to go on expensive prescription drugs to control noncommunicable illnesses such as high blood pressure, intestinal and heart diseases, arthritis, and diabetes. Just about every participant knows someone who is either on prescription drugs, on the verge of needing prescription drugs, or at some point was informed by their doctor to consider prescription drugs. Yet, I argue that while biomedical recommendations may help alleviate the diet-related illnesses such as high blood pressure, diabetes, and obesity, they do not and cannot address the root causes because many of these symptoms are also related to the environmental conditions in which one lives (Guthman 2011). For many colonized peoples, the diet-related illnesses they now face are not simply the result of bad food choices but also the result of cultural imperialism, oppression, colonization, and the intentional destruction of traditional nutritional knowledge (Salmón 2012).

Today, we are witnessing the resurgence and cultural revival of traditional foods that heal the physical bodies of colonized peoples while nourishing their histories, cultures, and ways of knowing and being. In this chapter, I resist the temptation to call the diets taken up by LMV home gardeners traditional because in some instances they have nothing to do with any one tradition. Rather, following the lead of Alisha Gálvez (2018), I refer to them as "milpa-based diets" or "milpa-based cuisine." This approach relies heavily on fresh and local vegetables commonly found in milpa farming, such as corn, squash, beans, and chilies. Such a move gestures toward food as medicine by challenging the prevailing logic that Mexican food is inherently unhealthy (Calvo and Esquibel 2016; Rodriguez 2013).

For home gardeners in this book, an important first step to healthy eating and living is conviviality. The shared experience of cooking does more than constitute a good meal, it constitutes the living, breathing experience of comida. This embodied practice is both life sustaining and culturally reaffirming. Gustavo Esteva and Madhu Suri Prakash explain that *"comida* defines a social condition in which power remains in the hands of the people. It is their source of solidarity and conviviality, their antidote to ragged, lonely individualism" (1998, 66). Comida remains a practical, relevant, and powerful resource for gardeners at the margins because it enables direct access to their social reproduction.

This chapter elaborates on a variety of ways that people learn and relearn the healing power of growing, eating, and cooking through the life-sustaining practices of comida. Home gardeners navigate their precarious financial conditions and evade Western biomedical remedies through the living memory of comida. While some home gardeners may choose to take prescription drugs to control noncommunicable illnesses, this choice often comes with a variety of risks often overlooked by health care professionals (see Holmes 2013; Gálvez 2011). Health care professionals are often blinded by the truth claims of biomedicine and neglect to see how such a worldview demonizes not just traditional knowledge, but difference as well. As explained by both Holmes and Gálvez, many recent immigrants avoid health professionals all together because they do not want to lose their culture (e.g., language, norms, values, and traditional practices) in the process. To avoid these risks, many participants in this ethnography reported turning to a milpa-based diet as their first line of defense against the mounting inequalities in access to health care and fresh and affordable foods.

Racialization of Health and Wellness

For many of the people in this study, noncommunicable illnesses such as type 2 diabetes, obesity, and high blood pressure are common conditions they face on a daily basis. In fact, people of color in the United States are far more likely to be confronted with diet-related illnesses than are their white counterparts and are also less likely to have health coverage to ameliorate those diseases (Russell 2010). This recent understanding has led to a heightened focus on the eating habits of ethnic minorities. The Office of Minority Health in the United States Department of Health Human Services has attempted to intervene through a variety of programs. A greater focus on cultural sensitivity, language, religion, and cultural norms offers opportunities for those hardest hit by this latest wave of diet-related illnesses.

While this heightened focus has improved the lives of many people, it has also normalized noncommunicable illnesses and unhealthy living habits in non-white communities (Montoya 2011; Hatch 2016). This occurs when public health is viewed as a "discourse" (Cloos 2015), or as a set of institutions, norms, values, types of classification, and modes of categorization (see Foucault 1982). Discourse shapes how we see the world, and in turn it shapes how we act in it. The data show that African Americans are one and a half times more likely than whites to be obese.[1] The data also show that Hispanics/Latinos are twice as likely as non-Hispanic whites to have type 2 diabetes.[2] However, when those data are interpreted as discourse, it normalizes (a) that minorities are more likely to have diet-related health issues, (b) that whites are healthier, and (c) that a healthy diet is a white (or European) one.

There are nuances to the health data collected by the Centers for Disease Control. Asian Americans have less heart disease than whites and Hispanic men have lower rates of hypertension than white or black men. The survey notes other factors like poverty and access to Medicaid contribute to higher rates of chronic diseases in these communities (Blackwell, Lucas, and Clarke 2014). Nevertheless, what we interpret as healthy eating and living is often fueled by perception. We need look no further than the media's attraction to the Mediterranean diet to see how healthy eating and living are often coded as white (Hayes-Conroy and Hayes-Conroy 2013; Nabhan 2013). When a healthy lifestyle that is projected as white (i.e., the Mediterranean diet) becomes the health standard, it becomes what everything and everyone else is measured against. There are, of course, anomalies, such as the Okinawan

---

1. US Department of Health and Human Services, "Obesity and African Americans," Office of Minority Health, access January 31, 2022, https://minorityhealth.hhs.gov/omh/browse.aspx?lvl=4&lvlid=25.

2. Centers for Disease Control and Prevention, "National Diabetes Statistics Report" accessed January 31, 2022, https://www.cdc.gov/diabetes/data/statistics-report/index.html.

diet, rich in seafood, or Afro-Caribbean dishes, rich in legumes and greens. Sadly, those are not commonly understood as simply healthy diets but rather healthy *ethnic dishes.*

This is what Teresa Mares (2012) was referring to when she critiqued Michael Pollan, who claims in his book *Food Rules* (2009), "Don't Eat Anything Your Great-Grandmother Wouldn't Recognize as Food," and then several chapters later says, "Eat Kale." Mares questions Pollan by asking, "[W]hat if your great-grandmother hails from central Mexico and would never recognize kale . . . but would recognize *huauzontles*?" (2012, 351), an annual crop well known in Mexico for with nutritional value. Food rules like this carry different weight in transnational and immigrant communities because of how it normalizes power/knowledge. Breeze Harper (2011) also took on the normalization of a healthy diet when she critiqued veganism's failure to engage in antiracism or critical whiteness awareness activism despite its goal to challenge human privilege. Such racialized knowledge produces a binary either/or, non-white/white ordering of the world that cannot deal with complexity, hybridity, or change. This approach is problematic because home gardeners inhabit the interstitial spaces between modernity and tradition, white and black, right and wrong.

The truth of the matter is that the social, cultural, and economic environment of the barrio is far different from that of a predominantly white suburb or gentrified inner city, and thus, public health analyses that use population studies detached from a group's sociohistorical context in which they live, or from the power/knowledge in which information is delivered, can contribute to the racialization, or the ascribing of racial identities in relationship to a particular disease. Furthermore, such an analysis can naturalize the patterns of the distribution of disease as if they were unaffected by the environment or the contingent sociopolitical forces compelling changes in both social (class, race, gender) and spatial hierarchies that structure privilege at one end of the inequality spectrum and vulnerability (precarity) at the other end.

This, unfortunately, has reoccurred throughout history. Poor people of all races, ethnicities, and genders who are marginalized are always swept to the least fertile ground and can often only afford the least nutritious foods.[3] There

---

3. Alishia Gálvez (2018) explores this same phenomenon in Mexico and uncovers how NAFTA displaces local, seasonal foods and undermines the health and well-being of rural Mexicans by increasing the access to cheap, processed foods. Similarly, Otero (2018) explores the "neoliberal diet" by analyzing how the globalization of industrial food coincides with the globalization of noncommunicable illnesses, especially in low-income communities of color.

are famine foods, which have allowed peoples to survive on every continent, and while they are not always palatable, they provide the means for survival. Women often get the short end of the deal by giving the men the meat (Adams 2015) while also being the caretakers of the kitchen, garden, and children. In many ways, modernity has helped women and other oppressed peoples gain some benefits. Is it perfect? No. But this does not mean home gardeners reject it. As "border thinkers," they simply balance its contradictions.

The existing health inequalities in these communities can partially be explained by the lack of access to healthy and affordable foods, which is part of a broad structural problem that was brought on by "white flight" (Guthman 2011, 84). The same development practices that privileged suburbia during the era of "white flight" contributed to the declining quality of life and health conditions of the urban poor and working classes. As Michael Montoya points out, the existence of diabetes in Mexican communities can be partially attributed to "radical lifestyle disruptions, dispossessions, [and] poverty" (2011, 49), but it is more than that. It also has to do with the recurrence of events and circumstances that force vulnerable communities into radical lifestyle disruptions, dispossessions, and poverty. The environments in which people live are as much, if not more important to the production of many noncommunicable illnesses than are the biological factors, so any attempt to improve the health of minority communities must also pay close attention to the sociohistorical conditions that created the conditions in the first place.

While communities continue to suffer from these inequalities, they also assert their own forms and practices of autonomy to improve their health outcomes in environments steeped in the disparate impacts associated with the spatial politics of the dominant actors and agencies. For example, Kumar and Nair (2006) found that many Mesoamericans suffer from poverty, but their home gardens have helped them survive financial hardships while improving their well-being and livelihoods. Similarly, Bachmann (2009) found that the home gardens of Cubans in Havana do not provide the staple foods, that is, corn or wheat, but they do provide nutritional complements that are culturally relevant. This is one of the reasons that the Slow Food Movement sees food as a "complex science" (Petrini and Padovani 2006, 155), which takes an interdisciplinary approach to the study of health, culture, food safety, diet, farming, and history. A traditional knowledge perspective moves the discussion from disease prevention to wellness promotion because embedded within the practices of traditional knowledge is the validation of culture and tradition (Unnikrishnan and Suneetha 2012). This has also been illustrated by scholars working with the South Central Farmers in California (Peña 2005; Mares and Peña 2010, 2011) who emphasize the importance of recreating a sense of place through agroecological and ethnobotanical knowledge and practices for Mesoamerican home gardeners in the United States.

The Commonsense Logic of Self-Provisioning

For many of the home gardeners in this book, food is a "healing agent" (Shmid 1997, ix). This means that food contains more than just calories, but also the social and cultural meanings that allow people to heal by providing pathways toward social reproduction and autonomy. The physical health of these home gardeners coincides with healthy relationships with their food *and* community. The stories that follow demonstrate how home gardens encourage self-valorization on many epistemological and ontological levels. Some of their self-provisioning practices are ancient, and others are new. Central to their practices is how comida postures as emblematic of value by retaining its material, social, and discursive elements (see Collins 2017).

According to Esteva and Prakash, "the modern individual self is created as much by the food he or she is fed from birth, as s/he is by the school texts, computers, automobiles and other 'goods' manufactured by and for industrial eaters" (1998, 51). The authors interpret "industrial eaters" as people who reduce food to a simple commodity removed of any meaning. Stripped of meaning, people eat food from all over the world, regardless of how or where it is produced, and with a focus on its caloric content (as fuel for the body). Esteva and Prakash believe the process of healing our bodies, communities, and cultures, begins with comida because it is a social relationship beyond the individual self. In fact, through their research in Mexico, the authors find that there exists a clear difference between comida, which translates as "food" in Spanish, and *alimento*, which also translates as "food." For the peasants in their study, comida refers to "a very complex cultural relationship with their [the peasants] land" (1998, 58). In contrast, the authors find that middle-class students in Mexico City consume alimentos, and "are completely dependent on the institutions that give or sell them these alimentos [or foods]" (1998, 58). Part of the importance of comida is its ability to accomplish autonomy and self-determination. Comida is a "living memory" (1998, 67) because it is embedded in the practices of growing, preparing, and sharing foods. Comida is alive, evolving, and inviting. The voluntary simplicity of gardening and the humble act of cooking foster the use of these as tools of conviviality, which people can use under their own marginalized circumstances to transform the world into one they would like to participate in.

Grace

Grace has been diagnosed with type 2 diabetes. She is a soft-spoken Chinese immigrant who appears to speak only when she feels she has something important to say. Her warm smile encourages other home gardeners to converse with her and share knowledge. Grace is in her late fifties and has spent the past fifteen years living in the Santa Clara Valley. She once told me that she developed diabetes over time but did not realize it until she started losing her eyesight. "Diabetes," she said, "is just one of those things that happens." The way that she said this gave me the impression that it was just something that everyone had. I asked her if she knew anyone else with the disease, and she said yes. In fact, at a recent La Mesa Verde event, an organizer asked if anyone had a family member with diabetes, and all forty-five people in the room raised their hands.

For my first visit with Grace, I was invited over to her home to eat lunch with her in the garden. I arrived around eleven thirty in the morning because she likes to eat outside before it gets too hot. Her home is nestled in an old neighborhood in North San José. I entered her yard through a side gate where mint, thyme, rosemary, and goji berries lined the side of the house. When I arrived, she had our meals waiting for us on a table in her large backyard that contained a concrete slab in the center. At the far end of her garden she has large fig and persimmon trees. She had two raised garden beds and some crops directly planted in the backyard soil. She told me that she grows blueberries along the south side of her home so that she can make jam when the season gets late. She had several types of cucumbers, squashes, melons, and heirloom tomatoes. She also had an herb garden, which she used almost daily. As we ate lunch we talked about her life, health, and gardening. She made me homemade kung pao chicken, fried rice, roasted carrots, and an arugula and tomato salad. All the vegetables we ate that day came from her garden. Grace's garden produces a large quantity of vegetables, which allows her to spend a little extra cash on good grass-fed or free-range meats and dairy products.

She told me that her diet now makes her feel like she has more energy and because she produced it, eating the food feels more rewarding.

Before Grace was diagnosed with diabetes, she told me that she never really felt right; something was always off. Then one night, she got into her car to drive home, and her eyesight was blurry. She was frightened and unsure about what was happening to her. She saw a doctor who informed her that she had developed a severe case of diabetes and that blurry vision was a side effect. Grace lives by herself, so losing her ability to see was tragic. She took quick action and began looking at ways she could change her lifestyle. She said that it must have been fate, because soon after her diagnosis LMV volunteers, who were out canvasing door-to-door looking for people to join, visited her home to tell her about the program. She signed up on the spot. Within a year, Grace was growing most of her own vegetables, she was using the fruit trees in her backyard, and she shared her surplus with her neighbors. In addition, her doctor took her off prescription medication, and her vision returned to the point of allowing her to drive again.

Grace told me that she typically does not eat fried rice anymore, but she wanted to make me something that she remembered from her childhood. She has moved away from white rice and today eats more brown rice and other whole grains. She also grows herbs for tea and bitter melon to help lower blood sugar levels. For people with diabetes, one of the biggest concerns with processed foods is that they digest quickly. In fact, in many cases, they digest too quickly. Grace has moved away from the diet she remember as a child, which often consisted of fried white rice and meat and has moved toward a diet full of whole grains (closer to Pollan's *Food Rules*), which are digested more slowly (Schmid 1997). As the stomach digests carbohydrates, it coverts food into glucose, a type of sugar, to fuel the body's energy needs. The faster a food digests in the stomach, the higher levels of glucose a person will have in their system at a given time. As glucose or blood sugar levels increase, the pancreas release insulin. Insulin is used by the body to allow glucose to enter into the cells and provide the body with energy. The type 2 diabetic, on the other hand, often has fat deposits, which limit the insulin's ability to allow glucose into the cells. The cells then send a signal to the pancreas to produce more insulin and to the liver to release more glucose.

Eventually the body reaches a point where both the insulin and glucose levels are so high that the body crashes. The inability to absorb glucose results in high blood sugar and high insulin levels, and over time, the overworked pancreas may stop functioning and create insulin deficiency. The individual may then become dependent on insulin injections. While this is an oversimplified version of what happens in the digestive system, the important point is that foods rich in fiber and low in carbohydrates tend to digest slower. These foods are the original "slow food." For many in these home gardeners, slow food is not about dining at an exclusive restaurant with a well-known chief using locally sourced produce but rather, eating with intention and cultivating awareness of the body.

Lupe

I first visited Lupe's home with one of University of California's master gardeners. I was invited to follow the master gardener to observe and record how she interacts with the LMV community. On that day, we visited three homes, and Lupe's was the last visit that day. She had a magnificent garden with an abundance of diverse crops. She had heirloom sweet corn growing along her back fence, and she had created a trellis for her chayote to climb and provide shade for strawberries, arugula, mustard greens, and red leaf lettuce. She told me that this is what her mother did back in Mexico, so it was only common sense that she do it as well. On the day I visited Lupe, she had only been with LMV for one year, which is why she still had a master gardener visiting her garden once a month. The irony is Lupe does not, nor did she ever, need a master gardener, but, as she told me, "I like the master gardeners because they help me out with things I don't know about. They also show me new things." Like many other recent immigrants in the program, Lupe benefits more from gaining access to resources such as drip irrigation than she does from the knowledge of a master gardener.

After touring Lupe's garden, she prepared us a meal of chayote, onion, tomato, with stuffed jalapeños and homemade limonada. She walked us through her step-by-step process because she wanted to be sure that we understood how to follow the recipe and gastronomical practices required to prepare this delicious treat for our families. She explained to us how hard it is for her family to stay healthy. She makes almost every meal and snack from scratch and uses few processed ingredients. Throughout the summer she makes traditional Mexican aguas frescas from strawberries, melons, hibiscus (referred to as *jamaica* in Mexico), lemons, and limes grown in her backyard. "That way," she told us, "it has no added sugar."

Just over a year before I met Lupe, she had developed an intestinal condition. She visited the doctor on several occasions, but they could not pin down what exactly was occurring in her digestive system. Over the course of several visits she was prescribed different medications and even antibiotics, but none of them worked. She was then told to change her diet and begin consuming low-fat dairy and whole grain bread. Still nothing. She grew irritated because she was spending money on drugs that she thought had no effect. So, she simply stopped taking them and, although she did not inform her doctor, returned to the milpa-based diet she had before crossing over to the United States. She integrated chayotes, tomatoes, and chilies into meals almost every day. She stopped buying soda and juices but continued to regularly drink homemade aguas frescas from her garden. Within a few short weeks, her intestinal maladies were resolved. When she returned to visit the doctor, he told her the medication must have worked and what was surmised to be an infection was gone. When she told him she had stopped taking the medication several weeks earlier he was shocked and asked why. She told him that with medication her body was always off and only through food could she achieve some sort of balance. Satisfied with her answer, he said, "Whatever you're doing is working, so keep doing it."

Lupe's experience with health professionals was very similar to the Mixtec migrant farmworkers documented by Holmes (2013) in Washington State whereby their marginality encouraged further vulnerability and the silencing of that vulnerability. Immigrants confront the health care system differently and experience the structural violence embedded in the health system at different levels than many Americans because immigrant health care often operates as a form of socialization (see Gálvez 2011). The power/knowledge relationships experienced by immigrants in the medical setting can challenge traditional practices of healing and well-being by forcing immigrants to negotiate between the received knowledge of medical professionals and the passed-down wisdom of elders. Lupe was forced to make a choice of what was best for her and her life circumstances. As Alisha Gálvez explains, this negotiation is present for many immigrants to the United States because its health care system is seen as a model of modernity, and the quest for modernity (whether job or well-being) is often one of the many reasons people end up in the United States in the first place. Lupe's case provides insight into the failures of modernity. As Lupe finished telling me her story she looked to my plate and said, "*come sus jalapeños, especia es saludable*/eat your jalapeños, spice is healthy."

Following the wisdom of age-old *curanderas*, Ronald Schmid argues, "nature cures," however, "for nature to cure, one must understand what nature is—what is natural—and live by it" (1997, 1). While determining what is "natural" and what is not can sometimes be difficult; for Lupe it was simple. As she told me, "When I eat from my garden, I feel good." She told us that when she eats food from her garden, she knows where it comes from, and how it was produced, and that it gives more meaning to her food. Among home gardeners, Lupe is considered to be one of the best cooks. She attributes this reputation to the fact that she combines what she has in her garden with harvest techniques based on seasonal cycles. She knows when a particular crop is ready for a particular recipe, and the decision about when to harvest is a choice made with the vital gastronomical or culinary qualities in mind. The best-known example of this is "green tomatoes," which can be the same varietal as any given vine-ripened tomato plant but are selected at an earlier stage for culinary reasons. She experiments with food and crops because she wants to grow and eat as much as she can from her garden, and she does this in a mindful way, tuned into the life cycle of the various crops.

Lupe's garden is a site of food production and social reproduction. When talking about Lupe and her restorative and seasonal approach to gardening, cooking, and eating, it is easy to get overly "romantic" about self-provisioning and forget how hard it is for her to maintain such a lifestyle. Lupe does not work for a wage; she looks after her two children and a few other kids in the neighborhood. Yet just because she has time to work in the garden does not mean that her children want to eat from the garden. "I don't know what my kids eat at school," she told me. She makes them a homemade meal every day, but her son often informs her that he trades things to get soda or candy. Lupe is one of the most outspoken members of the community when it comes addressing school lunches.

Her passion is very similar to the view championed by Janet Poppendieck, who believes that "schools are the place to influence children's eating habits," (2010, 12). Alice Waters, the owner of Chez Panisse Restaurant in Berkeley, is an advocate for educational experiences in the garden. Her edible schoolyard program at Martin Luther King Jr. Middle School in Oakland sparked international interest and continues to spread throughout many cities across the country (see Waters 2008). The relationship between schools and the family

FIGURE 13 Roasted tomatillo salsa. Photo courtesy of the author.

are mutually reinforced; a school can only do so much in the development of a child if the family does not follow through on its obligations. Likewise, Lupe's actions only mean so much if her children go to school and are then provided with cheaply processed and unhealthy foods, something former First Lady Michelle Obama, celebrity chief Jamie Oliver, and many others have taken up.

Conviviality and Healing with Comida

There is no doubt that food is a central aspect of social life (Counihan and Van Esterik 2008), and nearly every home visit during this study involved food as a central element. While the garden visits and interviews were part of the task of data gathering, the interactions, conversations, and subsequent collaborations led to an invitation for me to become part of a web of convivial relationships. I have been given food from harvests; I have eaten with families at their tables and in their gardens; I have helped to weed and prune and pick and cultivate; and I have been part of large potlucks at La Mesa Verde community events. In each of these instances, I have been humbled by the ways the community uses food as a healing agent and as a transformative medium for more radical social change by a multitude of convivial subjectivities.

Grace and Lupe grow, share, and consume comida, albeit in slightly different ways. Their gardens generate options to escape a mode of production that has contributed to them developing diet-related illnesses, but comida, as an expression of their social relationships, allows them to live on their own terms by challenging how society is organized. Karl Marx (1920) believed that social relations are closely tied to the mode of production. The productive forces of industrial capital that are reliant on private property, the accumulation and hoarding of wealth, and the exploitation of wage-labor are challenged by the existence of comida. By growing, sharing, and consuming comida that is removed from the capitalist mode of production, Grace is able to divest in a system that puts her at odds with her health. She exerts her autonomy by growing food in a slightly different way than Lupe. While both Grace and Lupe are clear examples of the of how the neoliberal diet can wreak havoc on our bodies, they devise different, but equally important ways to confront it.

When Grace arrived in the United State some twenty years ago, she did not have any signs of diabetes, it slowly developed as time passed. Perhaps it was the speed of life in the Silicon Valley that encouraged her to opt for convenience, or maybe it was the manner in which highly processed Chinese American food replaced the traditional foods she grew up with in Sichuan province. In either case, Grace has been led to believe that Chinese food is inherently bad for her health. White rice and fried foods, she insisted, were for special occasions. Grace uses her garden not to return to "traditional food" but to adhere to a diet that more closely resembles a milpa-based diet predicated on whole grains, vegetables, and very little meat. Grace views traditional foods with nostalgia, not as something she would eat on a daily basis. In her context, comida represents a social process of learning what is "right" to eat for her right now. Laura Newcomer explains nutrition as a process of "re-teaching myself how to eat on a regular basis. . . . The authority to define and re-define what 'just right' means, on a daily basis, for my body and for me . . . [is] listening" (2013, 196). The practice of learning and re-learning, defining and re-defining, allows Grace the ability to navigate the unsteady and ever-shifting terrain of nutrition to figure out what is "just right" to eat.

Lupe on the other hand, rejects modern Western science by turning to comida to heal. The failures of modern Western science forced her to look to her past for answers. Chayotes and chilies are powerful not only because of their chemical compounds, but because they are vital sources of situated knowledge for immigrant women like Lupe. Hegemonic nutrition (Hayes-Conroy and Hayes-Conroy 2013) is often the approach to health by modern Western science, and it has the power to erase centuries of embodied knowledge that exists in comida. But as Lupe's story illustrates, recipes for comida are not found in cookbooks; rather, "like any living language, comida reflects the living memory of routine or ritualized practice" (Esteva and Prakash 1998, 67). Lupe is that ritualized practice.

Esteva and Prakash insist that comida is communal memory (1998, 67) because it lives on in daily action, not in texts. Both of these women approach comida from different positionalities, yet because this embodied practice remains "alive in the flesh" (Esteva and Prakash 1998, 67), comida is always changing, never fixed. Marx (1977) insists that the capitalist mode of production that typifies much of daily life produces our social, political, and intellectual life. Gardens at the margins offer escapes from that way of life by engineering alterNative modes of production rooted in comida. Grace, Lupe, and many others in this book more closely resemble postcapitalist futures by reframing the value of food, labor, and community that acquire new (or perhaps restore old!) productive forces that enable them to restore their social relations and health.

The Living Memory of Comida

In August 2014, LMV held its annual harvest festival. At the festival, over one hundred families attended the all-day event at Frank Bramhall Park in Willow Glen. It was a bright sunny San José day, and the families gathered under a group of oak trees that provided shade from the heat. Two things stood out to me on that day. First, having a harvest festival brought people together to share their experiences throughout the year. Meeting outside of Sacred Heart changed the atmosphere and encouraged informal social interaction. Second, the festival showcased the produce grown in their home gardens. As we set up for the event, we lined four full-length park tables end-to-end to accommodate all of the food. As guests showed up, they placed the dishes on the tables and found a seat at the surrounding dinner tables. The variety of dishes displayed both cultural diversity and plant diversity present in their gardens. While some of the food was store-bought, people would often add crops from their harvests to enhance a dish. Families made as much as they could from what was being produced in their garden. There were salads, salsas, casseroles, tamales, empanadas, beans, aguas frescas, including jamaica, flour and corn tortillas, lasagnas, enchiladas, chiles rellenos, cakes, and ice creams; you name it, it was there. People shared recipes, seeds, and leftovers. The event provided gardeners an opportunity to cook, share, and eat food from the many cultures enacting the socioecological spaces of home gardens.

Toward the end of the event, several people got up to talk and reflect with the others on what the program meant to them and their families. One man sang a corrido to explain his gratitude to one of the program coordinators who was leaving to attend graduate school on the East Coast and to wish her luck in all future endeavors. Everyone clapped, and the teary-eyed singer and coordinator hugged and exchanged thanks. After he sat down, and the applause calmed, Lupe got up to speak. She spoke in Spanish while one of the organizers translated into English. She told stories of how it was before she had a garden. She expressed gratitude for having help in starting a garden because this allowed her to gain "a sense of freedom" and encouraged her to remember and revalue the traditional practices of her childhood spent in rural Mexico. Upon finishing, Lupe said, "Don't stop, we can't stop. We must continue to grow our own food. We must continue to share with our neighbors. We must continue to respect our Mother Earth."

As she walked off the stage people applauded and several expressed agreement with her sentiments. Soon after, the event ended, and people packed their things. As I drove home that evening, I thought about what Lupe had said; there were so many layers to it. I have spoken with Lupe several times since then and have eaten at her home; we have shared some great stories over wonderful meals embodying the meaning of comida. She might be one of the most dedicated home gardeners in the study because she believes in the transformative potential of home gardens. There are so many levels to health and even more to healing, yet the mundaneness of growing food offers an unlimited opportunity to challenge the alienating and upsetting aspects of the neoliberal capitalist food system. Lupe told me one day that gardening might not be able to change the world in an instant, but she emphasized that change will come one day, "poco a poco," she told me—little by little.

Gardening allows home gardeners to improve their well-being on two fronts. Their home gardens provide them with improved access to healthy organic foods, thus enabling and encouraging them to change their dietary habits to improve their physical bodies. On another, this network of home gardeners improves their collective well-being because it encourages the community to envision and enact the possibility of many futures. Wendell Berry argues, "the industrial economy does not see itself as a little economy; it sees itself as the only economy" (1987, 64). As the only economy, the industrial (or capitalist) economy transforms people and places by making them dependent on high-input farming practices and the "financialization" of the entire food chain. But as a gardener told me, "you don't have to be rich to be a good gardener, you just have to be patient." The home garden economy is not against the "industrial" economy. In fact, in many ways it benefits from it. Having a garden allows people to negotiate between economies while privileging the circumstances and resources of each household's own assets.

Conclusion

Health is not a one-dimensional outcome existing in some social, political, and environmental vacuum. Our current health system, like the food system, is imbricated with biopolitical technologies that are designed to privilege capitalist market rationalities and to subordinate the subject to a regime of self-financed (or insured) self-care. This mechanism prices most working class and immigrant households out of effective and equitable health care, including, especially, preventative care (see Berenson et al. 2012). Home gardeners respond to the inequities of the food and health systems by cultivating food in their own gardens because it is a practical tool to challenge the prevailing uses of land, soil, knowledge, and seed in the corporate-dominated American food system. But more than that, gardening also allows them to cultivate new subjectivities by providing access to the means of their own production and social and cultural reproduction (i.e., a return to milpa-based cuisines and traditional ingredients). Gardening moves us from alienated labor to unalienated labor while attending to our bodies, communities, and environments. That is the power of comida. Regardless of the unavoidable contradictions embedded in urban agriculture (McClintock 2014), comida can set us free.

The sharing and enjoying of comida is central to the healing practices of many colonized peoples because it can offer an escape from the oppressive norms of the industrial food system. The neoliberal diet places profit over people (Otero 2018), but when gardens at the margins emerge in contrast, new worlds of possibility emerge. Peña and his colleagues insist that

> Food is who we are, and how we grow, share, and consume our food informs us of the people we want to be, the places we wish to coinhabit, and the worlds we work to create. Decolonial food is not just a radical restructuring of our food system; it is the radical restructuring of the meaning of our food.

It is the resurgence of a way of being human that celebrates ancestral practical knowledge while engaging in the acts of making and sharing food and expanding accountability across the food chain. We are not only dismantling hierarchies of power and privilege but working to bring dignity back into all of our food practices by providing pathways to healing through transformative, everyday lived experiences and direct action. (2017, 365)

The everyday humble actions of home gardeners dismantle hierarchies of power and privilege by restructuring the meaning of food and pursuing a way of being human that expands beyond the self. This process creates new and imagined worlds, it allows for the self-determination of people and the renewal of their capacity for a sense of self by grounding it in place, culture, and dignity. More importantly, when food is understood as part of a complex web of relationships and not a mere commodity or the sum its individual nutrients, vitamins, and other components, it becomes part the "vibrant matter" that makes us who we are.[4] Comida is a source of solidarity and conviviality because it is shared and celebrated with others. Home gardeners understand this, and each passing meal is twofold. First, the sharing of comida continues the legacy of how to care for our communities, bodies, and landscapes in ways that also nourish and maintain cultural knowledge. Second, the sharing of comida ensures the survival, or even the commoning, of a convivial revolutionary subjectivity that is grounded in the vernacular values of simplicity, sustenance, dignity, and respect.

---

4. Gyorgy Scrinis (2015) refers to this school of thought as "nutritionism," or a reductive way of understanding health whereby food is valued less for its totality and more for its individual nutrients, minerals, and vitamins. This narrow appreciation of health is based on reductionist science and disregards the cultural value of what food can do for people beyond its molecular structure.

CHAPTER 5

"We're not just growing tomatoes"

Cultivating Revolutionary Subjectivities at the Margins

> We're actually a really big farm full of a lot of mini-plots.
>
> —*Luis*

In September of 2015, I met Luis at Roy's Station Coffee & Tea in San José's Japantown. It is a busy place at nine o'clock in the morning, one of those community coffee shops where you better know what you want before your turn comes because people are on the move. The city was waking up, and I expected the trendy coffee shop to be full of dot-comers and hipsters, which it was, but it was a lot more than that. Roy's served as a place where community members, social activities, academics, and politicians all congregated. The day I met with Luis there, I saw several people I have met with throughout the study all mingling. When Luis arrived, I ordered two cups of coffee for us, and we found a place outside in the shade to sit and talk.

As we sipped on our coffee, Luis explained how important gardening was in his life. Reminiscent of Grandma and Alfonso, gardening is not just something to do as a hobby but something that allows him to live life in a way that corresponds with his values and ethics of community, land, and self. The problem, he described to me, was that home gardens and community gardeners were now being presented as progressive. "I hate the word progressive," Luis told me with a shrug, "because I'm not progressive. Just because you grow food, doesn't mean you're progressive, because what we are doing is nothing new," he finished and took a sip of his black coffee. "I didn't really want to look for the political, but it's there whether I like it or not. And if I want to relax and enjoy life, I have to grow food." Luis paused for a moment and looked toward his watch. Both of us were nearing the limit on our parking meters. "I got two minutes," he said. "Yeah," I replied, "I got three."

Luis and I had talked many times throughout this study, and each time he stressed the fact that while so many people wanted to push the idea that growing food is always political, for him, it was less of a political move and more about living well. "And to tell you," he started to say as he stood up from his chair,

> You know, I just really enjoy growing vegetables, it's the truth. And really, that is what I'm doing, I really am. I enjoy this. I feel really good. I lost some weight, and I get to do some really fun stuff, like growing things I didn't know about. I looked things up, talked with other gardeners, and started growing heirloom tomatoes, then squash. You start to realize that we're [the gardeners in La Mesa Verde] like a real organism. We're actually a really big farm full of a lot of mini plots. And on the big stage, we grow a ton of food.

Throughout this study, gardeners consistently referred to their actions not as political acts but as acts of enjoyment. Does this mean conviviality itself has become a political and even maybe a decolonial move? Perhaps. In the *Economic and Philosophical Manuscripts of 1844*, Karl Marx commented on alienated labor by insisting that the "*devaluation* of the human world grows in direct proportion to the *increase in value* of the world of things" (Fromm 1966, 95). Gardens at the margins offer options to escape the dehumanizing and alienating processes of industrial capitalism through collective engagements of conviviality because as Franco Berardi insists, "wealth does not mean a person who owns a lot, but refers to someone who has enough time to enjoy what nature and human collaboration place within everyone's reach" (2009, 169). "And ultimately," Luis informed me, "it [having a home garden] will result in actions where people will experience what it is like to go against the grain, and they'll be like 'Whoa, that feels great!' Because someday we will have to go against the grain, whether we like it or not." While gardening as a way of life might help individuals achieve specific outcomes like weight loss or diabetes prevention, it also weds them to others in unexpected ways. The convivial subjectivities of home gardeners are part of a more considerable project of social transformation because, as Luis informed me, "We're not just growing tomatoes."

FIGURE 14 A La Mesa Verde garden full of biodiversity. Photo courtesy of the author.

Emerging Radical Political Subjectivities from the Margins

Evelyn lives alone in a converted studio apartment in South San José. As a white woman growing up in the suburbs of Chicago, she always wanted to move to California. In the late 1960s, she accomplished her goal and moved to Sonoma and learned to farm and grow her own food. Like many others, Evelyn's current condition is the result of a series of events often beyond her control. After raising her family in Sonoma, Evelyn moved to San José to be closer to her children, but living on her own was not what she expected. She has developed fibromyalgia, type 2 diabetes, and chronic fatigue syndrome. In an attempt to avoid high-priced prescription drugs to control her illnesses, Evelyn attended diabetes prevention and wellness classes at the Indian Health Center in San José. However, like so many in her situation, she learned that the food she was encouraged to eat, which was a diet high in fresh organic foods, was out of her price range.

When I talked with Evelyn in 2014, we sat in her apartment and shared a pot of tea made from herbs from her garden as she explained to me her current living situation. Her apartment is a simple one-bedroom granny unit located in Campbell, just west of San José. The property was shared with a family who was renting the house, which had a pool beyond the fence. Evelyn was quick to the point that out because they share a water bill. The front door led into a kitchen, which was clearly the center of the home. There were still plates in the sink left from breakfast and a bowl of sweet cherry tomatoes drying from being freshly rinsed. Over the sink, a window that looked into her two raised garden beds. Just past the kitchen was a small two-person table with matching chairs. Just to the left was the living room was a small couch with a reclining chair and a small, neatly placed coffee table. The house was homey, comfortable, and inviting. She had a small television that was not often used, and pictures of family and friends on the walls. As we took a seat at the table, Evelyn described what life is like for her living in the valley.

"I live off social security, but because of my disabilities, I don't receive full benefits," she said with a sense of frustration. "I get a supplemental income from the government that makes it actually harder to live." Evelyn makes so little from social security that she qualifies for a government program called Supplemental Security Income (SSI). The program awards her money so that she can have more to live on, but if she receives SSI, she does not receive food stamps. So, the supplemental income that is provided to her combined with her social security gives her just enough money for rent (around $1,200 per month), but because she does not receive food stamps, she must find other ways to get food. "At first, I went to food pantries, but the food they offer was discouraged for diabetes patients. Food banks are full of processed foods," she told me as she poured herself another cup of tea. She set the teapot down when her cup was full, took a sip, paused, and then continued.

> I was unable to meet my dietary needs. For a long time, I was nutrient deficient because of the food I was forced to eat from the food bank. You see, some people [the working poor] have higher incomes and can receive food stamps, but because I'm disabled and can't work, I make less and put less into social security. So, I receive a supplemental income just to get by. My allowance actually disallows me to receive food stamps. I'm literally too poor to receive help.

Evelyn's supplemental income bumps up her income just enough to make her ineligible for the SNAP program. The high cost of living in the area consumes much of her income, which leaves very little for healthy foods. Her story further confirms that noncommunicable illnesses like diabetes are not always wealthy people overeating, but poor people not eating enough of the right kinds of food (Patel 2007; Brownell 2004).

Evelyn's compounding illnesses of fibromyalgia, type 2 diabetes, and chronic fatigue syndrome feed off of each other, and there are limited times where she feels in control of her body and health. At one point in her life, she was so tired of living day to day with the help of nurses and family members that she got a full-time job. She made good money and lived in a beautiful place, but within a few months she developed sores all over her body, her taste buds were inflamed, and her body was slowly resisting and shutting down. She continued to work for nine months, until one day she just said enough. It took her body years before she felt like it had recovered.

"My garden is not just an important part of my life, it is vital to my survival. It's my main food source," she told me. While she eats almost everything her garden produces, she shares what she can. Her daughter helps her buy food throughout the weeks, mainly in the winter, when the garden is less productive. Evelyn understands that because of her health condition, she cannot overextend herself. When she can, she shares her surplus at LMV events with neighbors, family, and community. Evelyn is proud that she can give a piece of herself and does so because she also understands the need to support communal values.

After we finished the tea, Evelyn wanted to show me her garden. She rose from her chair and slowly made her way across the kitchen to the door. Exiting the front door, Evelyn took a moment while holding onto the door jam and then continued toward the garden. "The old ways need to come back," she said as she sat in a chair in the shade near her garden. It was clear that she had placed the chair in that particular spot, and I got the sense that she spent a lot of time simply relaxing there. Like many others in this book, Evelyn's garden plays a central role in sustaining her lifestyle. Evelyn's home garden relationships create mutual reliance and provide the basis for understanding an "ethic of care." According to Joan Tronto, "care helps us rethink humans as interdependent beings," and thus, it allows us "to move toward a more just and caring society" (1993, 21). But mutual reliance is not just about caring for each other on the premise of love. In fact, Peter Kropotkin argues that "to reduce animal sociability to love or sympathy means to reduce its generality and its importance" (2006, xi). When acts of mutual reliance are reduced to a narrow understanding of love or personal sympathy, it detracts from morality as a whole. Thus, acts of sharing and mutual reliance do not fit into a narrow definition of love, but rather arise from the innate human instinct of solidarity (see Anton and Schmitt 2012).

Could the fundamental drivers of society be solidarity and cooperation rather than competition? Evelyn's actions might encourage us to thinks so, and many others would agree with her (e.g., Boehm 2012; Bowles and Gintis 2011). In fact, that is exactly what Peter Kropotkin argued over one hundred years ago in his seminal work *Mutual Aid* where he states "the ideal of the ethical man is to limit his freedom of action to a sphere in which he does not interfere with the freedom of others" (2006, 273). As Evelyn explained to me, "Without the help of others, I couldn't plant my garden." Through cooperation and mutual reliance, Evelyn sustains a level of autonomy that supports her ability for social reproduction.

On another occasion with Evelyn, I helped her plant her fall garden. I was volunteering with La Mesa Verde to help plant gardens for those who could not, and Evelyn's name came up. I was happy to pay her a visit. As we planted, she sat in that same wooden chair in the shade as she told me what to plant and where to plant it. Evelyn often used gardening as a metaphor to explain and understand life, and slowly, our conversation turned that direction. "Through gardening, you can learn a lot about life," she insisted. "Our brains are now trained for an instantaneous reaction. We no longer take time to think, we just act," she continued as I was planting broccoli. "I'm afraid of where we're headed. I feel like I'm headed upstream, against the current. But I don't want to go with the current because it seems to me like it's headed to some sort of cesspool. Gardening can help change the direction we are headed," she asserted. "Everyone should have a garden. It can reconnect us to a slower pace. We need to realize that no matter what we need to accomplish, there is a pace to it that is natural," she said as she articulated her philosophy of sustainability. "You can't build quality quickly. It's not lasting, not sustainable." Evelyn often moved at a slower pace, and at first, I thought it was because of her fibromyalgia, but as I got to know her, I think it was less about her illnesses and more because she moved with intent. "The first thing you learn when gardening," she said, "is that gardens need a lot; water, sun, nutrients. Just like real relationships, you need to invest yourself."

Evelyn's garden subjectivity challenges the one-off society in which we live, which, according to Zygmunt Bauman (2000), is one that encourages its subjects to be consumers rather than producers. This logic encourages people to act on their own best interests while avoiding the consequences of their choices and sidestepping any responsibility that may be tied to the effects of one's own actions. In our contemporary world, risks are created by society and experienced by individuals. The "liquid times" experienced today are a result of a social system that praises the individual at the cost of the community (Bauman 2007). The neoliberal logic that has created such a society allows the state to abandon responsibility while placing those most vulnerable at the mercy of the inherent unpredictability of market forces. The individualized market forces division rather than unity (Bauman 2000, 148) and compels the consuming subject to "perceive the world as a container full of disposable objects, objects for one-off use; the whole world—including other human beings" (2000, 162). However demoralizing these "economies of abandonment" might be, as Povinelli (2011) shows, these spaces of social abandonment can be transformed into new areas of possibilities, just as Evelyn and others in this book have done.

Evelyn, and many others introduced in this book, have been growing food for several years and are deeply connected to other home gardeners. Many of these gardeners have been a part of La Mesa Verde for several years and have seen it change. "When I first started growing food with LMV, it was a one-year thing," Evelyn told later that morning after we finished in the garden. "You get seeds, beds, education, and plants. Then you're done." Unexpectedly, however, after the first year, several people wanted to stay connected. Gardeners met regularly, they shared experiences, traded recipes, and voted for speakers and classes. The program has been trying to create some type of community in the wake of neoliberal policies that have left the social safety net in tatters and forced many residents to build walls between neighbors rather than bridges. According to Evelyn, the community sought by LMV is always shallow because certain people are more invested than others.

While gardening has connected people to others they may never have been connected with otherwise, it also created an artificial community. This is part of the problem of "organized garden projects" (Pudup 2008) like LMV and inherent in the contradictory practices of urban agriculture (McClintock 2014). The structural adjustments initiated through neoliberal policies eroded social safety nets in such a way that it redistributed wealth and power upwards, creating the need and opportunity for urban agriculture to emerge. Still, urban agriculture, while empowering, allows the government to sidestep responsibility because people are already taking care of themselves. Projects like LMV are, on the one hand, spaces of social and political resistance because gardeners are working together to challenge the inequalities embedded in the food system. On the other, they are "spaces of neoliberal governmentality, that is, spaces in which gardening puts individuals in charge of their own adjustments(s) to economic restructuring and social dislocation through self-help technologies centered on personal contact with nature" (Pudup 2008, 1229).

Evelyn told me that the logic for many gardeners is, "Why should I do something if I'm always still going to get plants." She was referring to the funding structure of LMV, which receives funding and gives away seedlings and starters to anyone registered without asking for much in return. LMV would like to require its members to regularly volunteer, and if one does not, they would be dropped from the program. However, the reality is that LMV needs gardeners and numbers to continue to receive funding. While this contradiction continues to persist, gardeners like Evelyn think differently about the "free-rider" problem because her survival depends on the mutual reliance other LMV gardeners.

The last time I met with Evelyn, she gave me a watering tip that she learned from years of gardening, and even though it goes against the logic of the many master gardeners, she says it works. She explained to me the practice of "deep watering" is giving more water to a plant but doing so at longer intervals. This trains the roots to go deep into the soil where more moisture resides. As the plant matures, its roots go deep, and the plant requires less water over time. The top few inches of soil usually receive the most water, but that is also where the water is most likely to evaporate. Deep watering allows the water to be retained in the soil for longer. "The key to it all," she told me, "is healthy soil." I took her agroecological knowledge of deep watering to infer a metaphor about the social relationships and social networks created by these home gardeners. Deep watering takes time, and it is during that time that roots are created and established. The strength of roots for plants is as important as the strength of roots for social relationships.

All organizational forms have their limits, and while these home gardens have helped many of the people I interviewed, there is constant stress and pressure from outside forces. Many in this study cannot escape the biopolitical context of empire explained by Hardt and Negri (2000). The reality of health in this community is that, in spite of all of their collective efforts, they are still susceptible to the chaos of capitalism. Yet, remarkably, despite all that is wrong, home gardeners continue to find and create what is good. Evelyn told me one day that she feels like she is always going against the grain because to go with the flow of society is to move in a direction she unwilling to go. Evelyn's narrative unveils a radical political subjectivity that helps to form part of the struggle for food sovereignty. As she informed me, "People have lost their ability to critically think, but the garden forces us to slow down. [In today's speed-driven society] . . . people forget that there is no relationship you can build without spending time. We no longer slow down to make relationships." The radical political subjectivity embodied by Evelyn is one of a multiplicity of voices and cultures that have coalesced to create spaces for the self-organization and self-determination of needs, wants, and desires. This is what Antonio Negri refers to as the highest form of class-consciousness, which "consists in the realization that power resides not in a representative or a delegate but in the class itself" (1991, 204).

Gardens on the Brink

When I first met Nancy in 2012, she and her husband lived close to Sacred Heart and were among the first families to join the LMV program. Over time she had become extremely invested in the program and volunteered as much as she could. Nancy and her husband are both in their late fifties and are white. When they began the program, they both suffered from what medical experts term "social anxiety disorder." A doctor never officially diagnosed Nancy because her anxiety prohibited her from leaving the house. She did her own research and felt that the symptoms presented were very close to how she felt. Nancy also suffers from type 2 diabetes. Their son was the only person who stopped by to drop off groceries and visit with them every few days. Both she and her husband were out of work, depressed, and lived almost entirely on disability. One day, LMV organizers came to her door to ask if she wanted to be a part of the program. At first, she wanted nothing to do with the program, but her son thought it would be good for them, so they joined. Within months both Nancy and her husband had dramatically changed. For the first time in a long time, Nancy wanted to interact with people, inviting them to see her garden and what she was growing. She started a blog, and when news reporters wanted to write stories, they would often showcase her garden. "The smallest of changes can have lifelong implications," Nancy told me one day while we talked at a nearby coffee shop. "You have to understand," she continued, "this is more than a garden. This garden has literally changed my life."

Her garden reconnected her to food, provided a greater understanding of food and health-related issues, and, most of all, she felt more connected with herself and her community. Despite the challenges she confronted daily as a result of being unemployed and trying to navigate an industrial food system while living in a food desert, her garden was a place where she could find a sense of peace and stimulate personal growth. Gardening allows her to reversed decades of alienated labor. Over a few years, Nancy reduced the effects of her diabetic condition and had integrated herself into a community of home gardeners. "Some families," she let me know, "are afraid to come out, and gardening can help alleviate that."

In 2012, Nancy lived in an old Victorian-style home that needed repair. The living room was cluttered with paperwork and boxes, many windows and even porch lights were either cracked, broken, or no longer worked, but the kitchen and dining room were full of life. When I visited, there was always fresh fruit on the table, and during the summer months, the warm glow from the sun would light up what I took to be the most essential room in the house, the kitchen. The house was far too big for two people but cheap enough for them to afford. The backyard was optimal for growing food. It received well over eight hours of sunlight, but it also had areas of filtered light where she grew crops that required less sun, like cabbage, carrots, cauliflower, celery, chard, endive, and escarole. In the far corner of the yard, just beyond an abandoned truck that she hoped to someday plant food in its bed, was her compost pile. "I make compost the lazy farmer way," she said. "I just put it there and turn it every so often. But it works well." Nancy makes use of what she had access to, whether it be the bed of a truck or the chain-link fence where she grows tomatoes. Her homegrown food improved her own well-being, sense of place, and relations with other home gardeners.

Nancy's story is particularly poignant. It reveals how class inequality and the process of enclosure, privatization, and displacement driven by gentrification in the Bay Area are interrelated. While she saw tremendous beneficial changes in her health and social well-being while participating in garden sharing networks, she was recently forced to move and lost her garden. The South Bay is one of the most expensive places to live in the United States, and Nancy's rent rose to a price that she could no longer afford. At the time I finished this research, she and her husband had yet to secure full-time jobs and now live in a low-income housing complex where all they have is a room, a bathroom, and a hotplate. The loss of her garden has meant that Nancy has been forced back into the "food junkyard" and must often buy cheap, processed foods. She currently works the night shift at a packaging facility, but during the day, I often see her volunteering to do paperwork, making phone calls, or running errands for the LMV staff.

Nancy tries to maintain her garden networks, but because she works nights, many of her ties have weakened. She told me that she no longer feels like the person she was when I first visited her. She sleeps most of the day to work all night and misses her garden. Yet, Nancy is not letting her circumstances stop her. She is well aware of the countless other people in similar situations, which is why she does not allow the temporality of her garden to diminish her hope for change. "LMV wants to start a movement," she explained one day at an LMV event, "but they don't realize they already have. The roots are underground, and the implications are life-long." Nancy's precarious status reveals how class is also a factor creating the conditions for the illness and draws attention to the alienation that many lower-income people experience when they confront the neoliberal capitalist food system.

Many gardens emerge from the spaces of neoliberal neglect and then disappear without notice. When home gardens like Nancy's emerge from the aftermath and violence of life in spaces of neoliberal neglect, they are far more than gardens. They are temporary autonomous zones (Bey 2003; Bishop and Williams 2012) that allow people to reterritorialize space and community based on an "imaginary of local autonomy" (Appadurai 2003, 345). Their temporality is what enables their creativity and innovation because these gardens are connected through strong social networks. Nancy's story demonstrates how social networks can also be temporary and fragile for individuals who may lose their gardens due to conditions out of their control, such as rising rents, drought, and the cost of living.

Beneath the social networks created by these gardeners lies a far more extensive, far more complex, "rhizomatic" network of home garden economies that offer a multiplicity of alterNative norms, values, and worldviews as well as spaces of agroecological and social innovation. These hidden networks connect neighbors and families; they connect Santa Clara Valley to communities around the globe. These networks are built upon layers of moving bodies, knowledges, and seeds. Despite over four years of ethnographic fieldwork, interviews, and oral histories, I have only begun to understand the complexity of this organizational form and the shifting political subjectivities associated with it. As Amy Trauger explains,

> These potentially subversive political uses of space appeal to neither the state nor capital for solutions and instead rely on spaces of bounded autonomy in the margins. These spaces allow for dissent and a refusal to participate in "statism," and they foster the "unthinkable" in the form of self-sufficiency and mutual forms of relations. These contested struggles for autonomy might function as a kind of oppositional "state of exception" against the biopolitical control of the state—even if only temporarily. (2017, 56)

Nancy informed me that home gardening is about two things; promotion of the self and connection to others. The unique subjectivity ignited by acts of gardening, and acts of conviviality with others, assures that while these gardens may always be on the brink of enclosure by the biopolitical forces of industrial capitalism, they are also constantly on the brink of being reimagined.

Most of the home gardeners in this book are renters and are well aware that rising rents may one day force them to leave, but they do not let that stop their desire to grow food and attain a level of autonomy. The attachment to place that many of these home gardeners feel is not to a fixed place but to a reterritorialized space, which is why their ability to establish autotopographic gardens is essential. The earlier story of Davíd further expresses this reality. These home gardens are part of what Gibson-Graham refers to as the "politics of possibility in the *here* and *now*" (2006, xxvi) because they do not wait for justice to occur. Instead, they create their own version of justice through their shared sense of community and autonomy. Their attachments are mobile because they are memories of home, seeds passed down and shared, and ways of being that exist outside and de-linked from Western modernity. While the diasporic immigrants from Mexico in this study are clear examples of "place-makers in motion" (see Mares 2012; Mares and Peña 2011), so too are the many low-income white and Latinx families that continually experience displacement through gentrification. Experiences of food and health while diverse are also very similar because of the conditions imposed on people at the margins.

Nancy's narrative demonstrates how gardens at the margins encourage radical spatial and temporal subjectivities. Many of the gardens in this story are on the brink of being lost. Each one is exceptionally fragile, yet remarkably resilient. The gardener's ability to stay connected to and informed by this rhizomatic network helps to explain why gardens are lost and then resurface for various reasons that are always circumstantial. There are families who have been forced to leave the area because of rent increases, the loss of a job, or because a job opportunity arises elsewhere. In other cases, families stopped gardening because a family member experienced an illness or was deported, and the effort to maintain a garden became too burdensome. Gardening at the margins is always a biopolitical struggle often threatened by forces beyond the garden walls. Developing a sense of place is always a contested arena for gardeners in La Mesa Verde. For reasons like this, I have referred to such gardens as "gardens of sabotage" (Valle 2015) because they work to radically transform the status quo and create opportunities and escapes for people at the margins. Nancy's story illustrates how gardens of sabotage exist at the margins and can be found at the very core of industrial capitalism when home gardeners utilize their marginality to foster spaces of innovation, opportunity, and transformation to create new worlds of possibility. However, it also illustrates the vulnerability of such gardens and the chaos of capitalism.

A Space for Convivial Subjectivities

"I have been in San José all my life, and I have always known that the soil here is really good. I mean, it's obvious," Luis told me one day in the fall of 2014. He continued:

> [Growing up], I picked strawberries three blocks from my house. I went to hills to pick cherries and black berries. There were a lot of small framers on the Westside near Minnesota and Alma [roads]. This used to be farmland. Further south, there used to a giant pig farmer. Growing up around here, you couldn't help but to see things coming out of the ground.

Luis is nostalgic but also extremely practical about what he remembers growing up in the Santa Clara Valley. "As a child, my family always had a garden, but as I grew up and left home, I had little need for one . . . until I developed type 2 diabetes," he told me.

Around the same time, about five or six years ago, Luis converted his forgotten front yard into an abundant home garden.

> I found a little patch of dirt with a perfect amount of sunshine, but it had been used as a dumping ground by the previous owner, a tile guy. So, I had

to go through this little 3×5 patch with a rake, metal detector, all kinds of shit. It was the only ground I had because around here, on this side of town, there was a whole lot of cement laid. So that was all I had, and I dug it up and got going.

One thing is sure about Luis, once he starts something, he goes all in. "I hate starting something and not finishing it," he told me. "Also," he continued, "I hate taking advantage of something just because I can." When Luis made this comment, we were talking about his home garden networks and the issue of free riders, but that goes against everything he stands for. In many respects, society is set up for individuals to succeed, not for communities and groups to thrive. This group of home gardeners is looking to change that because at the heart of their motivation is not the pursuit of individual self-interest but the vernacular values of dignity, trust, and respect. Luis is doing more than engaging in a postcapitalist alternative food system, he is participating in a collective struggle for dignity (also see Madrigal 2017). The food grown in Luis's garden, and many others in this study, is guided by a way of living that supports community economies based on ethical decisions of how to live well (Gibson-Graham, Cameron, and Healy 2013).

Luis's convivial subjectivity is doing far more than reclaiming rights to food, or even to land. He is reclaiming his right to be human, or his humanness. Moving beyond rights and reclaiming his humanness, Luis is reclaiming his dignity. Emerging from this decolonial move is a convivial subjectivity created "in common" with others that offers a pathway toward restoring dignity.

This is an essential move for people like Luis because dignity is always self-determining. Dignity is awarded at birth and is based on a decolonial idea of humanity, whereas rights are granted by the state and are based on the imperial concept of citizenship. After all, "the conditions for citizenship are still tied to a racialized hierarchy of human beings that depends on universal categories of thought created and enacted from the identitarian perspectives of European Christianity and by white men" (Mignolo 2006, 313). The forced communities of birth ushered in by the idea of citizenship present in the Silicon Valley oftentimes clash with the organic communities of social citizenship (Del Castillo 2002) found in the Santa Clara Valley.

Labor, Value, and the Liberation of Convivial Subjectivities

The home gardeners in this book never once used the phrase "food sovereignty," yet their struggle for health, food, autonomy, and well-being aligns well with food sovereignty struggles around the world. In fact, Amy Trauger insists that food sovereignty is, on the one hand, material and, on the other, figurative. As she sees it, those who practice food sovereignty need physical space to grow food and political space to live life. While food sovereignty may not be able to thrive under the current model of state governance, "its theory and practice outline the contours of an alternative political space in which life can flourish" (Trauger 2017, 7). Luis told me that he never wanted to look for the political while growing food, yet, regardless, it was always present. In other words, whether we like it or not, growing food is always political, irrespective of how much joy or pain it may cause. Today, Luis is deeply rooted in what he refers to as a "homegrown food system," which is one possible version of what a food system could or should be.

The radical subjectivities articulated in this book come about through the struggle to create food sovereignty from meaningful experiences with community and the landscape. Trauger explains, "these struggles [for food sovereignty] take place all over the world, in backyards, in community gardeners, on squatted land, on lakes, in seed banks, and on small scale farms. This is the political practice at the margins, the places often overlooked in search of grander stories or more politically palatable narratives" (2017, 2). Such radical subjectivities arise at the margins because the margins are where worlds collide, where diversity is encouraged for survival and well-being. These are places of resilience. Mistinguette Smith insists that such sites are ecotones, "where built and natural ecologies meet and are in tension, creating places where diverse forms of life compete and cooperate" (2016, 138). These are places and spaces of abundance that may lead to non-capitalist global futures.

From a distance, gardens like the ones at La Mesa Verde appear to be about recreation, in fact, that is often how they are framed for funders seeking to bring "justice" to the barrio or ghetto, but for home gardeners, a garden is so much more (see Mougeot 2005; Eyzaguirre and Linares 2010). In fact, the social and political transformation initiated by place-based struggles like those in this book work to create a collective effort mobilized around

FIGURE 15 La Mesa Verde gardens are about more than growing food. Photo courtesy of the author.

food and the struggle for land and health (also see Peña et al. 2017). The joint struggle at the margins is often experienced "off the books" and part of the informal economy. For LMV home gardeners, informality is a process for individuals to pursue well-being and survival while at the same time intentionally and unintentionally working to control their social reproduction through an assemblage of informal networks that foster solidarity, trust, and cooperation.

The convivial labor of home gardeners that arises in these practices of informality has the potential to transform larger systems and institutions because it works to restructure the very basis of value theory. As Hardt and Negri insist, "a new theory of value has to be based on the powers of economic, political, and social innovation that today are expressions of the multitude's desire" (2009, 319). This is exactly what home gardeners have the potential to accomplish. They make up part of the multitude by expressing their desire for equality, liberation, and autonomy. The escapes created by gardens at the margins offer home gardeners a means for achieving their aspirations. These "gardens of sabotage" (Valle 2015) threaten the economic basis of value theory because people restore their dignity through their labor, or what Hardt and Negri call "labor-power against exploitation" (2009, 319). When home gardeners restore dignity to their labor, they challenge the very use-value of labor and throw off the balance between the biopolitical process (abstract labor) and the structure of biopower (self-valorizing labor) itself.

Luis spent time with union organizers in Santa Clara Valley and has a good understanding of the potential of removing his labor from the circuits of capital. When I asked him what the promises of growing his own food might be in the long run, he replied,

> Right now, a lot of people [in the food movement] don't know if that if we keep going down this street, we're going to start going up against some big corporate lawyers, big corporate lobbyers threatening our lives. But what can we do? We're gonna make big changes because I don't see it coming from the top. I don't see congress, at all, doing that shit. But here, locally, *we grow [food] in the margins, wherever we can.*

The real revolutionary potential of a garden subjectivity is that the measure of value is determined in relationship with others as an exercise of the common. That is, when home gardeners restore the dignity of self-valorizing labor, gardens at the margins become a voice for the multitude, assuring their wants, needs, and desires in their pursuit of liberation. La Mesa Verde may only be a small assemblage of actors in a little corner of the world, but they are part of a far larger global struggle against the rational choice logic of economic theory. "Value is created when resistance becomes overflowing, creative, and boundless and thus when human activity exceeds and determines a rupture in the balance of power" (Hardt and Negri 2009, 319). The narratives of Evelyn, Luis, and Nancy illustrate that going against the grain is not easy, but it is a necessary step to challenge the balance of power. Gardens at the margins restructure both the economic value of labor by turning spaces of neoliberal neglect into thriving refugias of life and diversity and the biopolitical value of labor by replacing the alienated labor of the industrial economy with the convivial labor of the community economy (also see Gibson-Graham 2006).

Conclusion
Giving Back to the Body and Land

Planting a seed is a humble act, yet the implications of planting extend into the histories of cultural, social, and ecological change and deep into the social and political makeup of larger structures of power. By sowing seed, we are not merely seeking to grow a plant. Instead, we are continuing the legacy of our ancestors by prolonging the continuity of alternative values and practices of comida. Each seed contains within it the memory of life. These memories are biological and cultural. They remind us of who we are, where we come from, and where we will go. Embedded within a seed is not just a genetic code, but a map that connects a place and a time to a multitude of other places and times. Each time we plant a seed or share the knowledge of how to care for and cultivate a plant, we continue the ancient tradition of agroecological exchanges that expand our biological and cultural well-being.

When I was first invited into the homes of this community of home gardeners, I was surprised by the biological, economic, and cultural diversity present in their gardens. Years later, these gardens truly remain forms of "vibrant matter" and retain the same levels of convivial intensity, biocultural diversity, and social complexity. Both human and more-than-human actors are always in motion in these spaces of urban transformation unleashed and tapped by these home gardeners. People move and return; plants cycle through the seasons; and gardeners continue mold and fertilize new political subjectivities through the practices of growing, sharing, and consuming food. A central aspect of this political subjectivity is the commitment to create and innovate escapes through tools of conviviality. This mobilizes home gardeners to support collective action strategies that build a future worth living.

Recently, the farmer and social critic Wendell Berry wrote a short article explaining his views on the future of climate change logic. He states, "If we think the future damage of climate change to the environment is a big problem only solvable by a big solution, then thinking or doing something, in particular, becomes more difficult, perhaps impossible" (Berry 2015, para. 22). He is not arguing that climate change is not a big problem, or that we do not need big solutions. In fact, he believes that large-scale governmental policies have their place. However, he believes that regulatory policy is always dependent on the future, a future that has progressively become more precarious by the day. Whereas small solutions, he explains, "do not wait upon the future. Insofar as they are possible now, exist now, are actual and exemplary now, they give hope" (2015, para. 22). In other words, small solutions are practical, useful, and effective in their immediacy. Throughout my research, the humble intentions of gardening at the margins have given me hope for the possibility of radical social transformation. As late neoliberal modernity continues to push people into the cruelest conditions of precarity, society at large faces an uncertain future. Yet those most marginalized continue to transform themselves and their communities in the most innovative and sustainable of ways.

Gardens of Love

Today, Indigenous, oppressed, and displaced people around the world are retooling themselves not by mirroring forms of social organization, forms of resistance, or ideas of justice presented to them by the dominant classes but by smashing the mirror altogether. They are not settling for the binary, either/or world offered to them because they are not demanding justice or individual rights as traditional social movements have in the past. Instead, there are no demands. There is only the struggle and praxis to assert autonomy and pursue dignity.

This may be part of what Chela Sandoval refers to as the "apparatus of love" (2000, 2), which allows one to break through "whatever controls in order to find understanding and community" (2000, 140). The "madness of economic reason" (see Harvey 2017) that guides our current food and economic system and produces individuals in constant competition with others is not the norm, but the exception. Love, trust, cooperation, and conviviality are not merely part of some utopian fantasy but deeply rooted in human evolution (Bowles and Gintis 2011; Boehm 2012). Many people are beginning to realize and return to these alterNative values of simplicity, sustenance, dignity, and respect.

Home gardeners enact spaces of autonomy in ways based on preexisting patterns of social organization they brought with them from their dislocations. As such, diasporic and displaced peoples use their multiple, shifting subjectivities to re-envision justice, equity, and autonomy. This is the story of how precarious and vulnerable communities make use of the margins to innovate, create, and transform orthodox notions of value, labor, and sociality. Gardening at the margins is a proactive experiment where people pursue well-being at the edges of center to valorize their social relationships with each other, their food, and the land. Home gardeners in this book are part of the multitude and what Hardt and Negri refer to as "singularities that act in common" (2004, 105). They embrace a relational approach to identity formation and do not let identity politics get in the way of social transformation. Such a worldview, "neither excludes nor includes but *spreads*" (Ingold 2018, 50). The revolutionary subjectivity of home gardeners seek to find common ground with others who, despite difference, work together to pursue simplicity, sustenance, dignity, and respect.

The collective response of these home gardeners is part of a larger global "network struggle" taking place in different locations around the globe. The movement takes different forms in different sites because the "multitude is an irreducible multiplicity . . . and can never be flattened into sameness, unity, identity, or indifference" (Hardt and Negri 2004, 105). This is truly what makes this leaderless, grassroots, international movement so powerful—it forces us to consider a plurality of life-forms. The food movement is not merely about food security, food access, or food sovereignty. It embraces life in all its manifestations. Human well-being, animal welfare, and biocultural diversity are all central to the movement because competition is not a given. Many in the food movement understand this, which is why this inclusive, flexible, and nonviolent movement has such tremendous potential.

Cooperation, Mutual Aid, and the End of Individualistic Rationalities

Change is rarely an easy process, especially when referring to larger social institutions. So, where do we begin? How does challenging the food system become something that can actually be done? When does the food system become less of a global hyperobject and more situated in local contexts, cultures, and ways of living? How can we de-link from the norms, histories, and rationalities of the current food system that are so deeply rooted in colonialism? I do not have the answers to these questions, but perhaps part of the solution resides in humility. La Mesa Verde strives to "raise consciousness" among its members about the food system and the inequality and degradation it perpetuates. A significant first step, especially if the practices follow the "pedagogies of the oppressed" (see Freire 1984) and respects the teachings of "original instruction" (Nelson 2008a). But I think there is more to it. In fact, Taiaiake Alfred insists, "awakening people is both a spiritual movement and a political mobilization" (2009, 63). Becoming aware of what lies beyond the assumptions of modernity reveals an oppressive logic that burdens the livelihoods of those who reject it. But there are escapes, and the heightened sense of awareness of just how "un-normal" normal is provokes people to act. It is my hope that this book and the narratives it holds contribute to the spiritual movement that is needed while also encouraging others to engage in political mobilization.

I began this study with a set of questions deemed useful and relevant by the gardeners themselves: What practices do home gardeners engage in to protect against vulnerability, attain social mobility, improve health and well-being, and strengthen ties to the neighborhood and community? Many of these practices have been discussed already, but I now wish to reflect on a deeper level and revisit questions about the rationality underlying the formation of human morals and the processes involved in the determination of what situated subjects define as value.

Throughout my time with home gardeners, I have witnessed the testimony of those with the least giving the most. Perhaps part of this can be explained by what Peter Kropotkin refers to as the unwritten rules of "human solidarity" (2006, xvi) or what Shawn Wilson more recently calls "relational accountability" (2008, 8). It is not just love or the moral obligation of sacrifice that forces one to act in solidarity with others but abeyance to an underlying principle of mutual aid. Kropotkin states, "In the practice of mutual aid, which we can retrace to the earliest beginnings of evolution, we . . . find the positive and undoubted origin of our ethical conceptions; and we can affirm that in the ethical progress of man, mutual support—not mutual struggle—has had the leading part" (2006, 247). This ethical stance helps uncover what it means to garden for the people in this book. The importance of the principle of mutual aid, seen on a canvas of a much larger set of implications, is borne out of contemporary accounts by evolutionary anthropologists who affirm that cooperation rather than competition is the more significant driver of human productive and reproductive adaptations to uncertainty (see, e.g., Hammerstein 2003; Boehm 2012; Bowles and Gintis 2011).

Given the context of a food system dominated by capitalist corporations, in which access to food is presumably determined by the invisible hand of consumer purchasing power and individual choices, the mutual aid option can only emerge as a political project if it undermines the dominant regime. This occurs not by seeking to "reform" that system but by enacting spaces of autonomy created through direct action and mutual aid by the members of informal networks like those nurtured by home gardeners in this book. The stories and accounts of these home gardeners provide persuasive examples of how cooperation (and mutual aid) emerge as a strategy among those of us who are facing the conditions of uncertainty produced by precarious work in toxic and diminished environments.

It is worth recalling the epigraph used by the late Elinor Ostrom (1999) in an article addressing the role of collective action in the evolution of "social norms." Ostrom, who disdained the idea that competition somehow *always* trumps cooperation, was also dismissive of rational choice theory's obsession with demonstrating how cooperation would only become possible if it was subordinated to individualized utilitarian interests. The quote she opens with is from Mancur Olson, a key proponent of (ir)rational choice theory: "[U]nless the number of individuals in a group is quite small, or unless there is coercion or some other special device to make individuals act in their common interest, *rational, self-interested individuals will not act to achieve their common or group interests*" (1965, 2; Ostrom's emphasis). Ostrom countered that one cannot predict any outcomes of such a determination without knowing the "history" of the participants in any given game-theoretic situation. Through culture previously hidden norms are revealed. There is no universal "rational egoist." The lessons from these home gardeners show how the uses of home garden networks are dependent on the gardener's life circumstances, yet the culture of the community is what guides and shapes the norms of cooperation. The utilitarian ethic and concept of the individual are relatively recent inventions across the broader span of human evolution, showing greater normative diversity. The cultural frame is what ultimately contains a multitude of possibilities in which cooperation is enacted and mutual aid rendered as a driving force of adaptation and transformation.

Culture also informs cooperating groups on how the problem of free riders might be addressed.

Among these gardeners, the free-rider is viewed as more endemic to a system in which the value set is defined by untenable neoliberal individualistic behaviors and values—that is, selfishness, greed, disinterest in sharing, commitment to unfettered accumulation, indifference to dispossession, etc. For example, *vergüenza* (or shame) can be used as a form of normative consensus and avoidance of graduated sanctions in organizations like La Mesa Verde. This is what home gardeners implied when they referred to the need to foster norms of accountability. This includes those who use social norms like reciprocity, trust, and fairness, which prefigures the type of member willing to sustain a commitment to such a collective ethos. This is forcefully illustrated by the tendency to coalesce around a membership that values honesty and reciprocity as the social norms underlying the commitment to become a member of a convivial sharing economy.

The resurgence of social norms like cooperation and mutual aid is something that must be seen in the context of more substantial and more encompassing food justice and food sovereignty struggles. Leading scholars in food justice and food sovereignty discourses often refer to people like those in this book as struggling *against* the food system to create some type of sovereignty over their food and health. But from what I have witnessed, this group is far different. Many of the home gardeners do not refer to the food system as something they are struggling against even as they recognize it imposes conditions of precarity on them. I believe that the reason is related, at least in part, to their perception of a food system that is "so big" and "so vast" that it becomes a "hyperobject" (see Morton 2013) rather than any system that can be remade or controlled by humans.

This does not mean that people do not act, because they do, and in the case of these home gardeners, this is realized on the basis of alterNative social norms corresponding to the ascendency of cooperation and conviviality. In fact, this study demonstrates that the myriad of practical ways in which people act to cooperate are also very humble. The newly appointed director of the Economic and Self-Sufficiency Programs at Sacred Heart Community Services recently explained to me how the food system has a tendency to victimize people who use the services provided by Sacred Heart. He described how some people want to use their garden to challenge larger structural forces imposed on the community. However, he believes that the organization and its people are motivated more by the desire to create an *alternative* food system, one that allows for escapes from the precarious condition of their positions in the dominant class and racial formation. He called this alternative a "homegrown food system." The director explained to me how by helping people grow their own food LMV is less concerned about challenging the structure of power from within the food system and more interested in fostering alternative "homegrown" spaces to emerge. This is precisely what the theory of autonomy suggests as well. These gardeners are not engaging in a mutual struggle against the food system. Instead, they are participating in the process of mutual support through formal and informal institutions of collective action to bring about something new—perhaps the beginning of a daring escape from the dominant food system. In doing so, they are encouraging their own version of a community economy with "collective actions in place" (Gibson-Graham 2006, 166). They are supporting the affirmation of their cultures, languages, environments, knowledges, customs, and people through the revival of one of the principal targets of neoliberal governmentality, the institutions of *meaningful* collective action sustained by the informal networks of everyday life in civil society.

While I have seen the potential of social transformation stemming from these home gardens, I am conscious of the power of late neoliberal modernity as the pervasive form of sovereign power in the Silicon Valley. Yet these home gardeners, and many others around the world, have the strength and resilience that comes from the informal exchange of knowledge about traditional plants, farming, and gardening. As I was told countless times, gardening is nothing new. In fact, it is ancient. The future we face as a society must call upon that ancient wisdom to heal the wounds caused by the neoliberal diet. Movements like the one started here can help to shatter the demoralizing and alienating effects of the neoliberal regime that privileges individualism by discounting the interconnectedness of both human and more-than-human actors and replacing it with forms of convivial labor that enable people to rehumanize labor and control their means of social reproduction. Gardens are not passive observers, and they, too, have the power to influence change. Planting a seed is a humble act, but how we choose to grow, prepare, share, and consume foods that nourish our minds, bodies, soils, and communities can truly become the first of many revolutionary acts unleashed by the living "form-giving fire" of emancipated labor giving life back to the body and the land.

Acknowledgments

This book began as a dissertation project many years ago and evolved over the years. I never thought this project would be read beyond the walls of Suzzallo Library or Denny Hall, but many people saw its potential. I owe a debt of gratitude that I can never fully repay. This book is the result of years of research, conversations, discussions, and feedback in which I have been aided in my time at the University of Washington as a graduate student; at the University of Washington, Bothell as a teaching fellow; and as faculty at California State University, San Marcos.

I am grateful for the countless mentors, students, colleagues, organizers, gardeners, and farmers whom I have been able to work with over the years. Devon Peña, you have been there since day one. You helped nourished this project from a seed, and I value your continued mentorship. Lucy Jaroz and Ann Anagnost helped transform this book from a dissertation to a manuscript through constant encouragement.

I am especially grateful to the community of La Mesa Verde who allowed me to learn from their deep understanding of the land and invited me to be a part of their lives. Without you, this research would not be possible. Thank you for your meals, lessons, and insights into how to grow food and live life. You taught me how find joy and love in ways I never thought possible. I am humbled by you. Thank you Malin Ramirez, Jamie Chen, Hector Ochoa, and Jackie Rivera. You invited me to be part of something special, and I hope this book does justice to your work.

I am eternally gratefully to my family for your continued love and support. Lastly, none of this would be possible without the support from my loving wife and our two boys. Thank you.

Appendix A
Home Garden Agrobiodiversity

Gardens	Employment status	Self-identification/ ethnicity	Multi-generational house	Place of birth	Number of crops	Household size
1	employed	white	yes	U.S.	30	6
2	employed	white	no	U.S.	48	5
3	employed	African American	yes	U.S.	33	3
4	employed	white	no	U.S.	28	3
5	not employed	Mexican	yes	MEX	44	5
6	not employed	Peruvian/white	no	PER/U.S.	57	2
7	employed	white/Native American	no	U.S.	43	2
8	employed	Filipino	yes	PHL	56	4
9	not employed	Mexican	yes	MEX	44	5
10	employed	Mexican	yes	MEX	53	5
Average	70 percent employed		60 percent multi-generational		41.8	

Appendix B
Garden Agrobiodiversity

These surveys focus on the agrobiodiversity present in the La Mesa Verde gardens and do not take into consideration the amount of plants present in each garden. The names of these plants, herbs, and crops derive from the knowledge of the gardeners. Each survey is not in alphabetical order; they are listed exactly how the gardener walked me through their garden. In cases where a number is listed, it indicates the number of different varieties of that particular corp.

*Unknown heirloom or domesticated variety.

Garden 1

Plant Name	Scientific Name	Plant Uses	Uses of Surplus
Roma tomato	*Solanum lycopersicum*	consumption	preserve
beefsteak tomato	*Solanum lycopersicum*	consumption	preserve
*heirloom tomato	*Lycopersicon esculentum*	consumption	preserve
cherry tomato	*Solanum lycopersicum var. cerasiforme*	consumption	preserve
eggplant	*Solanum melongena*	consumption	share
bell pepper	*Capsicum annuum*	consumption	share
zucchini	*Cucurbita pepo var. cylindrica*	consumption	share
pattypan squash	*Cucurbita pepo*	consumption	share
cucumber	*Cucumis sativus*	consumption	share
*cantaloupe	*Cucumis melo*	consumption	share
onions	*Allium cepa L.*	consumption	share
garlic	*Allium sativum*	consumption	share
spearmint	*Mentha spicata*	herb	n/a
parsley	*Petroselinum crispum*	herb	n/a
oregano	*Origanum vulgare*	herb	n/a
basil	*Ocimum basilicum*	herb	n/a
rosemary	*Rosmarinus officinalis*	herb	n/a
kumquat	*Fortunella crassifolia*	consumption	share
lemon tree	*Citrus limonum*	consumption	share
fig tree	*Ficus carica*	consumption	share
orange tree	*Citrus sinensis*	consumption	share
apple tree	*Malus domestica*	consumption	share
nectarine tree	*Prunus persica*	consumption	share
sunflower	*Helianthus annuus*	consumption	n/a
marigold	*Tagetes minuta*	pest management	n/a
radishes	*Raphanus sativus*	consumption	share
*grapes	*Vitis vinifera*	consumption	share
peach tree	*Prunus persica*	consumption	share
cilantro	*Coriandrum sativum*	herb	n/a
delicata squash	*Cucurbita pepo*	consumption	share

Garden 2

Plant Name	Scientific Name	Plant Uses	Uses of Surplus
kabocha	*Cucurbita maxima*	consumption	n/a
eggplant	*Solanum melongena*	consumption	n/a
butternut squash	*Cucurbita moschata*	consumption	n/a
pattypan Squash	*Cucurbita pepo*	consumption	n/a
*zucchini	*Cucurbita pepo var. cylindrica*	consumption	n/a
*pumpkin	*Cucurbita pepo*	Halloween	Halloween
mint (lemon balm)	*Melissa officinalis*	herb	n/a
mint	*Mentha longifolia*	herb	n/a
spearmint	*Mentha spicata*	herb	n/a
sage	*Salvia officinalis*	herb	n/a
chives	*Allium schoenoprasum*	herb	n/a
green onion	*Allium fistulosum*	consumption	n/a
oregano	*Origanum vulgare*	herb	n/a
thyme	*Thymus vulgaris*	herb	n/a
basil	*Ocimum basilicum*	herb	n/a
cilantro	*Coriandrum sativum*	herb	n/a
cherry tomato	*Solanum lycopersicum*	consumption	share
beefsteak tomato	*Solanum lycopersicum var. cerasiforme*	consumption	n/a
*melon (6)	*Cucumis melo*	consumption	n/a
sunflower	*Helianthus annuus*	consumption	n/a
strawberry	*Fragaria × ananassa*	consumption	n/a
artichoke	*Cynara scolymus*	consumption	n/a
sweet potato	*Ipomoea batatas*	consumption	n/a
Anaheim pepper	*Capsicum annuum* 'Anaheim'	consumption	n/a
jalapeño	*Capsicum annuum* 'Jalapeño'	consumption	n/a
bell pepper	*Capsicum annuum*	consumption	n/a
radish	*Raphanus sativus*	consumption	n/a
red kale	*Brassica napus subsp. pabularia*	consumption	n/a
pole beans	*Phaseolus coccineus*	consumption	n/a

(*continued*)

Garden 2 (continued)

Plant Name	Scientific Name	Plant Uses	Uses of Surplus
red lettuce	*Lactuca sativa*	consumption	n/a
arugula	*Eruca sativa*	consumption	n/a
bok choy	*Brassica rapa* subsp. *chinensis*	consumption	n/a
collard greens	*Brassica oleracea* var. *medullosa*	consumption	n/a
Armenian cucumber	*Cucumis melo* var. *flexuosus*	consumption	n/a
cucumber	*Cucumis sativus*	consumption	n/a
chard	*Beta vulgaris* subsp. *vulgaris*	consumption	n/a
parsley	*Petroselinum crispum*	herb	n/a
stripped zucchini	*Cucurbita pepo* var. *cylindrica* 'Italian Striped'	consumption	n/a
chayote squash	*Sechium edule*	consumption	n/a
*watermelon	*Citrullus lanatus*	consumption	n/a
*cantaloupe	*Cucumis melo* var. *cantalupensis*	consumption	n/a
asylum flower	*Alyssum maritimum*	pest management	n/a
magnolia	*Magnolia virginiana* L.	pest management	n/a
beets	*Beta vulgaris*	consumption	n/a
cauliflower	*Brassica oleracea* var. *botrytis*	consumption	n/a
*grapes	*Vitis vinifera*	decorative	n/a
plums	*Prunus domestica*	consumption	share
*chicken eggs	n/a	consumption and waste	share

Garden 3

Plant Name	Scientific Name	Plant Uses	Uses of Surplus
*grapes	*Vitis vinifera*	consumption	wine
green beans	*Phaseolus vulgaris*	consumption	share w/ neighbors & church
eggplant	*Solanum melongena*	consumption	share w/ neighbors & church
*tomato (10 varieties)	*Solanum lycopersicum*	consumption	preserve
*peppers (9 varieties)	*Capsicum annuum*	consumption	share w/ neighbors & church
okra	*Abelmoschus esculentus*	consumption	share w/ neighbors & church
basil	*Ocimum basilicum*	herb	share w/ neighbors & church
*squash	*Cucurbita pepo*	consumption	share w/ neighbors & church
parsley	*Petroselinum crispum*	herb	share w/ neighbors & church
cilantro	*Coriandrum sativum*	herb	n/a
mint	*Mentha longifolia*	herb	n/a
sage	*Salvia officinalis*	herb	n/a
peach tree	*Prunus persica*	consumption	can
orange tree	*Citrus sinensis*	consumption	juice/preserve
cherry tree	*Prunus serotina*	consumption	preserve
apricot tree	*Prunus armeniaca*	consumption	preserve
*apple tree (3 varieties)	*Malus domestica*	consumption	preserve/apple butter
persimmon	*Diospyros kaki*	consumption	wine
lemon	*Citrus limon*	consumption	share w/ neighbors & church
Myers lemon	*Citrus × meyeri*	consumption	share w/ neighbors & church
cucumber	*Cucumis sativus*	consumption	share w/ neighbors & church
strawberry	*Fragaria × ananassa*	consumption	share w/ neighbors & church

(*continued*)

Garden 3 (continued)

Plant Name	Scientific Name	Plant Uses	Uses of Surplus
avocado	*Persea americana*	consumption	share w/ neighbors & church
blueberry	*Vaccinium corymbosum*	consumption	share w/ neighbors & church
blackberry	*Rubus fruticosus*	consumption	share w/ neighbors & church
chard	*Beta vulgaris subsp. vulgaris*	consumption	share w/ neighbors & church
plum tree	*Prunus domestica*	consumption	preserve
Stevia	*Stevia rebaudiana*	herb	n/a
onions	*Allium cepa L.*	consumption	share w/ neighbors & church
collard greens	*Brassica oleracea var. medullosa*	consumption	share w/ neighbors & church
mustard greens	*Brassica juncea*	consumption	n/a
*watermelon	*Citrullus lanatus*	consumption	share w/ neighbors & church
*potato	*Solanum tuberosum*	consumption	share w/ neighbors & church

Garden 4

Plant Name	Scientific Name	Plant Uses	Uses of Surplus
green bell pepper	*Capsicum annuum*	consumption	share
yellow bell pepper	*Capsicum annuum*	consumption	share
Dahlia	*Dahlia*	decorative	n/a
jalapeño	*Capsicum annuum* 'Jalapeño'	consumption	share
crono di toro chile	*Capsicum annuum*	consumption	share
green chard	*Beta vulgaris* subsp. *vulgaris*	consumption	share
sungold tomato	*Solanum lycopersicum*	consumption	share
cherry tomato	*Solanum lycopersicum* var. *cerasiforme*	consumption	share
early girl tomato	*Solanum lycopersicum* 'Early Girl'	consumption	share
celebrity tomato	*Solanum lycopersicum* 'Celebrity'	consumption	share
diva cucumber	*Cucumis sativus*	consumption	share
zucchini	*Cucurbita pepo* var. *cylindrica*	consumption	share
Italian basil	*Ocimum basilicum*	consumption	n/a
thyme	*Thymus vulgaris*	consumption	n/a
sage	*Salvia officinalis*	consumption	n/a
rosemary	*Rosmarinus officinalis*	consumption	n/a
chives	*Allium schoenoprasum*	consumption	n/a
yellow wax beans	*Phaseolus vulgaris*	consumption	share
yellow pattypan squash	*Cucurbita pepo*	consumption	share
heirloom tomato (German green)	*Lycopersicon esculentum*	consumption	can
heirloom tomato (top of the world)	*Lycopersicon esculentum*	consumption	can
heirloom tomato (Ed's millennium)	*Lycopersicon esculentum*	consumption	can
heirloom tomato (carbon tomato)	*Lycopersicon esculentum*	consumption	can
gold star cantaloupe	*Cucumis melo*	consumption	share

(*continued*)

Garden 4 (continued)

Plant Name	Scientific Name	Plant Uses	Uses of Surplus
pumpkin	*Cucurbita pepo*	consumption	share
Hale's best cantaloupe	*Cucumis melo var. cantalupensis*	consumption	share
strawberry	*Fragaria × ananassa*	consumption	share
mint	*Mentha longifolia*	consumption	n/a

Garden 5

Plant Name	Scientific Name	Plant Uses	Uses of Surplus
kale	Brassica oleracea var. sabellica	consumption	share
basil	Ocimum basilicum	herb	n/a
marigold	Tagetes minuta	pest management	n/a
cauliflower	Brassica oleracea var. botrytis	consumption	share
serrano pepper	Capsicum annuum 'Serrano'	consumption	dry
jalapeño pepper	Capsicum annuum 'Jalapeño'	consumption	dry
yellow pepper	Capsicum annuum 'Yellow'	consumption	share
cherry tomato	Solanum lycopersicum var. cerasiforme	consumption	preserve
beefsteak tomato	Solanum lycopersicum	consumption	preserve
sungold tomato	Lycopersicon esculentum	consumption	preserve
tomatillo	Physalis philadelphica	consumption	share
green beans	Phaseolus vulgaris	consumption	share
eggplant	Solanum melongena	consumption	share
lemon tree (2)	Citrus limon	consumption	share
zucchini	Cucurbita pepo var. cylindrica	consumption	share
nopal (8)	Opuntia ficus-indica	consumption	sell
pumpkin (and flower for quesadilla)	Cucurbita pepo	consumption	share
red amaranth	Amaranthus tricolor	consumption	n/a
fig tree (2)	Ficus carica	consumption	preserve
peach tree	Prunus persica	consumption	share
orange tree	Citrus × sinensis	consumption	share
squash	Cucurbita pepo	consumption	share
onion	Allium cepa	consumption	share
garlic	Allium sativum	consumption	share
gala apple tree	Malus domestica 'Gala'	consumption	share

(continued)

Garden 5 (continued)

Plant Name	Scientific Name	Plant Uses	Uses of Surplus
iris	*Iris germanica*	decorative	n/a
poppy	*Eschscholzia californica*	decorative	n/a
dill	*Anethum graveolens*	herb	n/a
carrot	*Daucus carota* subsp. *sativus*	consumption	share
sunflower	*Helianthus annuus*	decorative	n/a
aloe vera (3)	*Aloe vera* var. *chinensis*	medicinal	n/a
cilantro	*Coriandrum sativum*	consumption	n/a
repollo (cabbage)	*Brassica oleracea* var. *capitata*	consumption	share
guava	*Psidium guajava*	consumption	share
epazote (purslane)	*Dysphania ambrosioides*	herb	n/a
persimmon	*Diospyros kaki*	consumption	share
granada (pomegranate)	*Punica granatum*	consumption	share
mint	*Mentha longifolia*	herb/medicinal	n/a
Easter lily	*Lilium longiflorum*	decorative	n/a
oregano	*Origanum vulgare*	herb/medicinal	n/a
verdolaga (purslane)	*Portulaca oleracea*	consumption	share
mastuerzo (garden cress)	*Lepidium sativum*	medicinal	n/a
strawberry	*Fragaria × ananassa*	consumption	share
rubella	*Arenaria rubella*	consumption	n/a

Garden 6

Plant Name	Scientific Name	Plant Uses	Uses of Surplus
quinoa	*Chenopodium quinoa*	consumption	n/a
epazote	*Dysphania ambrosioides*	herb	share
sunflower	*Helianthus annuus*	decorative	n/a
eggplant	*Solanum melongena*	consumption	share
onion	*Allium cepa*	consumption	share
cherry tomato	*Solanum lycopersicum var. cerasiforme*	consumption	preserve
beefsteak tomato	*Solanum lycopersicum*	consumption	preserve
heirloom tomato	*Lycopersicon esculentum*	consumption	preserve
alyssum	*Alyssum maritimum*	pest management	n/a
Swiss chard	*Beta vulgaris* subsp. *vulgaris*	consumption	share
cucumber	*Cucumis sativus*	consumption	share
Myers lemon	*Citrus × meyeri*	consumption	share
bay leaf	*Laurus nobilis*	herb	dry
lime	*Citrus × aurantiifolia*	consumption	n/a
peach	*Prunus persica*	consumption	share
persimmon	*Diospyros kaki*	consumption	share
*squash	*Cucurbita pepo*	consumption	share
strawberry	*Fragaria × ananassa*	consumption	preserve
celery	*Apium graveolens*	consumption	share
black mint	*Mentha longifolia*	herb/medicinal	preserve
kumquat	*Fortunella crassifolia*	consumption	share
blueberry	*Vaccinium corymbosum*	consumption	preserve
passionfruit	*Passiflora edulis*	consumption	preserve
apricot	*Prunus armeniaca*	consumption	preserve
red raspberry	*Rubus idaeus*	consumption	preserve
fingerling potato	*Solanum tuberosum L.*	consumption	share
Yukon potato	*Solanum tuberosum L.*	consumption	share
purple potato	*Solanum tuberosum L.*	consumption	share
basil	*Ocimum basilicum*	herb	n/a
sorrel	*Rumex acetosa*	herb/medicinal	n/a
ruby red grapefruit	*Citrus × paradisi*	consumption	share

(*continued*)

Garden 6 (continued)

Plant Name	Scientific Name	Plant Uses	Uses of Surplus
thornless blackberry	*Rubus canadensis*	consumption	preserve
iris	*Iris germanicaL.*	decorative	n/a
zucchini	*Cucurbita pepo var. cylindrica*	consumption	share
serrano pepper	*Capsicum annuumSerrano*	consumption	share
jalapeño pepper	*Capsicum annuum'Jalapeño'*	consumption	share
cayenne pepper	*Capsicum annuum 'Cayenne'*	consumption	share
navel oranges	*Citrus × sinensis*	consumption	share
oregano	*Origanum vulgare*	herb	n/a
thyme	*Thymus vulgaris*	herb	dry
rosemary	*Rosmarinus officinalis*	herb	dry
plum	*Prunus domestica*	consumption	preserve
Easter lily	*Lilium longiflorum*	decorative	n/a
rocoto (hot pepper)	*Capsicum annuum*	consumption	share
*grape	*Vitis vinifera*	consumption	share
aloe vera	*Aloe vera var. chinensis*	medicinal	n/a
kaffir lime	*Citrus hystrix*	consumption	share
lime	*Citrus × aurantiifolia*	consumption	share
kumquat	*Fortunella crassifolia*	consumption	share
*banana	*Musa*	consumption/decorative	n/a
orchid	*Orchidaceae*	decorative	n/a
strawberry	*Fragaria × ananassa*	consumption	preserve
sage	*Salvia officinalis*	herb	n/a
blood orange	*Citrus × sinensis 'Blood orange'*	consumption	share
*apple	*Malus domestica*	consumption	share
white peach	*Prunus persica*	consumption	share
Myers lemon	*Citrus × meyeri*	consumption	share

Garden 7

Plant Name	Scientific Name	Plant Uses	Uses of Surplus
poke salad (pokeweed)	*Phytolacca americana*	medicinal	n/a
pineapple mint	*Phytolacca americana 'Variegata'*	medicinal	dry/share
spearmint	*Mentha spicata*	medicinal	dry/share
peppermint	*Mentha × piperita*	medicinal/consumption	dry/share
lemon mint (lemon beebalm)	*Monarda citriodora*	medicinal	dry/share
mint	*Mentha*	medicinal/consumption	dry/share
lemongrass	*Cymbopogon*	medicinal/consumption	share/trade
blackberry	*Rubus fruticosus*	consumption	can/share/trade
blueberry	*Cyanococcus*	consumption	can/share/trade
red raspberry	*Rubus idaeus*	consumption	can/share/trade
cucumber	*Cucumis sativus*	consumption	share/trade
stinging nettle	*Urtica dioica*	medicinal	dry/share
lemon balm	*Melissa officinalis*	medicinal	dry/share
verdolaga (purslane)	*Portulaca oleracea*	medicinal/consumption	n/a
watercress	*Nasturtium officinale*	medicinal/consumption	n/a
southern mustard greens (wheatgrass)	*Thinopyrum intermedium*	medicinal/consumption	n/a
Italian bell pepper	*Capsicum annuum*	consumption	share/trade
jalapeño pepper	*Capsicum annuum 'Jalapeño'*	consumption	share/trade
serrano pepper	*Capsicum annuum 'Serrano'*	consumption	share/trade
Anaheim pepper	*Capsicum annuum 'Anaheim'*	consumption	share/trade
basil	*Ocimum basilicum*	consumption	n/a
alyssum	*Alyssum maritimum*	pest control	n/a
beefsteak tomato	*Solanum lycopersicum*	consumption	can/share/trade

(continued)

Garden 7 (continued)

Plant Name	Scientific Name	Plant Uses	Uses of Surplus
cherry tomato	*Solanum lycopersicum var. cerasiforme*	consumption	can/share/trade
Sungold tomato	*Lycopersicon esculentum*	consumption	can/share/trade
eggplant	*Solanum melongena*	consumption	share/trade
cilantro	*Coriandrum sativum*	consumption	share/trade
wild oregano	*Origanum vulgare*	medicinal	share/trade
carrots	*Daucus carota subsp. sativus*	consumption	share/trade
parsley	*Petroselinum crispum*	consumption	n/a
*potato	*Solanum tuberosum*	consumption	share/trade
*pumpkin	*Cucurbita pepo*	consumption	share/trade
spaghetti squash	*Cucurbita pepo*	consumption	share/trade
strawberry	*Fragaria × ananassa*	consumption	share/trade
aloe vera	*Aloe vera var. Chinensis*	medicinal	share/trade
tangerine	*Citrus tangerina*	consumption	glean/share/trade
peach	*Prunus persica*	consumption	glean/share/trade
avocado	*Persea americana*	consumption	glean/share/trade
green apples	*Malus domestica*	consumption	glean/share/trade
oranges	*Citrus × sinensis*	consumption	glean/share/trade
grapefruit	*Citrus × paradisi*	consumption	glean/shade/trade
lemon	*Citrus × limon*	consumption	glean/share/trade
lime	*Citrus × aurantiifolia*	consumption	glean/share/trade

Garden 8

Plant Name	Scientific Name	Plant Uses	Uses of Surplus
blueberry	*Cyanococcus*	consumption/medicinal	preserve
blackberry	*Rubus fruticosus*	consumption/medicinal	preserve
goji berry	*Lycium barbarum*	consumption/medicinal	preserve
strawberry	*Fragaria × ananassa*	consumption	preserve
*chilies (7)	*Capsicum annuum*	consumption	share
onions	*Allium cepa*	consumption	share
carrots	*Daucus carota* subsp. *sativus*	consumption	share
*olive tree (2)	*Olea europaea*	consumption	n/a
zucchini	*Cucurbita pepo* var. *cylindrica*	consumption	share
*roses	*Rosa*	decorative	n/a
kale	*Brassica oleracea* var. *sabellica*	consumption	share
radish	*Raphanus sativus*	consumption	share
*pumpkin	*Cucurbita pepo*	consumption	share
*sweet corn	*Zea mays*	consumption	share
green beans	*Phaseolus vulgaris*	consumption	share
sunflower	*Helianthus annuus*	decorative	n/a
okra	*Abelmoschus esculentus*	consumption	share
lettuce (Greek)	*Lactuca sativa*	consumption	share
*tomato (10)	*Solanum lycopersicum*	consumption	preserve
basil	*Ocimum basilicum*	herb	n/a
gardenia	*Gardenia jasminoides*	pest management	n/a
pinto beans	*Phaseolus vulgaris* Pinto Group	consumption	share
chrysanthemum	*Dendranthema grandiflorum*	pest management	n/a
cherry tree	*Prunus serrulata*	consumption	share
Myer lemon	*Citrus × meyeri*	consumption	share
key lime (Mexican lime)	*Citrus × aurantiifolia*	consumption	share
garlic	*Allium sativum*	consumption	share

(continued)

Garden 8 (continued)

Plant Name	Scientific Name	Plant Uses	Uses of Surplus
pomegranate	*Punica granatum*	consumption	share
plum	*Prunus domestica*	consumption	share
guava	*Psidium guajava*	consumption	preserve
persimmon	*Diospyros kaki*	consumption	share
figs	*Ficus carica*	consumption	preserve
henna	*Lawsonia inermis*	consumption/medicinal	n/a
mint	*Mentha*	herb/medicinal	n/a
summer squash	*Cucurbita pepo*	consumption	share
calamansi	*Fortunella japonica*	consumption	share
aloe vera	*Aloe vera var. Chinensis*	medicinal	n/a
cauliflower	*Brassica oleracea var. botrytis*	consumption	share
Asian pear	*Pyrus pyrifolia*	consumption	share
*apple (2)	*Malus domestica*	consumption	share
guamúchil (Nahuatl cuauhmochitl)	*Pithecellobium dulce*	consumption	share
camellia	*Camellia japonica*	decorative	n/a
geraniums	*Pelargonium*	decorative	n/a
*potatoes	*Solanum tuberosum*	consumption	share
*grapes	*Vitis vinifera*	consumption	n/a
tulips	*Tulipa*	decorative	n/a
peony	*Paeonia*	decorative	n/a
rosemary	*Rosmarinus officinalis*	herb	n/a
basil	*Ocimum basilicum*	herb	n/a
turmeric	*Curcuma longa*	herb	n/a
Dalia	*Dahlia pinnata*	pest management	n/a
beets	*Beta vulgaris*	consumption	share
kaffir lime	*Citrus hystrix*	consumption	share
sweet potato	*Ipomoea batatas*	consumption	share
eggplant	*Solanum melongena*	consumption	share
durian tree	*Durio zibethinus*	consumption/medicinal	n/a

Garden 9

Plant Name	Scientific Name	Plant Uses	Uses of Surplus
nectarine	*Prunus persica var. nectarina*	consumption	share
pomegranate	*Punica granatum*	consumption	share
white onion	*Allium cepa*	consumption	share
red onion	*Allium cepa*	consumption	share
oregano	*Origanum vulgare*	herb	dry
cilantro	*Coriandrum sativum*	herb	n/a
rosemary	*Rosmarinus officinalis*	herb	n/a
red raspberry	*Rubus idaeus*	consumption	share
apricot	*Prunus armeniaca*	consumption	share
cucumber	*Cucumis sativus*	consumption	share
zucchini	*Cucurbita pepo var. cylindrica*	consumption	share
*plum	*Prunus domestica*	consumption	share
apple	*Malus domestica*	consumption	share
*avocado	*Persea americana*	consumption	share
nopal	*Opuntia ficus-indica*	consumption	preserve
loquat	*Eriobotrya japonica*	consumption	share
kiwi	*Actinidia deliciosa*	consumption	share
chayote	*Sechium edule*	consumption	share
naranja agria	*Citrus aurantium*	consumption	share
ruda (common rue)	*Ruta graveolens L.*	consumption	n/a
yellow pepper	*Capsicum annuum 'yellow'*	consumption	share
serrano pepper	*Capsicum annuum 'serrano'*	consumption	dry
jalapeño pepper	*Capsicum annuum 'Jalapeño'*	consumption	dry
yellow peach	*Prunus persica*	consumption	share
white peach	*Prunus persica*	consumption	share
concord grape	*Vitis labrusca 'Concord'*	consumption	share
spearmint	*Mentha spicata*	herb/medicinal	n/a
yerba buena	*Mentha spicata*	herb/medicinal	n/a

(*continued*)

Garden 9 (continued)

Plant Name	Scientific Name	Plant Uses	Uses of Surplus
thyme	*Thymus vulgaris*	herb	n/a
yellow passionfruit	*Passiflora edulis*	consumption	share
purple passionfruit	*Passiflora edulis*	consumption	share
Myers lemon	*Citrus × meyeri*	consumption	share
guava	*Psidium guajava*	consumption	share
coro di toro tomato	*Capsicum annuum*	consumption	share
cherry tomato	*Solanum lycopersicum var. cerasiforme*	consumption	share
*heirloom tomato	*Lycopersicon esculentum*	consumption	preserve
beefsteak tomato	*Solanum lycopersicum*	consumption	preserve
eggplant	*Solanum melongena*	consumption	share
Wisconsin pepper	*Capsicum annuum*	consumption	share
parsley	*Petroselinum crispum*	herb	n/a
green onion	*Allium fistulosum*	consumption	n/a
mazama pepper	*Capsicum pubescens*	consumption	n/a
marigold	*Tagetes minuta*	pest management	n/a

Garden 10

Plant Name	Scientific Name	Plant Uses	Uses of Surplus
cherry tomato	Solanum lycopersicum var. cerasiforme	consumption	preserve
beefsteak tomato	Solanum lycopersicum	consumption	preserve
sungold tomato	Lycopersicon esculentum	consumption	preserve
*heirloom tomato	Lycopersicon esculentum	consumption	preserve
chard	Beta vulgaris subsp. vulgaris	consumption	share
white onion	Allium cepa	consumption	share
green onion	Allium fistulosum	consumption	share
bell pepper	Capsicum annuum	consumption	share
serrano pepper	Capsicum annuum 'serrano'	consumption	dry
jalapeño pepper	Capsicum annuum 'Jalapeño'	consumption	dry
kale	Brassica oleracea var. sabellica	consumption	share
yellow summer squash	Cucurbita pepo	consumption	share
green summer squash	Cucurbita pepo	consumption	share
pinto beans	Phaseolus vulgaris Pinto Group	consumption	dry
*avocado	Persea americana	consumption	share
*apple	Malus domestica	consumption	share
lemon	Citrus × limon	consumption	share
*orange	Citrus × sinensis	consumption	share
guava	Psidium guajava	consumption	share
nopal	Opuntia ficus-indica	consumption	preserve
apricot	Prunus armeniaca	consumption	preserve
nectarine	Prunus persica	consumption	preserve
mandarin	Citrus reticulata	consumption	share
eggplant	Solanum melongena	consumption	share
white peach	Prunus persica	consumption	share
aloe	Aloe vera var. chinensis	medicinal	n/a
chives	Allium schoenoprasum	consumption	n/a
garlic	Allium sativum	consumption	share

(*continued*)

Garden 10 (continued)

Plant Name	Scientific Name	Plant Uses	Uses of Surplus
rosemary	*Rosmarinus officinalis*	herb	n/a
thyme	*Thymus vulgaris*	herb	n/a
cilantro	*Coriandrum sativum*	herb	n/a
cucumber	*Cucumis sativus*	consumption	share
oregano	*Origanum vulgare*	herb	n/a
mint	*Mentha*	medicinal	n/a
yerba buena	*Mentha spicata*	medicinal	n/a

Appendix C
Recipes from the Garden

Over the course of this study, I have shared meals with many families who have told me their life histories, allowed me to conduct surveys of their gardens, and detailed expert knowledge about how to cook, garden, and live life. These are some of the recipes people have given me to share.

Chilacayote (Chiclayo) Beverage
Aka *Aqua de Chilacayote*

Chilacayote (known as fig-leaved gourd in the USA, shark fin melon in Asia, *cayote* in Argentina, *chila* or *gila* in Portugal, *potiron cheveux d'ange* in France, *calabaza de cabello de angel* [angel's hair] in Spain, *alcayota en chili*, and *chiclayo* in Peru) is a squash, not a melon, that grows as big as a watermelon. It is cooked like summer squash when it is young. When it is mature it is a hard winter squash/gourd with edible black and/or white seeds, which can last for years when stored in a dry place. The mature squash can be cooked in many ways, including as a candy, a pudding, and a beverage, for which a recipe follows.

Ingredients:
1 chilacayote squash (about 10–12 lbs.)
16 cups of water
1 piloncillo cone or 1 cup brown sugar

1 cinnamon stick (or 1 tsp. cinnamon)

1–2 limes and/or lemon (rind and juice), to taste

Fresh or canned pineapple (1 can optional)

Directions:

Wash the squash well and cut it into quarters. With a paring knife, chip off the hard shell of the squash. (Do not boil the squash with the shell because there is a bitter substance in it.) Chilacayote has the appearance of spaghetti squash. Remove most of the seeds and any yellowish strings/fibers, for these fibers will add a bitter taste to the drink. (It is not necessary to remove all the seeds at this point. They can be removed after boiling.) Cut each quarter in half and put all the pieces in a large stockpot, adding approximately 2 quarts of water. It is not necessary for the squash to be submerged.

Add the sugar to the pot, and simmer for 1 to 1 1/2 hours until tender. Remove squash from pot and let it cool. Save the water from the pot for later.

Remove seeds from the cooled pieces of squash, and process the pieces in a food processor or blender until smooth, adding liquid from the pot as needed. Pour into a large pitcher or container.

Add about 2 quarts of cool water to the pitcher. Add juice and rind (cut into pieces) of lime or lemon, and stir.

Pineapple is a nice addition and can be used to adjust the sweetness to your likeness. Either cut up the fruit into pieces or process it in a blender, and add to the pitcher. Makes about 4 quarts.

Serve cool or room temperature. Stir before pouring.

Zucchini Bread

Ingredients:

3 large eggs

1 cup (235 ml) olive or vegetable oil

1¾ (350 grams) cups sugar

2 cups grated zucchini

2 tsp. (10 ml) vanilla extract

3 cups (375 grams) all-purpose flour

1 tbsp. cinnamon

⅛ tsp. nutmeg

1 tsp. baking soda

½ tsp. baking powder

1 tsp. (6 grams) table salt

½ cup (55 grams) chopped walnuts or pecans (optional)

1 cup (115 grams) dried cranberries, raisins, or chocolate chips or a combination thereof (optional)

Directions:

Preheat oven to 350°F. Grease and flour two 8-by-4-inch loaf pans, liberally. (See those pictures of the cakes inside their nonstick pans? Yep, they're pretty much hanging out in there for the time being.) Alternatively, line 24 muffin cups with paper liners.

In a large bowl, beat the eggs with a whisk. Mix in oil and sugar, then zucchini and vanilla. Combine flour, cinnamon, nutmeg, baking soda, baking powder, and salt as well as nuts, chocolate chips, and/or dried fruit, if using. Stir this into the egg mixture. Divide the batter into prepared pans. Bake loaves for 60 minutes, plus or minus 10 minutes, or until a knife inserted into the center comes out clean. Muffins will bake far more quickly, approximately 20 to 25 minutes.

Yield: 2 loaves or approximately 24 muffins.

Ratatouille

Ingredients:

2 medium eggplant, cut into large dice (approx. 1-inch pieces)

About 3 tbs. olive oil

1 large onion, diced (approx. ½-inch pieces)

4 garlic cloves, minced

1 medium bell pepper red or green, cut into ½-inch pieces

2 medium zucchinis, cut into ¾-inch pieces

3–4 medium ripe tomatoes, diced, or 1 can diced tomatoes (26 oz.), with juice

1 tbs. dried oregano

Salt and pepper to taste

Optional:

Depending on your taste, 1 medium jalapeño or serrano pepper minced or a ½ tsp. dried chile flakes

Can substitute basil for oregano (fresh, chopped, or dried)

Can add meat (i.e., 1 lb. ground beef crumbled and browned with the onions and garlic; *normally, Ratatouille is vegetarian.*)

Finish with 2–3 tbs. chopped herbs (parsley, cilantro, basil)

Directions:

Heat a heavy-bottomed deep pan or pot. Add about 2 tbs. oil and the diced eggplant, lightly salt and pepper, and cook over medium heat until soft and medium brown; about 15 minutes. Use a spatula to prevent sticking and add a small amount of more oil if needed. Once browned and soft, remove and set aside. You will notice that the eggplant shrunk a bit. You can cook the eggplant in batches if the pot is not big enough.

Note: It is not necessary to salt or peel eggplant for bitter juices if the eggplant is relatively young. If you choose to, lightly sprinkle the diced eggplant with salt and put in a strainer to drain for approx. 30 mins. Dry off the eggplant with a paper towel before browning.

If adding ground beef to recipe, brown the meat in the same pot with salt and pepper and the remaining tablespoon of olive oil for about 5 minutes. Set meat aside for later. With the flame medium-low, add oil, then add the onions, hot peppers (fresh or dried), and garlic and cook until onions soften, about 2 minutes. Then add the chopped bell (sweet) pepper and cook 3–5 minutes. Add more oil if needed.

Stir in the zucchini, cooking for about 2 minutes, followed by the tomatoes (juice and all) and oregano. Adjust salt and pepper to taste. Simmer for about 5 minutes. Stir in the reserved eggplant and meat (if included in recipe). Simmer on low about 10 minutes more, stirring occasionally to prevent sticking of the vegetables. Add the optional 2–3 tbs. chopped fresh parsley, cilantro, or basil depending on your taste.

Serve this dish warm or cold; it is good served with a side of brown rice (especially if was made with meat) and tastes even better the next day. It can also be served mixed with pasta sauce.

Pomegranate and Persimmon Salad

Ingredients:

4–6 persimmons

1 pomegranate

1 jalapeño

Cilantro

Directions:
Peel the persimmons, then cut them in half and cut into ¼-inch slices. Place in salad bowl. Add about half of the pomegranate. Dice and deseed jalapeño. Add to bowl. Destem cilantro and add to your liking. Leave the salad at room temperature for around an hour to allow juices to mingle. Serve.

Veggie Guiso (stew)

Ingredients:
2 tbs. olive oil
2 onions, chopped
3–5 cloves garlic, minced
5 scallions, chopped
1 serrano chili
7–9 tomatoes, chopped
2 medium zucchinis, chopped (can substitute with 2–3 handfuls chard, purslane/verdolagas)
¼–½ tsp. salt
½ tsp. ground cumin
¾ cup cheddar cheese for garnish
5 sprigs cilantro, chopped for garnish

Directions:
Rinse, dry, and chop all vegetables. Add oil to a large skillet. When it's hot, add onions, garlic, scallions, chili, salt, and cumin. Cook 10 minutes, stirring occasionally, until onions are a deep caramelized brown. If the onions start to burn, turn the heat down. You want them sizzling but not blackened. Add tomatoes and cook until skins are softened, about 5 minutes. Stir in black beans and cook until heated through, about 2 minutes. Serve over quinoa or brown rice. Garnish with grated cheddar cheese and cilantro. Alternatively, serve the guiso with whole grain tortillas. Enjoy!

Chayote, Tomato, and Jalapeños

Ingredients:
2–3 chayotes, peeled and sliced
1 onion, roughly chopped
1 jalapeño, diced

2 garlic cloves, diced
2 ripe tomatoes, chopped
Olive oil
Cilantro for garnish
Salt to taste

Directions:

Over medium heat, warm olive oil. Add chayote and cook until soft, 8–10 minutes. Add onions and cook until fragrant, 3–5 minutes. Add garlic and jalapeño and cook for 3 more minutes. Add tomato and reduce heat and cook for another 5–8 minutes. Serve on a warm plate and garnish with cilantro. The perfect complement for this dish is fresh pinto beans and warm corn tortillas.

References

Abarca, Meredith E. *Voices in the Kitchen Views of Food and the World from Working-Class Mexican and Mexican American Women*. College Station: Texas A&M University Press, 2006.
Adams, Carol J. *The Sexual Politics of Meat: A Feminist-Vegetarian Critical Theory*. New York: Bloomsbury Publishing, 2015.
Agamben, Giorgio. *The Open: Man and Animal*. Translated by Kevin Attell. Palo Alto, Calif.: Stanford University Press, 2004.
Agyeman, Julian. *Sustainable Communities and the Challenge of Environmental Justice*. New York: New York University Press, 2005.
Alfred, Taiaiake. *Wasáse: Indigenous Pathways of Action and Freedom*. Toronto: University of Toronto Press, 2009.
Algert, Susan J., Aziz Baameur, Lucy O. Diekmann, Leslie Gray, and Diego Ortiz. "Vegetable Output, Cost Savings, and Nutritional Value of Low-Income Families' Home Gardens in San Jose, CA." *Journal of Hunger & Environmental Nutrition* 11, no. 3 (2016): 328–36.
Algert, Susan J., Aziz Baameur, and Marian J. Renvall. "Vegetable Output and Cost savings of Community Gardens in San Jose, California." *Journal of the Academy of Nutrition and Dietetics* 114, no. 7 (2014): 1072–6.
Alkon, Alison Hope, and Teresa Marie Mares. "Food Sovereignty in US Food Movements: Radical Visions and Neoliberal Constraints." *Agriculture and Human Values* 29 (2012): 347–59.
Allen, Patricia. "Reweaving the Food Security Safety Net: Mediating Entitlement and Entrepreneurship." *Agriculture and Human Values* 16, no. 2 (1999): 117–29.
Almaguer, Tomás. *Racial Fault Lines: The Historical Origins of White Supremacy in California*. Berkeley: University of California Press, 1994.
Altieri, Miguel A., and Susanna B. Hecht, eds. *Agroecology and Small Farm Development*. Boca Raton, Fla.: CRC Press, 1990.

Anderson, Kevin B. *Marx at the Margins: On Nationalism, Ethnicity, and Non-Western Societies*. Chicago: University of Chicago Press, 2010.

Anderson, M. Kat. "Indigenous Uses, Management, and Restoration of Oaks of the Far Western United States." United States Department of Agriculture, 2007.

Anton, Anatole, and Richard Schmitt. *Taking Socialism Seriously. Critical Studies on the Left*. Lanham, Md.: Lexington Books, 2012.

Anzaldúa, Gloria. *Borderlands / La Frontera: The New Mestiza*. San Francisco: Aunt Lute Books, 2007.

Anzaldúa, Gloria. "Let Us Be the Healing of the Wound: The Coyolxauhqui Imperative—la sombra y el sueño." In *Gloria Anzaldúa Reader: Latin America Otherwise*, edited by Ana Louise Keating, Walter Mignolo, Irene Silverblatt, and Sonia Saldívar-Hull, 303–17. Durham, N.C.: Duke University Press, 2009.

Appadurai, Arun. "Sovereignty without Territoriality: Notes for a Postnational Geography." In *The Anthropology of Space and Place: Locating Culture*, edited by Setha M. Low and Denise Lawrence-Zúñiga, 337–50. Malden, Mass.: Blackwell, 2003.

Arellano, Juan Estevan. "Convide: A Sustainable Philosophy." *Environmental and Food Justice* (Blog). March 26, 2010. https://ejfood.blogspot.com/2010/03/guest-blog-estevan-arrellano.html?q=convide.

Armstrong, Donna. "A Survey of Community Gardens in Upstate New York: Implications for Health Promotion and Community Development." *Health & Place* 6, no. 4 (2000): 319–27.

Auyero, Javier, and Debora Alejandra Swistun. *Flammable: Environmental Suffering in an Argentine Shantytown*. New York: Oxford University Press, 2009.

Ávila, Julia Vieira da Cunha, Anderson Santos de Mello, Mariane Elis Beretta, Rafael Trevisan, Pedro Fiaschi, and Natalia Hanazaki. "Agrobiodiversity and In Situ Conservation in Quilombola Homegardens with Different Intensities of Urbanization." *Acta Botanica Brasilica* 31, no. 1 (2017): 1–10. https://dx.doi.org/10.1590/0102-33062016abb0299.

Bachmann, Christine. "Cuban Home Gardens and their Role in Social-Ecological Resilience." *Human Ecology* 37 (2009): 705–21.

Baldwin, Jeff. "Life, Labor, and Value: Recreating Affective Food Ecologies Through Interspecies Cooperation." *Visions for Sustainability* 6 (2016): 6–22.

Barca, Stefania. "History." In *Keywords for Environmental Studies*, edited by Joni Andamson, William A. Gleason, and David N. Pellow, 132–35. New York: New York University Press, 2016.

Barbiero, Giuseppe. "Affective Ecology for Sustainability." *Visions for Sustainability* 1, no. 1 (2014): 20–30.

Barndt, Deborah. *Tangled Routes: Women, Work, and Globalization on the Tomato Trail*, 2nd ed. Lanham, Md.: Rowman & Littlefield, 2008.

Barthel, Stephan, Carl Folke, and Johan Colding. "Social-Ecological Memory in Urban Gardens—Retaining the Capacity for Management of Ecosystem Services." *Global Environmental Change* 20, no. 2 (2010): 255–65.

Barreiro, José, ed. *Thinking in Indian: A John Mohawk Reader*. Golden, Colo.: Four Colour Print Group, 2010.

Bauman, Zygmunt. *Liquid Modernity*. Malden, Mass.: Polity Press, 2000.
Bauman, Zygmunt. *Liquid Times: Living in an Age of Uncertainty*. Malden, Mass.: Polity Press, 2007.
Benner, Chris. *Work in the New Economy: Flexible Labor Markets in Silicon Valley*. Malden, Mass: Blackwell Publishers, 2002.
Benner, Chris, Gabriela Guista, Louise Auerhahn, Bob Brownstein, and Geffrey Buchanan. *Still Walking the Lifelong Tightrope*. Report by Working Partnerships, USA, 2018.
Bennett, Jane. *Vibrant Matter: A Political Ecology of Things*. Durham, N.C.: Duke University Press, 2010.
Berardi, Franco. *The Soul at Work: From Alienation to Autonomy*. Los Angeles: Semiotext(e), 2009.
Berenson, Julia, Michelle M. Doty, Melinda K. Abrams, and Anthony Smith. "Achieving Better Quality of Care for Low-Income Populations: The Role of Health Insurance and the Medical Home for Reducing Health Inequalities." *Issue Brief* 11 (2012): 1–18.
Berlant, Lauren. *Cruel Optimism*. Durham, N.C.: Duke University Press, 2011.
Berry, Wendell. *Home Economics*. San Francisco: North Point Press, 1987.
Berry, Wendell. "Wendell Berry on Climate Change: To Save the Future, Live in the Present." *YES! Magazine*, March 24, 2015. http://www.yesmagazine.org/issues/together-with-earth/wendell-berry-climate-change-future-present.
Bey, Hakim. *The Temporary Autonomous Zone: Ontological Anarchy, Poetic Terrorism*. 2nd ed. New York: Aotonomedia, 2003.
Bishop, Peter, and Lesley Williams. *The Temporary City*. London: Routledge, 2012.
Blackwell, Debra L., Jaqueline W. Lucas, and Tainya C. Clarke. "Summary Health Statistics for U.S. Adults: National Health Interview Survey," 2012. *Vital and health statistics*. Series 10: *Data from the National Health Survey*, 260 (2014): 1–161.
Blair, Dorothy, Carol C. Giesecke, and Sandra Sherman. "A Dietary, Social and Economic Evaluation of the Philadelphia Urban Gardening Project." *Journal of Nutrition Education* 23, no. 4 (1991): 161–67.
Blay-Palmer, Alison, and Betsy Donald. "A tale of Three Tomatoes: The New Food Economy in Toronto, Canada." *Economic Geography* 82, no. 4 (2006): 383–99.
Blomley, Nicholas. "Enclosure, Common Right and the Property of the Poor." *Social & Legal Studies* 17, no. 3 (2008): 311–31.
Boehm, Christopher. *Moral Origins: The Evolution of Virtue, Altruism, and Shame*. New York: Basic Books, 2012.
Bollier, David. *Think Like a Commoner: A Short Introduction to the Life of the Commons*. Gabriola Island, BC: New Society Press, 2014.
Bonfil Batalla, Guillermo. *Mexico Profundo: Reclaiming a Civilization*. Austin: University of Texas Press, 1996.
Bowles, Samuel, and Herbert Gintis. *A Cooperative Species: Human Reciprocity and its Evolution*. Princeton, N.J.: Princeton University Press, 2011.
Bowman, David M. J. S., and Simon G. Haberle. "Paradise Burnt: How Colonizing Humans Transform Landscapes with Fire." *Proceedings of the National Academy of Sciences* 107, no. 50 (2010): 21234–35.

Brescia, Steve, ed. *Fertile Ground: Scaling Agroecology from the Ground Up.* Oakland, Calif.: Food First Books, 2017.

Brisman, Avi. "Crime-Environment Relationships and Environmental Justice." *Seattle Journal for Social Justice* 6, no. 2 (2008): 727–817.

Broadway, Michael. "Growing Urban Agriculture in North American Cities: The Example of Milwaukee," *FOCUS on Geography* 52, no. 3/4 (2009): 23.

Brown, Cheryl, and Stacy Miller. "The Impacts of Local Markets: A Review of Research on Farmers Markets and Community Supported Agriculture (CSA)." *American Journal of Agricultural Economics* 90, no. 5 (2008): 1298–1302.

Brown, Kate H., and Andrew L. Jameton. "Public Health Implications of Urban Agriculture." *Journal of Public Health Policy* 21, no. 1 (2000): 20–39.

Brownell, Kelly D. *Food Fight: The Inside Story of the Food Industry, America's Obesity Crisis & What We Can Do About It.* New York: McGraw Hill Books, 2004.

Bullard, Robert D. *Dumping in Dixie: Race, Class, and Environmental Quality.* San Francisco: Westview Press, 1990.

Bullard, Robert D. "The Threat of Environmental Racism." *Natural Resources & Environment,* 7 no. 3 (1993): 23–56.

Bullard, Robert D., Paul Mohai, Robin Saha, and Beverly Wright. *Toxic Wastes and Race at Twenty 1987–2007: A Report Prepared for the United Church of Christ Justice & Witness Ministries.* Cleveland, Ohio: The United Church of Christ, 2007.

Byrd, Jodi A. *The Transit of Empire: Indigenous Critiques of Colonialism.* Minneapolis: University of Minnesota Press, 2011.

Cajete, Gregory, ed. *A People's Ecology: Explorations in Sustainable Living.* Santa Fe, N.Mex.: Clear Light Publishers, 1999.

Cajete, Gregory. *Native Science: Natural Laws of Interdependence.* Santa Fe, N.Mex.: Clear Light Publishers, 2000.

Calvet-Mir, Laura, Erik Gómez-Baggethun, and Victoria Reyes-García. "Beyond Food Production: Ecosystem Services Provided by Home Gardens: A Case Study in Vall Fosca, Catalan Pyrenees, Northeastern Spain." *Ecological Economics* 74 (2012): 153–60.

Calvo, Luz, and Catriona Rueda Esquibel. *Decolonize Your Diet: Plant-Based Mexican-American Recipes for Health and Healing.* Vancouver, BC: Arsenal Pulp Press, 2016.

Čapek, Stella. "The 'Environmental Justice' Frame: A Conceptual Discussion and an Application." *Social Problems* 40, no. 1 (1993): 5–24.

Carmin, Joann, and Julian Agyeman. *Environmental Inequalities Beyond Borders: Local Perspectives on Global Injustices.* Cambridge, Mass.: MIT Press, 2011.

Carney, Megan A. *The Unending Hunger: Tracing Women and Food Insecurity Across Borders.* Berkeley: University of California Press, 2015.

Carpenter, Novella. *Farm City: The Education of an Urban Farmer.* New York: Penguin Books, 2009.

Chan, Joana, Lisa Pennisi, and Charles A. Francis. "Social-Ecological Refugees: Reconnecting in Community Gardens in Lincoln, Nebraska." *Journal of Ethnobiology* 36, no. 4 (2016): 842–60.

Chandler, David, and Julian Reid. *The Neoliberal Subject: Resilience, Adaptation and Vulnerability*. Lanham, Md.: Rowman & Littlefield, 2016.

Chavez, Cesar. "Farmworkers at Risk." In *Toxic Struggles: The Theory and Practice of Environmental Justice*, edited by Richard Hofrichter, 169–70. Philadelphia: New Society Publishers, 1993.

Clark, Brett. "Metabolic Rift: Toward a Sociology of Ecological Crisis." PhD diss., University of Oregon, 2006.

Clark, Brett, and Richard York. "Rifts and Shifts." *Monthly Review* 60, no. 6 (2008): 13–24.

Cleaver, Harry. "The Uses of an Earthquake." *Commons Sense* 8 (1989): 17–21.

Cleaver, Harry. "The Inversion of Class Perspective in Marxian Theory." *Open Marxism* 2 (1992): 106–44.

Cleaver, Harry. *Reading Capital Politically*. San Francisco: AK Press, 2000.

Cloos, Patrick. "The Racialization of U.S. Public Health: A Paradox of the Modern State." *Cultural Studies ↔ Critical Methodologies* 15, no. 5 (2015): 379–86.

Cervantes, Lorna Dee. *Emplumada*. Pittsburgh, Pa.: University of Pittsburgh Press, 1982.

Collins, Jane L. *The Politics of Value: Three Movements to Change How We Think about the Economy*. Chicago: University of Chicago Press, 2017.

Cockrall-King, Jennifer. *Food and the City: Urban Agriculture and the New Food Revolution*. Amherst, Mass.: Prometheus, 2012.

Conklin, Harold C. "An Ethnoecological Approach to Shifting Agriculture." In *Environmental Anthropology: A Historical Reader*, edited by Michael R. Dove and Carol Carpenter, 241–48. Malden, Mass.: Blackwell Publishing, 2008.

Coulthard, Glen. "Indigenous Peoples and the Politics of Recognition." In *Sovereign Acts: Contesting Colonialism Across Indigenous Nations & Latinx America*, edited by Frances Negrón-Muntaner, 82–106. Tucson: University of Arizona Press, 2017.

Counihan, Carole, and Penny Van Esterik. *Food and Culture: A Reader*. 2nd ed. New York: Routledge, 2008.

County of Santa Clara. "Community Health Existing Conditions Report." Report Prepared by Raimi + Associates. San José, Calif.: 2013. https://stgenpln.blob.core.win dows.net/document/HealthElement_Existing_Health_Conditions_FINAL_May _2013.pdf.

Cronon, William. "The Trouble with Wilderness: Or, Getting Back to the Wrong Nature." *Environmental History* 1, no. 1 (1996): 7–28.

Crow, Consuelo. "Tracing Food Packs and Tuna Cans on *La Línea*: Food, Water, and Foodways during Transborder Travel." In *Mexican-Origin Foods, Foodways, and Social Movements: Decolonial Perspectives*, edited by Devon G. Peña, Luz Calvo, Pancho McFarland, and Gabriel R. Valle, 83–106. Fayetteville: University of Arkansas Press, 2017.

Cruikshank, Barbara. *The Will to Empower: Democratic Citizens and Other Subjects*. Ithaca, N.Y.: Cornell University Press, 1999.

Crumley, Carole L. *Historical Ecology: Cultural Knowledge and Changing Landscapes*. Santa Fe, N.Mex.: School of American Research Press, 1994.

Davis, Mike. *City of Quartz: Excavating the Future of Los Angeles*. New York: Verso, 2006.

De Angelis, Massimo. *The Beginning of History: Value Struggles and Global Capital*. London: Pluto Press, 2007.

Del Castillo, Adelaida R. "Illegal Status and Social Citizenship: Thoughts on Mexican Immigrants in a Postnational World." *Aztlán: A Journal of Chicano Studies* 27, no. 2 (2002): 11–32.

Dowie, Mark. *Conservation Refugees: The Hundred-Year Conflict Between Global Conservation and Native Peoples*. Cambridge, Mass.: MIT Press, 2009.

Doyle, Rebekah, and Marianne Krasny. "Participatory Rural Appraisal as an Approach to Environmental Education in Urban Community Gardens." *Environmental Education Research* 9, no. 1 (2003): 91–115.

Dumont, Louis. "On Value." Proceedings of the British Academy 66 (1980): 207–41.

Dunbar-Ortiz, Roxanne. *An Indigenous Peoples' History of the United States*. Boston: Beacon Press, 2014.

Egerer, Monika, and Hamutahl Cohen. *Urban Agroecology: Interdisciplinary Research and Future Directions*. Boca Raton, Fla.: CRC Press, 2021.

Eizenberg, Efrat. "Actually Existing Commons: Three Moments of Space of Community Gardens in New York City." *Antipode* 44, no. 3 (2012): 764–82.

Elkington, John. *Cannibals with Forks*. Stony Creek: New Society Publishers, 1998.

Emmons, Mark. "The Jungle: San José Shuts Notorious Homeless Encampment." *San José Mercury News*. December 4, 2014.

Ernwein, Marion. "Urban Agriculture and the Neoliberalisation of What?" *ACME: An International E-Journal for Critical Geographies*, 16, no. 2 (2017): 249–75.

Eschbach, Karl, Glenn V. Ostir, Kushang V. Patel, Kyriakos S. Markides, and James S. Goodwin. "Neighborhood Context and Mortality among Older Mexican Americans: Is There a Barrio Advantage?" *American Journal of Public Health* 94, no. 10 (2004): 1807–12.

Esteva, Gustavo. "Development." In *The Development Dictionary: A Guide to Knowledge as Power*, edited by Wolfgang Sachs, 6–25. New York: Zed Books, 2005.

Esteva, Gustavo, and Madhu Suri Prakash. *Grassroots Post-modernism: Remaking the Soil of Cultures*. New York: Zed Books, 1998.

Eyzaguirre, Pablo B., and Olga F. Linares, eds. *Home Gardens and Agrobiodiversity*. Washington, DC: Smithsonian Books, 2010.

FAO. "Small Family Farmers Produce a Third of the World's Food." Food and Agriculture Organization (FAO) of the United Nations. April 23, 2021. https://www.fao.org/news/story/en/item/1395127/icode/.

Farquhar, Judith. "Food, Eating, and the Good Life." In *Handbook of Material Culture*, edited by Chris Tilley, Mike Rowlands, Patricia Spyer, Susanne Kuechler, and Webb Keane, 145–60. London: SAGE, 2006.

Federici, Silvia. *Caliban and the Witch: Women, the Body and Primitive Accumulation*. Third printing. Brooklyn, N.Y.: Autonomedia, 2009.

Federici, Silvia. *Revolution at Point Zero: Housework, Reproduction, and Feminist Struggle*. Oakland, Calif.: PM Press, 2012.

Federici, Silvia. *Re-enchanting the World: Feminism and the Politics of the Commons.* Oakland, Calif.: PM Press, 2018.

Ford, Anabel, and Ronald Nigh. "The Milpa Cycle and the Making of the Maya Forest Garden." *Research Reports in Belizean Archaeology* 7 (2010): 183–90.

Foster, John Bellamy, Brett Clark, and Richard York, eds. *The Ecological Rift: Capitalism's War on the Earth.* New York: Monthly Review Press, 2010.

Foucault, Michel. *The Archaeology of Knowledge: And the Discourse on Language.* New York: Pantheon, 1982.

Fox, Steve. *Toxic Work: Women Workers at GTE Lenkurt.* Philadelphia: Temple University Press, 1991.

Francis, Richard C. *Epigenetics: How Environment Shapes our Genes.* New York: W. W. Norton & Company, 2011.

Freire, Paolo. *Pedagogy of the Oppressed.* New York: Continuum Publishing Corporation, 1984.

Fromm, Erich. *Marx's Concept of Man.* Translated by T. B. Bottomore. New York: Frederick Ungar Publishing, 1966.

Gálvez, Alyshia. *Patient Citizens, Immigrant Mothers: Mexican Women, Public Prenatal Care, and the Birth-Weight Paradox.* New Brunswick, N.J.: Rutgers University Press, 2011.

Gálvez, Alyshia. *Eating NAFTA: Trade, Food Policies, and the Destruction of Mexico.* Berkeley: University of California Press, 2018.

Gerodetti, Natalia, and Sally Foster. "'Growing Foods from Home': Food Production, Migrants and the Changing Cultural Landscapes of Gardens and Allotments." *Landscape Research* 41, no. 7 (2015): 808–19.

Gibson-Graham, J. K. *A Postcapitalist Politics.* Minneapolis: University of Minnesota Press, 2006.

Gibson-Graham, J. K., Jenny Cameron, and Stephen Healy. *Take Back the Economy: An Ethical Guide for Transforming Our Communities.* Minneapolis: University of Minnesota Press, 2013.

Giddens, Anthony. *Central Problems in Social Theory: Action, Structure, and Contradiction in Social Analysis.* Berkeley: University of California Press, 1979.

Giddens, Anthony. *Beyond Left and Right: The Future of Radical Politics.* Stanford: Stanford University Press, 1994.

Gilbert, Fabiola Cabeza de Baca. *The Good Life: New Mexico Traditions and Food.* 1949. Santa Fe: Museum of New Mexico Press, 2005.

Gilio-Whitaker, Dina. *As Long as Grass Grows: The Indigenous Fight for Environmental Justice, from Colonization to Standing Rock.* Boston: Beacon Press, 2019.

Gilligan, Carol. *In a Different Voice: Psychological Theory and Women's Development.* Cambridge, Mass.: Harvard University Press, 1982.

Gliessman, Stephen R. *Agroecology: The Ecology of Sustainable Food Systems.* Boca Raton, Fla.: CRC Press, 1990.

Gómez-Barris, Macarena. *The Extractive Zone: Social Ecologies and Decolonial Perspective.* Durham, N.C.: Duke University Press, 2017.

Gottlieb, Robert. *Forcing the Spring: The Transformation of the American Environmental Movement*. Washington, DC: Island Press, 1994.

Gottlieb, Robert, and Anupama Joshi. *Food Justice*. Cambridge, Mass.: MIT Press, 2010.

Gowdy-Wygant, Cecilia. *Cultivating Victory: The Women's Land Army and the Victory Garden Movement*. Pittsburgh, Pa.: University of Pittsburgh Press, 2013.

Graeber, David. *Anthropological Theory of Value: The False Coin of Our Own Dreams*. New York: Palgrave, 2001.

GRAIN. "Hungry for Land: Small Farmers Feed the World with Less than a Quarter of All Farmland." May 28, 2014. https://grain.org/article/entries/4929-hungry-for-land-small-farmers-feed-the-world-with-less-than-a-quarter-of-all-farmland.

Gramsci, Antonio. *Prison Notebooks*. Edited by Joseph A. Buttigieg and Antonio Callari. Translated by Joseph A. Buttigieg and Antonio Callari. New York: Columbia University Press, 1992.

Gray, Leslie, Patricia Guzman, Kathryn Michelle Glowa, and Ann G. Drevno. "Can Home Gardens Scale up into Movements for Social Change? The Role of Home Gardens in Providing Food Security and Community Change in San Jose, California." *Local Environment* 19, no. 2 (2014): 187–203.

Gregory, Christopher A. "The Competing Theories." In *Gifts and Commodities*, edited by Christopher Gregory, 10–28. London: Academic Press, 1982.

Gregory, Christopher A. "The Value Question." In *Savage Money: The Politics of Commodity Exchange*, edited by Christopher Gregory, 1–42. Amsterdam: Harwood Academic, 1997.

Grossinger, Robin M., Charles J. Striplen, Ruth A. Askevold, Elise Brewster, and Erin E. Beller. "Historical Landscape Ecology of an Urbanized California Valley: Wetlands and Woodlands in the Santa Clara Valley." *Landscape Ecology* 22, no. 1 (2007): 103–20.

Gullì, Bruno. *Labor of Fire: The Ontology of Labor between Economy and Culture*. Philadelphia: Temple University Press, 2005.

Guthman, Julie. *Weighing In: Obesity, Food Justice, and the Limits of Capitalism*. Berkeley: University of California Press, 2011.

Hammerstein, Peter. *Genetic and Cultural Evolution of Cooperation*. Cambridge, Mass.: MIT Press, 2003.

Hardt, Michael, and Antonio Negri. *Empire*. Cambridge, Mass.: Harvard University Press, 2000.

Hardt, Michael, and Antonio Negri. *The Multitude: War and Democracy in the Age of Empire*. New York: Penguin Books, 2004.

Hardt, Michael, and Antonio Negri. *The Common Wealth*. Cambridge, Mass.: Belknap Press, 2009.

Harper, Breeze A. "Vegans of Color, Racialized Embodiment, and Problematics of the 'Exotic.'" In *Cultivating Food Justice: Race, Class, and Sustainability*, edited by Alison Hope Alkon and Julian Agyeman, 221–38. Cambridge, Mass.: MIT Press, 2011.

Harrison, Jill Lindsey. *Pesticide Drift and the Pursuit of Environmental Justice.* Cambridge, Mass.: MIT Press, 2011.
Harvey, David. *Spaces of Capital: Toward a Critical Geography.* New York: Routledge, 2001.
Harvey, David. *Rebel Cities: From the Right to the City to the Urban Revolution.* New York: Verso, 2012.
Harvey, David. *Marx, Capital, and the Madness of Economic Reason.* New York: Oxford University Press, 2017.
Hatch, Anthony Ryan. *Blood Sugar: Racial Pharmacology and Food Justice in Black America.* Minneapolis: University of Minnesota Press, 2016.
Hayes-Conroy, Allison, and Jessica Hayes-Conroy, eds. *Doing Nutrition Differently: Critical Approaches to Diet and Dietary Intervention.* New York: Taylor & Francis Group, 2013.
Hedges, Chris, and Joe Sacco. *Days of Destruction, Days of Revolt.* New York: Nation Books, 2012.
Held, Virginia. *The Ethics of Care: Personal, Political, and Global.* New York: Oxford University Press, 2006.
Heraty, Joanne M., and Norman C. Ellstrad. "Maize Germplasm Conservation in Southern California's Urban Gardens." *Economic Botany* 70, no. 1 (2016): 37–48.
Holifield, Ryan. "Defining Environmental Justice and Environmental Racism." *Urban Geography* 22, no. 1 (2001): 78–90.
Holland, Leigh. "Diversity and Connections in Community Gardens: A Contribution to Local Sustainability." *Local Environment* 9, no. 3 (2004): 285–305.
Holloway, John. "Zapatismo and the Social Sciences." *Capital & Class* 78 (2002): 153–60.
Holmes, Seth. *Fresh Fruit, Broken Bodies: Migrant Farmworkers in the United States.* Berkeley: University of California Press, 2013.
Holt-Giménez, Eric, ed. *Food Movements Unite! Strategies to Transform our Food System.* Oakland, Calif.: Food First Books, 2011.
Holt-Giménez, Eric, and Yi Wang. "Reform or Transformation?: The Pivotal Role of Food Justice in the U.S. Food Movement." *Race/Ethnicity: Multidisciplinary Global Contexts* 5, no. 1 (2011): 83–102.
Howard, Patricia L. "Gender and Social Dynamics in Swidden and Homegardens in Latin America." In *Tropical Homegardens: A Time-Tested Example of Sustainable Agroforestry*, edited by Kumar, B. M., and P. K. R. Nair. Dordrecht, Netherlands: Springer, 2006.
Hylkema, Mark G. *Santa Clara Valley Prehistory: Archaeological Investigations at CA-SCL-690 The Tamien Station Site, San José, California.* Davis, Calif.: Center for Archaeological Research at Davis, 2007.
Illich, Ivan. *Tools for Conviviality.* New York: Marion Boyars Publishers, 2009a.
Illich, Ivan. *Shadow Work.* New York: Marion Boyars Publishers, 2009b.
Ingold, Tim. *Anthropology: Why It Matters.* Medford, Mass.: Polity Press, 2018.

Jalbert, Kirk, Anna Willow, David Casagrande, and Stephanie Paladino, eds. *ExtrACTION: Impacts, Engagements, and Alternative Futures*. New York: Routledge, 2017.

Jarosz, Lucy. "The City in the Country: Growing Alternative Food Networks in Metropolitan Areas." *Journal of Rural Studies* 24, no. 3 (2008): 231–44.

Johnston, Barbara Rose, and Holly M. Barker. *Consequential Damages of Nuclear War: The Rongelap Report*. Walnut Creek, Calif.: Left Coast Press, 2008.

Juárez, Rufina. "Indigenous Women in the Food Sovereignty Movement: Lessons from the South Central Farmers." In *Mexican-Origin Foods, Foodways, and Social Movements: Decolonial Perspectives*, edited by Devon G. Peña, Luz Calvo, Pancho McFarland, and Gabriel R. Valle, 27–40. Fayetteville: University of Arkansas Press, 2017.

Katz, Sandor Ellix. *The Revolution Will Not Be Microwaved: Inside America's Underground Food Movements*. White River Junction, Vt.: Chelsea Green Publishing, 2006.

Keeley, Jon E. "Native American Impacts on Fire Regimes of the California Coastal Ranges." *Journal of Biogeography* 29, no. 3 (2002): 303–20.

Kohn, Eduardo. *How Forests Think: Toward an Anthropology beyond the Human*. Berkeley: University of California Press, 2013.

Komarnisky, Sara. "Suitcases full of mole: Traveling food and the connections between México and Alaska." *Alaska Journal of Anthropology* 7, no. 1 (2009): 41–56.

Kropotkin, Peter. *Mutual Aid: A Factor of Evolution*. Mineola, N.Y.: Dover Publications, 2006.

Kuehn, Robert R. "A Taxonomy of Environmental Justice." *Environmental Law Reporter* 30, no. 9 (2000): 10681–703.

Kumar, B. M., and P. K. R. Nair, eds. *Tropical Homegardens: A Time-Tested Example of Sustainable Agroforestry*. Dordrecht, Netherlands: Springer, 2006.

Ladner, Peter. *The Urban Food Revolution: Changing the Way We Feed Cities*. Gabriola Island, BC: New Society Publishers, 2011.

LaDuke, Winona. *Recovering the Sacred: The Power of Naming and Claiming*. Cambridge, Mass.: South End Press, 2005.

Latour, Bruno. "On Actor-Network Theory: A Few Clarifications." *Soziale Weflt* 47, no 4 (1996): 369–81.

Lavelle, Marianne, and Marcia Coyle. "Unequal Protection: The Racial Divide in Environmental Law." *National Law Journal* 15, no. 3 (1992): 1–12.

Lawson, Laura J. *City Bountiful: A Century of Community Gardening*. Berkeley: University of California Press, 2005.

Lazarus, Richard J. "Pursuing 'Environmental Justice': The Distributional Effects of Environmental Protection." *Northwestern University Law Review* 87, no. 3 (1993): 787–857.

LeClere, Felicia B., Richard G. Rogers, and Kimberley D. Peters. "Ethnicity and Mortality in the United States: Individual and Community Correlates." *Social Forces* 76, no. 1 (1997): 169–98.

Lefebvre, Henri. *The Production of Space*. Cambridge, Mass.: Blackwell, 1991.
Leopold, Aldo. *Sand County Almanac and Sketches Here and There*. New York: Oxford University Press. First published in 1987 by Oxford University Press, 1949.
Lerner, Steve. *Sacrifice Zones: The Front Lines of Toxic Chemical Exposure in the United States*. Cambridge, Mass.: MIT Press, 2010.
Leventhal, Alan, Les Field, Hank Alvarez, and Rosemary Cambra. "The Ohlone Back from Extinction." In *The Ohlone Past and Present: Native Americans of the San Francisco Bay Region*, edited by Lowell John Bean, 297–336. San José, Calif.: Ballena Press. Anthropological Papers, 1994.
Linebaugh, Peter. *The Magna Carta Manifesto: Liberties and Commons for All*. Berkeley: University of California Press, 2009.
Linebaugh, Peter. *Stop, Thief!: The Commons, Enclosures, and Resistance*. Oakland, Calif.: PM Press, 2014.
Lope-Alzina, Diana G., and Patricia L. Howard. "The Structure, Composition, and Functions of Homegardens: Focus on the Yucatán Peninsula." *Etnoecológica* 9, no. 1 (2012): 17–41.
Lowder, Sarah K., Marco V. Sánchez, and Raffaele Bertini. "Which Farms Feed the World and Has Farmland Become More Concentrated?" *World Development* 142 (2021): 105455. https://doi.org/10.1016/j.worlddev.2021.105455.
Lowe, Lisa. "The Intimacies of Four Continents." In *Haunted by Empire: Geographies of Intimacy in North American History*, edited by Ann Laura Stoler, 191–212. Durham, N.C.: Duke University Press, 2006.
Ludwig, David S., and Mark I. Friedman. "Increasing Adiposity: Consequence or Cause of Overeating?" *JAMA* 311, no. 21 (2014): 2167–168.
Lyson, Thomas A. *Civic Agriculture: Reconnecting Farm, Food, and Community*. Medford, Mass.: Tufts University Press, 2004.
Madrigal, Tomás. "We Are Human!: Farmworker Organizing across the Food Chain in Washington." In *Mexican-Origin Foods, Foodways, and Social Movements: Decolonial Perspectives*, edited by Devon G. Peña, Luz Calvo, Pancho McFarland, and Gabriel R. Valle, 235–90. Fayetteville: University of Arkansas Press, 2017.
Maffi, Luisa. "Biocultural Diversity and Sustainability." In *The SAGE Handbook of Environment and Society*, edited by Jules N. Pretty, 267–77. Los Angeles: SAGE, 2007.
Mares, Teresa, "Tracing Immigrant Identity through the Plate and the Palate," *Latino Studies* 10, no. 3 (2012): 334–54.
Mares, Teresa, and Devon Peña. "Urban Agriculture in the Making of Insurgent Spaces in Los Angeles and Seattle." In *Insurgent Public Space: Guerrilla Urbanism and the Remaking of Contemporary Cities*, edited by Jeffrey Hou, 253–67. New York: Routledge, 2010.
Mares, Teresa, and Devon Peña. "Environmental and Food Justice: Toward Local, Slow, and Deep Food Systems." In *Cultivating Food Justice: Race, Class, and Sustainability*, edited by Alison Hope Alkon and Julian Agyeman, 197–219. Cambridge, Mass.: MIT Press, 2011.

Marris, Emma. *Rambunctious Garden: Saving Nature in a Post-Wild World.* New York: Bloomsbury Publishing, 2011.
Marx, Karl. *A Contribution to the Critique of Political Economy.* Moscow: Progress Publishers, (1977). https://www.marxists.org/archive/marx/works/1859/critique-pol-economy/preface.htm.
Marx, Karl. *Capital: A Critique of Political Economy.* Vol. 3. Translated by D. Fernbach. New York: Penguin, 1981.
Marx, Karl. *Capital: A Critique of Political Economy.* Vol. 1. Translated by Ben Fowkes. New York: Penguin Classics, 1990.
Marx, Karl. *Grundrisse.* Translated by Martin Nicolaus. New York: Penguin Classics, 1993.
Marx, Karl, and E. J. Hobsbawm. *Pre-capitalist Economic Formations.* New York: International Publishers, 1964.
Marx, Karl, and Friedrich Engels. *The Poverty of Philosophy.* Translated by H. Chicago: Charles H. Kerr & Co, 1920.
Mauss, Marcel. *The Gift: Forms and Functions of Exchange in Archaic Societies.* New York: Norton, 1990.
McClintock, Nathan. "Why Farm the City?: Theorizing Urban Agriculture through a Lens of Metabolic Rift." *Cambridge Journal of Regions, Economy and Society* 3, no. 2 (2010): 191–207.
McClintock, Nathan. "From Industrial Garden to Food Desert: DemarcatedDevaluation in the Flatlands of Oakland, California." In *Cultivating Food Justice: Race, Class, and Sustainability*, edited by Alison Hope Alkon and Julian Agyeman, 98–120. Cambridge, Mass.: MIT Press, 2011.
McClintock, Nathan. "Radical, Reformist, and Garden-Variety Neoliberal: Coming to Terms with Urban Agriculture's Contradictions." *Local Environment* 19, no. 2 (2014): 147–71.
Meah, Angela. "Reconceptualizing Power and Gendered Subjectivities in Domestic Cooking Spaces." *Progress in Human Geography* 38, no. 5 (2014): 671–90.
Merchant, Carolyn. *Ecological Revolutions: Nature, Gender, and Science in New England.* Chapel Hill: University of North Carolina Press, 1989.
Méndez, Ramón Mariaca. *El Huerto Familiar del Sureste de México.* Mexico: D. R. Secretaría de Recursos naturales y Protección Ambiental del Estado de Tabasco, 2012.
Mignolo, Walter. "Citizenship, Knowledge, and the Limits of Humanity." *American Literary History* 18, no. 2 (2006): 312–31.
Mignolo, Walter. "Epistemic Disobedience, Independent Thought and De-Colonial Freedom." *Theory, Culture & Society* 26, no. 7–8 (2009): 1–23.
Mignolo, Walter. *The Darker Side of Western Modernity: Global Futures, Decolonial Options.* Durham, N.C.: Duke University Press, 2011a.
Mignolo, Walter. "Epistemic Disobedience and the Decolonial Option: A Manifesto." *Transmodernity: A Journal of Peripheral Cultural Production of the Luso-Hispanic World* 1, no. 2 (2011b): 44–66.

Mihesuah, Devon Abbott. *Recovering Our Ancestors' Gardens: Indigenous Recipes and Guide to Diet and Fitness*. Lincoln: University of Nebraska Press, 2005.

Milbourne, Paul. "Everyday (In)Justices and Ordinary Environmentalisms: Community Gardening in Disadvantaged Urban Neighborhoods." *Local Environment* 17 no. 9 (2012): 943–57.

Mohai, Paul, and Bunyant Bryant. "Race, Poverty, and the Environment." *EPA Journal* 18 (1992): 6–8.

Mohawk, John. "From the First to the Last Bite: Learning from the Food Knowledge of Our Ancestors." In *Original Instruction: Indigenous Teachings for a Sustainable Future*, edited by Melissa K. Nelson, 170–79. Rochester, N.Y.: Bear & Company, 2008.

Morton, Timothy. *Hyperobjects: Philosophy and Ecology after the End of the World*. Minneapolis: University of Minnesota Press, 2013.

Montoya, Michael J. *Making the Mexican Diabetic: Race, Science, and the Genetics of Inequality*. Berkeley: University of California Press, 2011.

Mougeot, Luc J. A., ed. *Agropolis: The Social, Political, and Environmental Dimensions of Urban Agriculture*. London: Earthscan, 2005.

Munn, Nancy. *The Fame of Gawa: A Symbolic Study of Value Transformation in a Massim (Papua New Guinea) Society*. New York: Cambridge University Press, 1986.

Nabhan, Gary Paul. *Coming Home to Eat: The Pleasures and Politics of Local Foods*. New York: W. W. Norton & Company, 2002.

Nabhan, Gary Paul. *Food, Genes, and Culture: Eating Right for your Origins*. Washington, DC: Island Press, 2013.

Nabhan, Gary Paul, ed. *Ethnobiology for the Future: Linking Cultural Diversity and Ecological Diversity*. Tucson: University of Arizona Press, 2017.

Nazarea, Virginia D. *Heirloom Seeds and Their Keepers: Marginality and Memory in the Conservation of Biological Diversity*. Tucson: University of Arizona Press, 2005.

Nelson, Melissa K., ed. *Original instructions: Indigenous teachings for a sustainable future*. Rochester: Collective Heritage Institute, 2008a.

Nelson, Melissa K. "Preface: Remembering the Original Instructions." In *Original Instructions: Indigenous Teachings for a Sustainable Future*, edited by Melissa Nelson, xxi–xxiv. Rochester, N.Y.: Collective Heritage Institute, 2008b.

Nelson, Melissa K. "Re-Indigenizing Our Bodies and Minds through Native Foods." In *Original Instructions: Indigenous Teachings for a Sustainable Future*, edited by Melissa Nelson, 180–95. Rochester, N.Y.: Collective Heritage Institute, 2008c.

Negri, Antonio. *Marx Beyond Marx: Lessons on the Grundrisse*. Brooklyn, N.Y.: Autonomedia, 1991.

Newcomer, Laura. "Nutrition is . . ." In *Doing Nutrition Differently: Critical Approaches to Diet and Dietary Intervention*, edited by Allison Hayes-Conroy and Jessica Hayes-Conroy, 191–96. New York: Taylor & Francis Group, 2013.

Nixon, Rob. *Slow Violence and the Environmentalism of the Poor*. Cambridge, Mass.: Harvard University Press, 2011.

Norgaard, Kari Marie, Ron Reed, and Carolina Van Horn. "A Continuing Legacy: Institutional Racism, Hunger, and Nutritional Justice on the Klamath." In *Cultivating*

Food Justice: Race, Class, and Sustainability, edited by Alison Hope Alkon and Julian Agyeman, 23–46. Cambridge, Mass.: MIT Press, 2011.

O'Connor, James. "On the Two Contradictions of Capitalism." *Capitalism, Nature, Socialism* 2, no. 3 (1991): 107–9.

Olson, Mancur. *The Logic of Collective Action; Public Goods and the Theory of Groups.* New York: Schocken Books, 1965.

Omi, Michael, and Howard Winant. *Racial Formation in the United States.* New York: Routledge, 1989.

Ong, Aihwa. *Neoliberalism as Exception: Mutations in Citizenship and Sovereignty.* Durham, N.C.: Duke University Press, 2006.

Ontiveros, Randy J. *In the Spirit of a New People: The Cultural Politics of the Chicano Movement.* New York: New York University Press, 2014.

Ostrom, Eleanor. *Governing the Commons: The Evolution of Institutions of Collective Action.* New York: Cambridge University Press, 1990.

Ostrom, Eleanor. "Collective Action and the Evolution of Social Norms." Paper presented at the Workshop in Political Theory and Policy Analysis, Department of Political Science, Indiana University, 1999.

Otero, Gerardo. *The Neoliberal Diet: Healthy Profits, Unhealthy People.* Austin: University of Texas Press, 2018.

Park Lisa Sun-Hee, and David N. Pellow. "Racial Formation, Environmental Racism, and the Emergence of Silicon Valley." *Ethnicities* 4, no. 3 (2004): 403–24.

Park, Lisa Sun-Hee, and David N. Pellow. *The Slums of Aspen: Immigrants vs. the Environment in America's Eden.* New York: New York University Press, 2011.

Pastor Jr., Manuel, Rachel Morello-Frosch, and James L. Sadd. "Breathless: Schools, Air Toxics, and Environmental Justice in California." *Policy Studies Journal* 34, no. 3 (2006): 337–62.

Patel, Raj. *Stuffed and Starved: The Hidden Battle for the World Food System.* New York: Melville House Publishing, 2007.

Pellow, David N. "Toward a Critical Environmental Justice Studies: Black Lives Matter as an Environmental Justice Challenge." *Du Bois Review: Social Science Research on Race* 13, no. 2 (2016): 221–36.

Pellow, David N. *What Is Critical Environmental Justice?* Medford, Mass.: Polity Press, 2018.

Pellow, David N., and Robert J. Brulle. *Power, Justice, and the Environment: A Critical Appraisal of the Environmental Justice Movement.* Cambridge, Mass.: MIT Press, 2005.

Pellow, David, and Lisa Sun-Hee Park. *The Silicon Valley of Dreams: Environmental Injustice, Immigrant Workers, and the High-tech Global Economy.* New York: New York University Press, 2002.

Peña, Devon G. "Tortuosidad: Shop Floor Struggles of Female Maquiladora Workers." In *Women on the U.S.-Mexico Border: Responses to Change*, edited by Viki Ruíz and Susan Tiano, 129–54. Boston: Allen & Unwin, 1987.

Peña, Devon G. *The Terror of the Machine: Technology, Work, Gender, and Ecology on the US-Mexico Border.* Austin: University of Texas Press, 1997.

Peña, Devon G., ed. *Mexican Americans and the Environment: Tierra y Vida*. Tucson: University of Arizona Press, 2005.
Peña, Devon G. "Autonomía and Food Sovereignty: Decolonizing across the Food Chain." In *Mexican-Origin Foods, Foodways, and Social Movements: Decolonial Perspectives*, edited by Devon G. Peña, Luz Calvo, Pancho McFarland, and Gabriel R. Valle, 5–26. Fayetteville: University of Arkansas Press, 2017a.
Peña, Devon G. "The Humming Bird and the Redcap." In *Wildness: Relations of People and Place*, edited by Gavin Van Horn and John Hausdoerffer, 89–99. Chicago: University of Chicago Press, 2017b.
Peña, Devon G., Luz Calvo, Pancho McFarland, and Gabriel R. Valle, eds. *Mexican-Origin Foods, Foodways, and Social Movements: Decolonial Perspectives*. Fayetteville: University of Arkansas Press, 2017.
Petrini, Carlo, and Gigi Padovani. *Slow Food Revolution: A New Culture for Dining & Living*. New York: Rizzoli International Publications, 2006.
Pezzullo, Phaedra C., and Ronald D. Sandler. *Environmental Justice and Environmentalism: The Social Justice Challenge to the Environmental Movement*. Cambridge, Mass.: MIT Press, 2007.
Pitti, Stephen J. *The Devil in Silicon Valley: Northern California, Race, and Mexican Americans*. Princeton, N.J.: Princeton University Press, 2003.
Pollan, Michael. *Food Rules: An Eater's Manual*. New York: Penguin Books, 2009.
Poppendieck, Janet. *Sweet Charity?: Emergency Food and the End of Entitlement*. New York: Penguin Books, 1998.
Poppendieck, Janet. *Free for All: Fixing School Food in America*. Berkeley: University of California Press, 2010.
Poot-Pool, Wilbert Santiago, Hans van der Wal, Salvador Flores-Guido, Juan Manuel Pat-Fernández, and Ligia Esparza-Olguín. "Home Garden Agrobiodiversity Differentiates Along a Rural-Peri-Urban Gradient in Campeche, México." *Economic Botany* 69, no. 3 (2015): 203–17.
Polanyi, Karl. *The Great Transformation*. New York: Farrar & Rinehart, Inc., 1944.
Posey, Darrel A. "Cultural and Spiritual Values of Biodiversity: A Complementary Contribution to the Global Biodiversity Assessment." In *Cultural and Spiritual Values of Biodiversity*, edited by Darrel A. Posey, 1–19. London: UNEP and Intermediate Technology Publications, 1999.
Povinelli, Elizabeth A. *Economies of Abandonment: Social Belonging and Endurance in Late Liberalism*. Durham, N.C.: Duke University Press, 2011.
Pudup, Mary Beth. "It Takes a Garden: Cultivating Citizen-Subjects in Organized Garden Projects." *Geoforum* 39 (2008): 1228–40.
Pulido, Laura. *Environmentalism and Economic Justice: Two Chicano Struggles in the Southwest*. Tucson: University of Arizona Press, 1996.
Pulido, Laura. "Rethinking Environmental Racism: White Privilege and Urban Development in Southern California." *Annals of the Association of American Geographers* 90, no. 1 (2000): 12–40.
Quijano, Aníbal. "Colonialidad y Modernidad/Racionalidad." *Perú Indígena* 13, no. 29 (1992): 11–20.

Quijano, Aníbal. "Coloniality of Power and Eurocentrism in Latin America." *Nepantla: Views from the South* 1, no. 3 (2000): 519–32.

Rai, Shirin, Jane Parpart, and Kathleen Staudt. "(Re)defining Empowerment, Measuring Survival." Paper prepared for Workshop on Empowerment: Obstacles, Flaws, Achievements. May 3–5, 2007. Ottawa, Canada: Carleton University.

Reynolds, Kristin, and Nevin Cohen. *Beyond the Kale: Urban Agriculture and Social Justice Activism in New York City*. Athens: University of Georgia Press, 2016.

Robbins, Joel. "Beyond the Suffering Subject: Toward an Anthropology of the Good." *Journal of the Royal Anthropological Institute* 19, no. 3 (2013): 447–62.

Robinson, Fiona. *The Ethics of Care: A Feminist Approach to Human Security*. Philadelphia: Temple University Press, 2011.

Robinson, James. *Toil and Toxics: Workplace Struggles and Political Strategies for Occupational Health*. Berkeley: University of California Press, 1991.

Rodriguez, Art. *East Side Dreams*. San Jose, Calif.: Chusma House Publications, 1998.

Rodriguez, Chris. "Another Way of Doing Health: Lessons from the Zapatista Autonomous Communities of Chiapas, Mexico." In *Doing Nutrition Differently: Critical Approaches to Diet and Dietary Intervention*, edited by Allison Hayes-Conroy and Jessica Hayes-Conroy, 199–217. Burlington, Vt.: Ashgate, 2013.

Rodríguez, Roberto Cintli. *Our Sacred Maíz is Our Mother: Indigeneity and Belonging in the Americas*. Tucson: University of Arizona Press, 2014.

Rojas, James Thomas. "The Enacted Environment: The Creation of "Place" by Mexican and Mexican Americans in East Los Angeles." PhD diss., MIT, 1991.

Rosas, Gilberto. *Barrio Libre: Criminalizing States and Delinquent Refusals of the New Frontier*. Durham, N.C.: Duke University Press, 2012.

Rosset, Peter M., and Miguel Altieri. *Agroecology: Science and Politics*. Black Point, Nova Scotia: Fernwood Publishing, 2017.

Rubin, Isaak Ilyich. *Essays on Marx's Theory of Value*. N.p.: Pattern Books, 2020.

Ruíz, Vicki. *Cannery Women, Cannery Lives: Mexican Women, Unionization, and the California Food Processing Industry, 1930–1950*. Albuquerque: University of New Mexico Press, 1987.

Russell, Lesley. "Fact Sheet: Disparities by Race and Ethnicity." Center for American Progress Fact Sheet, 2010.

Sahlins, Marshall. "The Original Affluent Society." In *Limited Wants, Unlimited Means: A Hunter-Gatherer Reader on Economics and the Environment*, edited by John Gowdy, 5–41. Washington, DC: Island Press, 1998.

Salmón, Enrique. *Eating the Landscape: American Indian Stories of Food, Identity, and Resilience*. Tucson: University of Arizona Press, 2012.

Saldivar-Tanaka, Laura, and Marianne E. Krasny. "Culturing Community Development, Neighborhood Open Space, and Civic Agriculture: The Case of Latino Community Gardens in New York City." *Agriculture and Human Values* 21, no. 4 (2004): 399–412.

Sandoval, Chela. *Methodology of the Oppressed*. Minneapolis: University of Minnesota Press, 2000.

Schmelzkopf, Karen. "Urban Community Gardens as Contested Space." *Geographical Review* 85, no. 3 (1995): 364–81.

Schlosser, Eric. *Fast Food Nation: The Dark Side of the All-American Meal*. Boston: Houghton Mifflin, 2001.

Schmid, Ronald F. *Traditional Food Are Your Best Medicine: Improving Health and Loving Native Nutrition*. Rochester, N.Y.: Healing Arts Press, 1997.

Scott, James C. *The Moral Economy of the Peasant: Rebellion and Subsistence in Southeast Asia*. New Haven, Conn.: Yale University Press, 1976.

Scott, James C. *Seeing Like a State: How Certain Schemes to Improve the Human Condition Have Failed*. New Haven, Conn.: Yale University Press, 1998.

Scott, James C. *The Art of Not Being Governed: An Anarchist History of Upland Southeast Asia*. New Haven, Conn.: Yale University Press, 2009.

Scott, James C. *Two Cheers for Anarchism*. Princeton, N.J.: Princeton University Press, 2012.

Scrinis, Gyorgy. *Nutritionism: The Science and Politics of Dietary Advice*. New York: Columbia University Press, 2013.

Sevilla-Buitrago, Álvaro. "Capitalist Formations of Enclosure: Space and the Extinction of the Commons." *Antipode* 47, no. 4 (2015): 999–1020.

Shiva, Vandana. *Monocultures of the Mind: Perspectives on Biodiversity and Biotechnology*. New York: Zed Books, 1997.

Shiva, Vandana. *Staying Alive: Women, Ecology, and Development*. Brooklyn, N.Y.: South End Press, 2010.

Shiva, Vandana. *Who Really Feeds the World?: The Failures of Agribusiness and the Promise of Agroecology*. Berkeley: North Atlantic Books, 2016.

Silici, Laura. "Agroecology: What It Is and What It Has to Offer." IIED Issue Paper. London: IIED, 2014.

Simopoulos, Artemis P. "Omega-3 Fatty Acids in Inflammation and Autoimmune Diseases." *Journal of the American College of nutrition* 21, no. 6 (2002): 495–505.

Smith, Linda Tuhiwai. *Decolonizing Methodologies: Research and Indigenous Peoples*. New York: Zed Books, Ltd., 2007.

Smith, Mistinguette. "Wild Black Margins." In *Wildness: Relations of People and Place*, edited by Gavin Van Horn and John Hausdoerffer, 137–44. Chicago: University of Chicago Press, 2016.

Solnit, Rebecca. *A Paradise Built in Hell: The Extraordinary Communities that Arise in Disasters*. New York: Viking, 2009.

Soule, Judith D., and Jon K. Piper. *Farming in Nature's Image: An Ecological Approach to Agriculture*. Washington, D.C.: Island Press, 1992.

Soursourian, Matthew. "Suburbanization of Poverty in the Bay Area." *Community Development Research Brief* (January 2012): 1–17.

Spies-Butcher, Benjamin. "Tracing the Rational Choice Origins of Social Capital: Is Social Capital a Neoliberal Trojan Horse?" *Australian Journal of Social Issues* 37, no. 2 (2002): 173–92.

Spies-Butcher, Benjamin. "Social Capital in Economics: Why Social Capital Does Not Mean the End of Ideology." *The Drawing Board: An Australian Review of Public Affairs* 3, no. 3 (2003): 181–203.

Standing, Guy. *The Precariat: The New Dangerous Class*. New York: Bloomsbury, 2011.

Sykes, Karen, ed. *Ethnographies of Moral Reasoning: Living Paradoxes of a Global Age*. New York: Palgrave, 2009.
Taylor, Dorceta E. *Toxic Communities: Environmental Racism, Industrial Pollution, and Residential Mobility*. New York: New York University Press, 2014.
Taylor, John R., Sarah Taylor Lovell, Sam E. Wortman, and Michelle Chan. "Ecosystem Services and Tradeoffs in the Home Food Gardens of African American, Chinese-Origin and Mexican-Origin Households in Chicago, IL." *Renewable Agriculture and Food Systems* 32, no. 1 (2017): 69–86.
Taylor, Michael. *Rationality and the Ideology of Disconnection*. Cambridge, Mass.: Cambridge University Press, 2006.
Travaline, Katharine, and Hunold, Christian. "Urban agriculture and ecological citizenship in Philadelphia." *Local Environment* 15, no. 6 (2010): 581–90.
Tezozomoc. "Fragmentary Food Flows: Autonomy and the 'Un-signified' Food Deserts of the Real.'" In *Mexican-Origin Foods, Foodways, and Social Movements: Decolonial Perspectives*, edited by Devon G. Peña, Luz Calvo, Pancho McFarland, and Gabriel R. Valle, 211–33. Fayetteville: University of Arkansas Press, 2017.
Tlostanova, Madina V., and Walter D. Mignolo. *Learning to Unlearn: Decolonial Reflections from Eurasia and the Americas*. Columbus: Ohio State University Press, 2012.
Toensmeier, Eric, and Jonathan Bates. *Paradise Lot: Two Plant Geeks, One-Tenth of an Acre and the Making of an Edible Garden Oasis in the City*. White River Junction, Vt.: Chelsea Green Publishing, 2013.
Trauger, Amy. *We Want Land to Live: Making Political Space for Food Sovereignty*. Athens, Ga.: University of Georgia Press, 2017.
Tronto, Joan C. *Moral Boundaries: A Political Argument for an Ethic of Care*. New York: Routledge, 1993.
Tronto, Joan C. "Interview with Joan Tronto." *Ethics of Care*. October 16, 2009. https://ethicsofcare.org/joan-tronto/.
Tronto, Joan C. "Partiality Based on Relational Responsibilities: Another Approach to Global Ethics." *Ethics and Social Welfare* 6, no. 3 (2012): 303–16.
Trouillot, Michel Rolph. *Global Transformations: Anthropology and the Modern World*. New York: Palgrave Macmillan, 2003.
Tsing, Anna. *The Mushroom at the End of the World*. Princeton, N.J.: Princeton University Press, 2015.
Tylor, Edward B. *Primitive Culture: Researches into the Development of Mythology, Philosophy, Religion, Language, Art, and Custom*. New York: G. P. Putnam's Sons, 1920.
United Christ Church. *Toxic Wastes and Race in the United States*. UCC Commission on Racial Justice, 1987.
Unnikrishnan, P. M., and M. S. Suneetha. "Biodiversity, Traditional Knowledge and Community Health: Strengthening Linkages." United Nations University and United Nations Environment Programme, United Nations University-Institute of Advanced Studies, Japan, 2012.
Valdovinos, María Guillen. "Travels of a Diaspora Community: From La Sierra Madre y Tierra Caliente to the Pacific Northwest." In *Mexican-Origin Foods, Foodways,*

and Social Movements: Decolonial Perspectives, edited by Devon G. Peña, Luz Calvo, Pancho McFarland, and Gabriel R. Valle, 169–87. Fayetteville: University of Arkansas Press, 2017.

Valle, Gabriel R. "Gardens of Sabotage: Food, the Speed of Capitalism, and the Value of Work." *Aztlán: A Journal of Chicano Studies* 40, no. 1 (2015): 63–86.

Valle, Gabriel R. "Food Values: Urban Kitchen Gardens and Working-Class Subjectivity." In *Mexican-Origin Foods, Foodways, and Social Movements: Decolonial Perspectives*, edited by Devon G. Peña, Luz Calvo, Pancho McFarland, and Gabriel R. Valle, 41–62. Fayetteville: University of Arkansas Press, 2017.

Wald, Sarah D. *The Nature of California: Race, Citizenship, and Farming since the Dust Bowl*. Seattle: University of Washington Press, 2016.

Wald, Sarah D., David J. Vázquez, Priscilla Solis Ybarra, and Sarah Jaquette Ray, eds. *Latinx Environmentalisms: Place, Justice, and the Decolonial*. Philadelphia: Temple University Press, 2019.

Waters, Alice. *Edible Schoolyard: A Universal Idea*. San Francisco: Chronicle Books, 2008.

Whyte, Kyle. "Settler Colonialism, Ecology, and Environmental Injustice." *Environment and Society* 9, no. 1 (2018): 125–44.

Wilson, Shawn. *Research Is Ceremony: Indigenous Research Methods*. Black Point, Nova Scotia: Fernwood Publishing, 2008.

Winne, Mark. *Closing the Food Gap: Resetting the Table in the Land of Plenty*. Boston: Beacon Press, 2008.

Winne, Mark. *Food Rebels, Guerrilla Gardeners, and Smart-Cookin' Mamas: Fighting Back in an Age of Industrial Agriculture*. Boston: Beacon Press, 2010.

Winson, Anthony. *The Industrial Diet: The Degradation of Food and the Struggle for Healthy Eating*. New York: New York University Press, 2013.

Ybarra, Priscilla Solis. *Writing the Goodlife: Mexican American Literature and the Environment*. Tucson: University of Arizona Press, 2016.

Zimmerman, Rae. "Issues of Classification in Environmental Equity: How We Manage Is How We Measure." *The Fordham Urban Law Journal* 21, no. 3 (1994): 633–69.

Zinn, Howard. *A People's History of the United States*. New York: Harper & Row, 1990.

Zlolniski, Christian. *Janitors, Street Vendors, and Activists: The Lives of Mexican Immigrants in Silicon Valley*. Berkeley: University of California Press, 2006.

Index

Agamben, Giorgio, 150; anthropological machine, 89; openness, 89; open whole, 89
agroecology, 7, 31, 110; defined, 7n1
Algert, Susan J., 17
alienation, 10; autonomy and self-valorization reduces, 91; contemporary capitalist economic system reproduces, 42; contradiction between gardening to counter, 109; conviviality as collective response to, 101; defined, 13; ecological destruction contributes to, 84; gardeners aim to move to autonomy, in place of, 10; gardening as counter to, 11, 109; gardening resists, 90; growing food can mend the wounds of, 101; historical legacy of, 14; illness draws attention to, 149; labor and, 108. *See also* autonomy; conviviality; Federici, Silvia; labor theory of value; Marx, Karl; reproduction; self-valorization; surplus value; Tsing, Anna
Alkon, Alison Hope, 17, 55
Alma, as mentor, 5; reputation for knowing everyone and everything, 4

autonomy, 20, 21n2, 47, 53, 64, 72, 80, 109, 125, 133, 144, 150; access to land can enable, 73; comida and, 126; enactment of, 94, 159, 161; encourages the self-constitution among those who practice, 75, 93; limitations of the state and existence of, 63; flexible labor supports self-determination and, 49; gardeners' capturing moments of, 22; gardeners desire for equality, liberation and, 155; gardeners pursue dignity while striving for, 35, 158; gardening and, 8, 18, 33–34, 92; gardening, self-valorization and, 91; gardens as temporary zones of, 149; gardens at the margins and, 4; gardens contain essential elements for social reproduction and, 35, 107, 126; growing food and, 70, 150; justice, equity, and, 159; justice, sense of community and, 150; local lives find and create spaces of, 32; objective of gardening to move from alienation to, 10; oppositional states of exception and, 150; spaces of bounded, 150; struggles for, 150; theory of, 163; a working class for itself asserts its, 108. *See also* comida; margins

Berardi, Franco, 14; on meaning of wealth, 140; refusal to work does not erase activity, 13
biopolitics, 109; of industrial capitalism, 35. *See also* Agamben, Giorgio; Foucault, Michel
bioremediation, 110
Bullard, Robert D., 19, 42, 69

civic agriculture: can contribute to individual and environmental well-being, 17; defined, 17; introduced by Lyson, Thomas, 17
Cleaver, Harry, 44, 108; self-valorization, 13, 93
comida (food), 10, 75, 157; alternative values and practices of, 157; as antidote to individualism, 122; collapses structure/agency dilemma, 9; communications with, 87; contrast with neo-liberal diet, 136; conviviality and healing with, 132; cooking and healing with, 121–37; diet-related illness, 9; distinction between *comida* and *alimento*, 126; expression of social relationships and, 132; food deserts, 9, 22, 33, 41, 92, 94; as healing agent, 126; living memory of, 126, 134–36; material realities and, 9; multiple factors shape the acquisition and consumption of, 10; recovering and (re)discovering value of, 34; shared experience of cooking, 122; situated knowledge and, 133; as social condition and power, 122; social reproduction and, 122; as source of solidarity and conviviality, 122; Spanish translation as *alimento*, 126. *See also* Esteva, Gustavo; food insecurity; gardens/gardening; Prakash, Madhu Suri
conviviality: convivial labor, ix, 12–16, 18, 34, 49, 53, 93–94, 102, 106, 116, 154–55, 163; convivial labor defined, 16; sharing economy and, 162. *See also* gardens/gardening; sharing
crop rotation, 3

decoloniality: conviviality and, 140, 152; decolonial move, 140; decolonial option, 30, 100, 115, 116; dignity, humanity and, 152; ethnography and, 30; food and, 136. *See also* conviviality; Mignolo, Walter; Smith, Linda
dispensability. *See* sacrifice zones

enclosure, 86, 92, 103, 116; aim to remove persons from their own means of production, 80; autonomous spaces at risk of, 79; biological and demographic impacts of, 84; colonial matrix of power and, 86; colonized people's experience with, 70–71; commoning as struggle against, 71; create a marketplace for labor and goods, 80; creation of heteronomous value regimes goal of, 79; defined, 80; and the disciplining of social organization through market expansion, 92; dispossession and deprivation at risk of, 79; dispossession of autonomous capacity for self-valorization and, 92; erasure and, 28, 70; gardeners always on the brink of, 150; gardening against, 80–85; home gardens as actions against, 71, 92; homogenization of space and values and, 71; Indigenous efforts to escape and resist, 28; interrelationship between displacement, privatization, gentrification, and, 148; Mexican-origin peoples and history of, 86; privatization and, 57; reoccurring process and, 71; self-regulation of capitalist operations and, 57; Spanish transformation of *gerguensun* into an, 83; U.S. neo-regulatory, 57. *See also* gardens/gardening; margins; precarity

Esteva, Gustavo, 126; *comida*, 122, 133–34; *comida* as changing and never fixed, 134; *comida* as communal memory, 134; *comida* reflects living memory of ritualized practice, 133; disengaging from the logic of the market, 93; human rights as Trojan horse, 21n2; new commons, 71, 93; self-creation and food, 126; struggles of the common man, 69. *See also* Prakash, Madhu Suri
ethic of care, 8; defined, 8; gardeners allowed to root themselves through an, 71; gardeners mutual reliance and interdependence as the basis of an, 143; innate human instinct of solidarity and an, 144; movement toward a more just and caring society aided by an, 143; place-attachments help generate an, 91. *See also* conviviality; place-attachments

Federici, Silvia, 12; capitalism's control of reproduction and mobility, 11; labor-power, 109–10; overlooks death of land, 110
flexible labor, 53; autonomy and self-valorization supported by, 49; choice and coercion in, 49; defined, 47, 53; essential to agribusiness and Silicon Valley, 47; part of the new work economy, 48; postindustrial economy driven by, 49; a source of precarity, 49; a source of self-valorization, 48; working-class struggles enabled and inhibited by, 49. *See also* conviviality; Silicon Valley
food insecurity, 5, 60, 98, 105; Village Harvest efforts to address, 105. *See also comida* (food)
food sovereignty, 147, 152, 153, 159; food justice and, 162; radical subjectivities and, 153. *See also* autonomy; *comida*; food insecurity; Trauger, Amy

Foster, John Bellamy, 12, 48n2; demands of capital and ecological problems, 41; ecological rifts, 41; Jevon's Paradox, 48n2; metabolic rift, 84; paperless office paradox, 48n2
Foucault, Michel, 123
funds of knowledge: gardening taps into preexisting, 28

Gálvez, Alyshia, 27n4, 34, 59, 69, 122, 130; diet-related illness, 9–10; NAFTA displacement of local food, 124n3
gardens/gardening (home/at margins): act of self-valorization, 35, 155, 159; allow the displacement of industrial economy with convivial labor, 155; autotopographic, 73, 87, 150; as both radical and neoliberal, 62; conditions for emergence, 33, 41; contribute to the social reproduction of home gardeners, 41; contribute to social and ecological resilience, 10; conviviality and, 9, 72; defined, 10–11; desire to create alternative food system, 163; emerge in response to ethic of care in, 8; enacted spaces where labor's form-creating fire, 41; fertilizing soil for future movements, 35; forms of resistance to capitalist enclosure, 75; foster alternative values, 15; fosters the move from alienated labor to unalienated labor, 136; gardeners and gleaning of fruit, 105; gardeners as revolutionaries, 60–62, 64, 139–55; gardeners communicate to and with their, 91; grounded in social and ecological relationships, 8; growing food as environmental justice, 34; healing and, 34; held together through relational accountability, 8; hidden in plain sight, 3–6; home gardeners resist precarity and vulnerability, 42, 44; *huertos familiares*, 75; importance of

gardens/gardening (*continued*)
sharing crop knowledge, 5; importance of sharing crops produced, 5; intergenerational learning and teaching, 7; involves a politics of recognition, 62; involves labor that is neither productive nor unproductive, but creative, 16; legacy and erasure of home, 75–80; marginalized, 22, 34; mutual interdependence in, 8; possibility of radical social transformation, 158; a proactive experiment, 159; production of social norms in, 5; reorganize reproductive work through discursive and subversive practices, 11; represent political statements, 101; reproduction at the heart of, 10; response to capitalism, 41, 62; sabotage and, 151, 155; seeds containing biological and cultural memories, 157; self-constitution and autonomy, 70; self-sufficiency and trust, 9; self-valorization and, 35, 63, 108, 126, 155; social reproduction of the community, 15; spaces for social reproduction, 17, 18, 21, 28, 34, 35, 41, 53, 72, 90, 107, 122, 126, 131, 144, 154, 163; strive for autonomy in pursuit of dignity, 35, 64; surface in response to metabolic rift, 41. *See also* autonomy; *comida*; conviviality; enclosures; margins; milpa-based production; precarity; rifts; self-valorization; sharing; value

gerguensun (Muweka Ohlone, the place of the oak tree), 80, 83; Ohlone view of, 83; site of Santa Clara Mission, 83

Graeber, David, 15, 18, 34; on value, 15, 103

Gramsci, Antonio: reading Marx as humanist, 12

Gray, Leslie, 17

Hardt, Michael, 42, 91, 92, 146, 154, 155, 159; labor-power against exploitation, 155; network struggle, 60; singularities that act in common, 159. *See also* Negri, Antonio

hegemonic nutrition, 133; defined, 123

industrial food system: externalization of costs to the most vulnerable, 60

Jungle, The (encampment known as): coexisted with the wealthy in Silicon Valley, 52; located near the Sacred Heart Community Services office, 52; one of the largest homeless encampment in the US, 52; removed in December 2014, 52

Kropotkin, Peter: animal/human sociability not reducible to love or sympathy, 143; on legacy of mutual aid, 160; on the limits of the concept of ethical man, 144; unwritten rules of human solidarity, 160

labor theory of value: defined, 12; insights from, 11. *See also* alienation; Cleaver, Harry; Federici, Silvia; Marx, Karl; reproduction; surplus value

La Mesa Verde (LMV) gardening project: diverse aims within members and Sacred Heart Community Services, 163–64; gardens at the margins, 4; initial creation and University of California Master Gardner Program, 28; members of, ix–xi; a project of Sacred Heart Community Services, 28. *See also comida* (food); gardening; margins; Sacred Heart Community Services; University of California Master Gardner Program

Mares, Teresa Marie, 17, 55, 73, 78, 79, 87, 126, 150; critique of Pollan, Michael, 124 margins: become centers, and centers become margins, 27; displaced, marginalized, and oppressed people at the, 10; diversity within, 10; emergence of radical political subjectivities at the, 34; gardeners use their marginality as a creative force, 22; gardens at the, 33, 35, 41; good life at the, 99–101; home gardeners use their marginalization as an inventive force, 42, 58, 62; life at the, 10; marginality as inventive force, 42; marginalization, 15, 42, 94; marginalized persons inhabit least fertile ground, 124; *milpas* at the, 65–67; overlooked, forgotten, and disenfranchised urban pockets, 4; precarious life at the, 34, 42; pursuit of dignity by persons at the, 101; unpredictability at the, 87. *See also* autonomy; gardening; precarity; value

Marx, Karl, 15, 18, 84, 113–14, 132, 134, 140; capitalist desire as vampire-like, 109; distinction between working class for itself, and in itself, 108; importance of labor to understand power, 13; labor as human life, 108; labor as liberating activity, 15; labor as the living, form-giving fire, 14, 16; labor power, 108; primitive accumulation, 80; social metabolism, 41, 108; theories of value, 13, 100; theory of alienation, 13; writings can be read differently, 12. *See also* Ricardo, David; Smith, Adam

Mauss, Marcel, 89, 99, 105, 113, 114

Mignolo, Walter, 22, 101, 152; border thinkers, 29; research and the decolonial option, 30, 100

milpa-based diet/cuisine, 69, 120; *chayotes con chiles* as, 120; cooking and healing with comida, 121–37; defined, 122. *See also* gardens/gardening

Muwekma Ohlone (Ohlone) peoples, 37, 81–82, 84, 85, 86; agroforestry among, 82, 83; diverse diet of, 82; experienced land enclosure, 83–84; forcefully removed from ancestral lands by European-settlers, 83; *gerguensun* is the site of Santa Clara Mission, 83; importance of acorns, 82; importance of oak trees, 82; labeled the oak savanna as *gerguensun* (the place of the oak trees), 83; leading cause of population decline was European diseases, 84; second leading cause of demographic decline was malnutrition and starvation, 84; segment of the community held captive at the Spanish Catholic missions of Dolores, San Jose and Santa Clara, 85. *See also* enclosures

Nabhan, Gary Paul, 78, 111, 119, 123

Negri, Antonio, 42, 91, 92, 146, 147, 154, 155, 159; labor-power against exploitation, 155; network struggle, 60; reading Marx as revolutionary, 12; self-valorization, 13, 93, 159; singularities that act in common, 159. *See also* Hardt, Michael

neoliberal food system: damaging to the environment, communities, and human bodies, 10; fosters alienation, 10; home gardens as actions to foster alternative food systems, 10; separates people from their very means of production, 10

Park, Lisa Sun-Hee, 19, 20, 26, 41, 46, 47; environmental privilege, 26. *See also* Pellow, David N.

Pellow, David N., 19, 20, 21, 23, 26, 41, 46, 47; environmental privilege, 26. *See also* Park, Lisa Sun-Hee

Peña, Devon G., 19, 29, 42, 48, 60, 70, 73, 76, 78, 79, 87, 93, 126, 136, 150, 152, 154; the relationality of wildness, 89 place-attachments, 91; aids the movement beyond ownership and toward relationality, 113; do not have monetary value, 91; ethic of care fostered by, 91; gardening aids, 91; relationship with nature as a form of, 113; reterritorialized space and, 150; sharing of seed and sharing of, 113, 116. *See also* ethic of care

Polanyi, Karl, 64

Prakash, Madhu Suri, 126; *comida*, 122, 133–34; human rights as Trojan horse, 21n2. *See also* Esteva, Gustavo

precariousness, 11, 42, 58, 99, 149, 158, 159, 161, 162; autonomy may exist despite position among the, 64; actions to address personal and community health among, 27; challenge and resistance to, 44, 87; considered beyond the suffering subject, 32; as contemporary condition, 28, 34, 62; convivial labor and, 49; flexible labor can produce, 49; food insecurity and, 10; gardening to ease, 63, 100, 116, 122; growing and sharing of food among persons facing, 11; harsh reality within, 35; a historical process, 44; marginalization and, 42; new work economy and the production of, 48; political cruelty and, 158; precariat class, 64; self-exploitation and, 48; state efforts to make permanent vulnerability and, 42; structural condition that increase, 107; uncertainty and, 41; vulnerability and, 159; vulnerability as, 124. *See also* conviviality; margins

primitive accumulation, 110; the body and labor-power as the original site of, 109; defined, 80; first occurred at the emergence of capitalism, 80; violence and, 114. *See also* Marx, Karl

Pulido, Laura, 20, 26; racism embedded in environmental policy, 20

Quijano, Aníbal, 86

reproduction: alienation and social, 10; capital, 75; community social, ix; crop cultivation and, 10; culture and conservative, 62; defined, 12; dynamic relationship between production and, 13; gardens as space of social, cultural and symbolic, 76; global capitalism continuously threatens, 11; at heart of home gardens, 10; not only concerns material needs, 12; production and social, and cultural, 136; social and symbolic, 12. *See also* alienation; Federici, Silvia; gardens/gardening

Ricardo, David: labor and value, 13, 100

rifts, 44, 62; autonomy and, 53; disruption of the Earth's natural cycles (metabolism), 33; disruption of metabolic interactions between humans and their environments 23; dual process of shifts and, 33; ecological, 41; efforts to restore, 44, 46; fostered by capitalism's shifts, 23, 41, 50; gardens/gardening as a response to, 46; individual, 41; metabolic, 41; movements for food justice a response to, 33; social, 41. *See also* shifts

Sacred Heart Community Services, 31, 52, 134, 147; collaborates with the University of California Master Gardener Program, 28; La Mesa Verde urban gardener program part of the Economic and Family Self-Sufficiency component, 28, 162; located in the Washington-Alma community in San José, 29, 38; sponsor of the La Mesa Verde urban gardening program, 28. *See also* La Mesa Verde project; University of California Master Gardener Program

sacrifice zones, 22–23, 42, 69; dispensability of persons/communities in, 23; explained, 19, 23, 42

Santa Clara Valley/County: capitalist industrial transformation of, 42–49, 64; City of San José' Guadalupe River as the most mercury-contaminated river in North America, 47; high cost of living in, 26; highest number of toxic waste sites located in, 46; racially segregated labor markets in, 26. *See also* gardens/gardening; *gerguensun*; Jungle, The; Silicon Valley

Scott, James C., 79, 107; art of not being governed, 64; contradiction in market-based ideologies, 106–7; emancipatory social change emerges from below, 62; social institutions designed to control the masses, 57; thick human locations, 8–9

Scrinis, Gyorgy (George), 137n4; nutritionism defined, 137n4

self-valorization, 13, 35, 48, 63, 93, 94, 126, 155; autonomous capacities for, 79; biopower, labor, and, 155; defined, 13; enclosures and dispossession of autonomy and, 92; flexible labor can be a source of, 48; healing of alienation a step toward autonomy and, 91; labor and, 108; remembering an act of healing, resistance, and, 86; self-defining, self-determining and, 93. *See also* Cleaver, Harry; gardens/gardening; Negri, Antonio

settler colonialism, 20, 84; conquest and, 85

Sevilla-Buitrago: definition of enclosure, 91; dispossession of communities has become highly methodical, 81; diverse materialities and morphologies in enclosures, 93; goal of commoning is to generate spatiality of difference, 71; goal of enclosures is to assert the primacy of the marketplace, 79; new spaces as the spatiality of difference, 93; reframing commoning beyond physical space, 91; suggest the term enclosure for commoning, 91. *See also* enclosures

sharing of crops/food, 6, 12, 20–21, 32, 34, 63, 76, 90, 110, 113, 115–16, 127, 133, 136–37, 148, 162; as act of liberation, 93; as an act of self-valorization, 108; alternative food systems and, 10; becomes part of local social norms, 5; celebratory aspects in, 90; collective action of growing, eating, and food, 15; community and individual survival, and, 15, 16; *convide* and, 115; convivial, 60; cooperation and, 114; cost of living and, 101; creation of revolutionaries and, 64; de-linkage from industrial capitalism involves, 16; as an effort against neoliberal capitalism, 11, 106; encourages autonomy, 18; encourages collective well-being, 6; everyday practices of survival involve, 10, 137; fostering dignity, 6; intergenerational, 92; mutual interdependence and, 8; political subjectivity and, 157–58; reasons for, 105, 143–44; reciprocal exchange, 34; reconfiguring neoliberal capitalist values through, 93; resisting empire and enclosure and, 92; restoration of bodies and communities through, 35, 137; restoration of dignity, 18; self and, 113; as strategy of resistance and cooperation, 6; subversion in, 31; traditional knowledge and, 92; what gardeners do, 5; what it means to be human and, 14, 15. *See also comida*; conviviality; gardens/gardening; margins

shifts, 50, 62; economic expansions and, 33; environmental problems, capitalism and, 23; intergenerational trauma and, 53; produce food deserts and diet-related illnesses, 33; produce rifts, 23; Silicon Valley produced by capitalism's, 44; violence and healing within, 23. *See also* rifts

Silicon Valley, 53, 58, 60, 100, 106, 112, 115, 133, 163; agricultural livelihoods of the area threatened by, 25; average cost of a house is $1.4 million in, 52; citizenship and, 152; contrast between Santa Clara Valley and, 24; creation of the silicon-gilded version of the American Dream, 84; dependent on flexible labor, 47, 53; gardeners and others navigate the worlds of Santa Clara Valley and, 25, 28, 101, 103; hegemonic forces of, 28; a heterotopia, 25; an imagined location, 25; lauded as a meritocracy but has one of the highest income gaps in the US, 52; located in the Muwekma Ohlone *gerguensun*, 80–86; metabolic rift fostered by, 42; Muir, John label of alley of your hearts delight, 24, 42, 47; neoliberal ordering in, 62; offshoring of hazardous products, 46–47; presumed to be a post-racial paradise, 25; production of a precariat class in, 64; racialized order of employment in, 46; same distinct geographic location of Santa Clara Valley and, 25; shifts and rifts created by, 44; widening chasm between wealth and poverty in, 64. *See also* flexible labor; *gerguensun*; rifts; sacrifice zones; shifts

Smith, Adam: labor and value and, 13, 100

Smith, Linda Tuhiwai: and decoloniality, 30. *See also* decoloniality; Mignolo, Walter

spatiality of difference. *See* Sevilla-Buitrago, Silvia

surplus value: central to capitalism, 12; division between those who produce and those who accumulate, 12; production of inequality and, 12. *See also* Cleaver, Harry; Federici, Silvia; labor theory of value; Marx, Karl; reproduction

Tlostanova, Madina V., 101

Trauger, Amy, 73, 93; on food sovereignty, 153; locations of struggles for food sovereignty, 153; oppositional state of exception, 150; political practice at the margins, 153; spaces of bounded autonomy, 149–50. *See also* food sovereignty

Treaty of Guadalupe Hidalgo (1848), 20

Tsing, Anna: haunting and legacy of alienation, 14; precarity as the condition of our time, 28. *See also* precariousness

University of California Master Gardner Program, 28, 129; distributes starter plants and seeds each season, 28; diversity in views between La Mesa Verde gardeners and the institution, 28–29; goal of the program was to teach low-income residents ways to grow food, 28. *See also* La Mesa Verde project; Sacred Heart Community Services

Valle, Gabriel R., 16, 93, 151, 155; application of environmental laws and regulation have a disproportionately unequal impact, 20; aspirations and escapes, 155; construction of possible solutions as escapes, 22, 35, 64, 134; critical environmental justice approach to the study of home gardens, 19–23; environmental policy riddled with racial inequality, 20; escapes can contain contradictions, 22; gardens of sabotage, 151, 155; limits of the research on the commons, 92; observation that those with the least giving the most, 160; volunteer at Sacred Heart Community Services, 31. *See also* Sacred Heart Community Services value: attachment to whole and to the individual, 14; *comida*, gardening and, 12, 34; food, 10; hegemonic, 15; not given but pursued, 114; reciprocal recognition shapes alternative, 15; role of the state in constructing, 15; Santa Clara Valley and Silicon Valley antagonistic forces shape, 103; shaped and reshaped by home gardens, 15; social norms created by, 15; a social phenomenon because it is created in a social context, 14. *See also* Graeber, David; Marx, Karl; Ricardo, Davis; Smith, Adam

Wald, Sarah D., 21, 60; Latinx environmentalisms, 21

Wilson, Shawn: relational accountability, 160

About the Author

Gabriel R. Valle is an associate professor of environmental studies at CSUSM. He received his PhD in anthropology from the University of Washington in 2016. His published work includes articles in peer reviewed journals such as *Food Ethics, Environment and Planning E: Nature and Space, Aztlán Journal,* and the *Journal of Environmental Studies and Sciences.* He is co-editor of the award-winning book *Mexican-Origin Foods, Foodways, and Social Movements.*